D0467550

SC

NO LONGER PROPERTY OF
SEATTLE PUBLIC LIBRARY

BUSINESS/SCIENCE

Seattle Public Library

Please note the date this item is to be returned
and keep the date due card in the pocket.

CORPORATE BLOODLINES

CORPORATE BLOODLINES

The Future of the Family Firm

by Barbara B. Buchholz
and Margaret Crane

338.642
B852C

A Lyle Stuart Book
Published by Carol Publishing Group

Copyright © 1989 Barbara B. Buchholz and Margaret Crane

A Lyle Stuart Book
Published by Carol Publishing Group

Editorial Offices
600 Madison Avenue
New York, NY 10022

Sales & Distribution Offices
120 Enterprise Avenue
Secaucus, NJ 07094

In Canada: Musson Book Company
A division of General Publishing Co. Limited
Don Mills, Ontario

All rights reserved. No part of this book
may be reproduced in any form, except by
a newspaper or magazine reviewer who wishes
to quote brief passages in connection
with a review.

Queries regarding rights and permissions
should be addressed to: Carol Publishing Group,
600 Madison Avenue, New York, NY 10022

Manufactured in the United States of America

Library of Congress Cataloging-in-Publication Data

Buchholz, Barbara Ballinger.
    Corporate bloodlines : the future of the family firm / by Barbara
B. Buchholz and Margaret Crane.
        p.   cm.
    "A Lyle Stuart book."
    Bibliography: p.
    ISBN 0-8184-0507-4 : $20.00
    1. Family corporations—United States—Case studies   I. Crane,
Margaret.   II. Title.
HD62.25.B83   1989   89-35673
338.6'42—dc20   CIP

To our husbands, Ed and Nolan, who embraced our book project with no less enthusiasm than we did. They unstintingly gave of their compassion, love and support. To our five children, Adam, Laura, Joanna, Tommy and Lucy, who tried so hard to understand why we were always "too busy" but now know everything about family business.

ACKNOWLEDGMENTS

Many people made this book possible. They agreed to be interviewed, suggested family businesses, supplied information, checked facts, performed calculations, took care of our children, fed our husbands, and gave us a place to stay far from home.

Our family business owners, members and non-family employees: For their cooperation, indulgence, hospitality and patience in answering our barrage of questions.

Our families: Mary Anne Rothberg Rowen for her ideas and keen editorial eye; Charlotte Ballinger, Estelle and Joseph Ballinger, Beatrice and Joseph Rothberg, Molly and Charlie Crane, Charlotte Buchholz.

Our Agent: Harvey Klinger, who loved the subject, liked our writing style and was determined to find the right publisher.

Our editor: Sandy Richardson for his editorial acumen, conscientiousness and cheerful support.

And to: The Auto Club of America (St. Louis), Glenn Bardgett, Albee Baker, Rabbi James Bennett, Lawrence Brody, Sharon K. Bower, Geoffrey Brooke, Rex Campbell, Cathie Burnes Beebe, Catholic Archdioceses of St. Louis and Chicago, Chateau Souverain Restaurant, Leon A. Danco, Dierberg's Markets, Julian I. Edison, Val Farmer, Fred W. Friendly, Al and Mimi Golbert, Mary Goede of Galaxy Travel Inc., Stephen and Alan Hassenfeld of Hasbro Inc. Toys, Becky Homan, Henry Howard, Susan and Larry Kessler, Richard Kodl, Ladue Video, Henry A. Lay, Robert E. Lefton, Lois Leith, Harry Levins, John Linstead, David Lipman, Kris Lotz, Rosetta Lloyd, Dana Zaret Luck, Glory McCamey, Father Thomas McQueeny, S.J., Eulan, Frances and Michael McSwain, William Monahan, Frankie Miller, Carole Nangle, John Morrison, Lloyd Palans, John E. Plummer, Lester Pollack, Rabbi Joseph Rosenbloom, Peter Ruane, Saint Louis Public Library (Reference and Research), Leslie Scallet, Martha Scharff, Alex and Harley Schuford, Debby and Allan Silverberg, Sisters of LaVerne Heights, Edna and Victor Soetaert, Ed Staley, Richard W. Stein, Robert Steyer, Paul Ullman, Judith VandeWater, Cynthia Vartan, Paul Weil, Barbara Walston, Barbara Wiley, Steve Wolff, William Woo and Alan Young.

Since we completed interviewing, five family business heads have died: Louis and Maria Balducci, Bruno Benziger, Jehiel Elyachar and Stephen Hassenfeld.

Contents

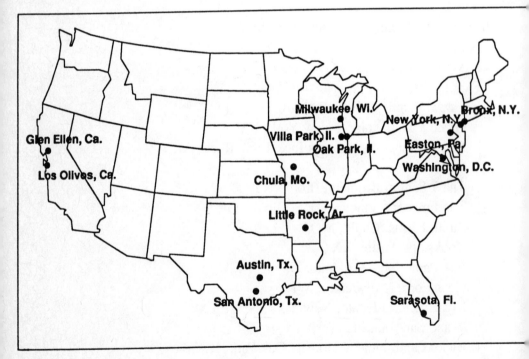

List of Family Businesses Profiled

Lazzara Optical
Courtyard Shopping Center
100-20 East Roosevelt Rd.
Villa Park, IL 60181
312-279-0505
Lucille Gioia, owner

Grace's Marketplace
1237 Third Ave.
New York, NY 10021
212-737-0600
Grace and Joe Doria, owners

Dillard Department Stores Inc.
900 West Capitol Dr.
Little Rock, AR 72203
501-376-5901
William T. Dillard,
chairman and chief executive

Bixler's
24 Centre Square
Easton, PA 18042
215-253-3589
Philip Mitman, president

The 7 Santini Brothers
1405 Jerome Ave.
Bronx, NY 10452
212-293-7000
Tino Santini, former president

The Firestone Vineyard
P.O. Box 244
Los Olivos, CA 93441
805-688-3940
A. Brooks Firestone, owner

Smith Farms
Route 1 North—Box 178
Chula, MO 64645
816-639-2175
Robert and Patty Smith, owners

Bookstop
6106 Baldwin
Austin, TX 78724
512-926-7001
Gary E. Hoover, chairman

Fox Photo Inc.
70 N.E. Loop 410
Suite 1100
San Antonio, TX 78216
512-341-1616
Carl Newton III, president

Koss Corp.
4129 North Port Washington Ave.
Milwaukee, WI
414-964-5000
John and Michael Koss,
chief executive and president

LHR Construction
Rolling Green South
Sarasota, FL
813-355-0612 (Fl.) or
(212)-697-9755 (N.Y.)
Daniel and Ralph Elyachar, owners

Blake-Lamb Funeral Homes
4727 West 103rd St.
Oak Lawn, IL 60453
312-636-1193
Matt and Dick Lamb, partners

Unified Services Inc.
2640 Reed St. NE.
Washington, DC 20018
202-785-3445
Jerry and Jean Davis, owners

Glen Ellen Winery
1883 London Ranch Rd.
Glen Ellen, CA 95542
707-996-1066
Bruno and Mike Benziger, owners

Dear Ann: When I read your column about the brothers who worked for their father in a family business, with the understanding that it would be theirs in the future, it rekindled the bitter resentment I felt in my heart after the unfortunate death of my father.

I am one of those sons who was told repeatedly by my father, "What I'm working so hard to build is going to be yours someday. Learn all you can and work your head off so when the time comes you'll be able to carry on."

Dad kept that carrot in front of me for many years to keep me from accepting other opportunities. I trusted him and it was a big mistake.

I am 50 years old. Dad passed away two years ago and left everything to my mother. She decided to run the business. I chased the carrot for 30 years and got whacked with the stick when my father's will was read. All I can do now, after 32 years of dedication and hard work, is start over.

My advice to children involved in family businesses is to ignore promises. Tell your father you trust him but you want everything in writing. If you can't get it, leave.

TOO LATE SMART

If all men who wrote to relate the same story were laid end-to-end they'd reach from Maine to California. (Are you listening, students?)

Unless your father is willing to relinquish some of his authority after you've been around for 10 years, it's safe to assume he intends to remain in the driver's seat until senility sets in. Face the facts and do accordingly.

INTRODUCTION

Mixing family and business has always been precarious. Most family businesses in this country fall faster than the Dow Jones Average on Black Monday. They have a life expectancy of less than 25 years. Only 30 percent survive to the second generation. Of those that do, only half make it to the third generation. Fourth, fifth and sixth generation family businesses are virtually non-existent.

I became interested in the dynamics and survival of family businesses after my husband entered our family wholesale wine and spirits company 13 years ago at the age of 33.

My family wholesale wine and spirits business had been successful and lucky through the years, avoiding the typical intergenerational bickering and sibling rivalries so prevalent among family firms. My dad, Joseph Rothberg, was the only family member working in the business that he started in 1950, after having been a chemist and production troubleshooter for various spirits companies. Through hard work and gumption, he built Manhattan Distributing Co., a tiny wholesale toy and novelty firm with a liquor license, into a multimillion-dollar corporation. He ran it single-handedly.

In less than 25 years, the company expanded beyond my father's grasp. With no heir apparent, Dad thought about selling out and had several good offers. But at age 57, he wasn't ready to sell or to retire. It occurred to him to invite my husband to join the family firm. Nolan, who had worked his way up the corporate ladder at two major public conglomerates, saw the family business as a chance to get ahead faster, insure a solid future and job security, live near family and work with his father-in-law, a kind, decent and generous man.

But in the rush to bring Nolan into the business, my father hadn't planned ahead. He didn't fully understand what it meant to bring in a relative—or partner. Less than a year after joining, feuding began when Nolan wasn't included in major decision making.

My mother and I were drawn into the battle. Hostilities flared. Just four years after joining the business, Nolan resigned. My dad, who had come to depend on Nolan's help, wanted to reconcile. The incident forced the two men for the first time to sit down and talk about the reasons for the friction. Reconciliation was made easier because just two family members were involved. They began communicating and divided responsibilities. Nolan was given the go-ahead to open a separate wine division.

Today, Dad is trying to step out of the business, but still has trouble relinquishing control. At times he longs to return to the "old days." Nolan assumes more responsibilities as Dad learns how crucial a clearly defined family succession is to the various wine and spirits companies Manhattan represents.

I decided that other families in business must have similar problems. I researched the issue, which had been barely covered except in academic business literature, came up with solutions about how family members working together could avoid major disagreements and wrote an article for *Inc.* magazine's February 1982 issue. It became a more significant story than expected. It was the first family business article the magazine published and the results were a deluge of long-distance telephone calls and letters to me seeking help, plus numerous requests to speak before industry groups that were comprised of family businesses.

Four years later the article was reprinted. Letters and phone calls again requested advice. But I was rusty. Some of the information in the *Inc.* article was obsolete. Shortly afterward, I discussed the possibility of a book with Barbara Buchholz, a former business and features reporter for the *St. Louis Post-Dispatch.* Barbara had written about many family firms in St. Louis.

We decided to pool our resources and write an in-depth book on one of America's oldest, most constant and most prolific institutions. Finding families in business was easier than we anticipated. Every time anything relating to the subject appeared in print, on television or cropped up in a conversation, we jotted down the names of the family members, the business and its address and added them to our growing list. We saw names in advertisements and commercials, in letters to the editor, on labels and on box tops.

A clothing ad for Raleigh's suits had the blurb: "My father . . . in 1932 had the courage and independence to found a securities firm. . . ." We wrote the family head to learn more about George M. Ferris Jr., chief executive, and more about his family firm, Ferris & Co. Inc.

In *Inc.* magazine, we read a letter from Lucille Lazzara Gioia, whose father initially wouldn't let her take control of the family optometry business. In this Italian family, it was tradition to hand down the business to the eldest son. Lucille finally got the chance to run the business after her brother almost ran Lazzara Optical into the ground.

We spotted a tag line on a bag of Charles Potato Chips that said, "Charles Chips is a Lancaster County, family owned company, dedicated to providing its valued customers with the finest quality snack foods attainable. . . ." It was the first of many times we saw family businesses using their names to connote quality.

Altogether we spent almost a year compiling close to 100 names. We gradually narrowed the list to a cross section of family businesses based on reasons for success or failure, industries, revenue—from tiny Mom and Pop producers to giant multigenerational dynasties, geographic locales, number of generations working together, cultural and ethnic backgrounds and religions. We sought family businesses that dealt extensively with the gamut of issues that most affect them: sibling rivalries, boundaries between business and family, corporate cultures, professionalism or the lack thereof, succession and tax and estate planning.

We decided to eliminate well-known large corporations and families whose lives have been well documented, such as the Crowns of Chicago, the Gallos of Napa Valley, the Binghams of Louisville, the Sebastianis of Sonoma.

We wrote to approximately 30 family business owners, asking if they, their families and key non-family employees would sit down and talk with us over a three-to-four-day period. We anxiously awaited the responses by letter and phone. Several families hemmed and hawed about being interviewed, such as Chicagoans Melvin and Ellen Gordon of Tootsie Roll Industries. Others gave us a flat-out "No." Donald Trump wrote that he was penning his own autobiography, *The Art of the Deal*, and that we should buy and read it. Andrew H. Tisch, a second-generation son of the family that owns CBS and Loews Corp., agreed to talk, but only off the record. That stipulation conflicted with our criteria. Edward R. Schwinn Jr. of the bicycle company that bears the family name said that he would cooperate, but only if he received a percent of royalties. Again, we declined.

But we had no problem securing enough "Yesses." In fact, we had to turn down many interesting family businesses as we further narrowed our list to 16 and planned our itinerary for eight months of travel across the country.

We hit the road in November 1987 armed with a list of 50 detailed and sensitive questions, a camera and tape recorder. We planned to talk to many other families for additional verification. We tromped through eight states and logged thousands of miles by car and plane by the time we completed our travels in June 1988. As we crisscrossed the country, we fine-tuned our interviewing technique: stepping into each family's life, meeting and grilling as many family members and employees as time permitted, checking their offices and homes, and, in many cases, even moving in with them, or in the case of the A. Brooks Firestone family, into their chic bunk house in Los Olivos, CA.

Our most memorable trip was to the struggling seventh-generation Robert Smith farm in Chula, MO. On a follow-up visit, we stayed overnight in the convent of LaVerna Heights in Savanna, MO, where the Sisters of St. Francis have lent support to area farmers. Darkness descended as we drove to the dark and eerie 100-year-old building, which appeared to have jumped from the pages of a Gothic novel with its long narrow dark corridors, squeaky wood floors and 20-foot-high ceilings. The rooms were impeccably clean and spartan, not much larger than a walk-in closet.

During each visit, conversations flowed easily as we arose at 5:00 A.M. to be at Grace's Marketplace in Manhattan as vendors delivered goods long before the doors to the gourmet take-out shop opened and stayed until closing. We went back several times to the headquarters of the 7 Santini Brothers in the Bronx, NY, to get a better handle on the unraveling of that troubled four-generation firm and family. Many business conversations turned into special social evenings such as dining at Phil Mitman's home in Easton, PA, where we discussed the eight-generation jewelry chain and watched the 1987 Winter Olympics on TV.

In every case, we have used real names, places, dates and anecdotes with permission of our subjects. In many cases, we quoted directly. In others, we relied on our subjects' detailed recollection of events and conversations, especially when a family member was no longer alive or refused to talk to us, which happened with the Andy Balducci family and with Jehiel Elyachar. In only two instances did the family heads ask to read our chapters to correct misinformation because of lawsuites they had been involved in. In only one case do we know that a family checked our credibility with the publisher.

Not every character is likable. In some chapters, the players may come across as greedy, self-centered and contentious. But each has contributed something positive to the understanding of the subject of family working together in a business.

Before starting the book, we had numerous preconceptions about families in business. After our first few interviews, some of these preconceptions were shattered. We expected many of the families to live in luxurious homes and have fancy business-paid cars, memberships in country clubs and liberal expense accounts. That wasn't always the case. Many lived modestly.

No sooner did we think we could generalize, however, than we pulled into the garage of the Blake-Lamb Funeral Homes in downtown Chicago and parked near a silver Rolls-Royce. It belonged to one of the two Lamb brothers who built the family business into one of the Midwest's largest. Matt Lamb owns not one but two Rollses, plus an elegant Chicago penthouse with a fabulous view of Lake Michigan and Lincoln Park.

We also assumed that heading a family business would offer a cushy lifestyle and was a primary reason for going into it. Kenneth Feld, 39, president, owner and producer of Ringling Bros. and Barnum & Bailey Combined Shows Inc., whom we interviewed over the phone, said that from the time he was five years of age he wanted to work with his father, who had bought the circus from John and Henry Ringling North. "My father lived to work. I knew that the only way I could spend time with him at home, on the road and at summer theater was to join his business."

It sounded to us like a panacea to be able to waltz into the top job in a company where the family always has its collective best interests at heart. How wrong we were. In many cases, greed and power superseded family loyalty. It becomes impossible at times to separate business from family. Nothing is more stressful. After his parents died, Kenneth, executor of his father's estate, was sued by his sister, Karen, over the will's validity. Kenneth and Karen settled with Kenneth gaining control of the business. What was never a good relationship worsened, Feld said.

Another assumption destroyed was that professional non-family managers were difficult to attract. We thought all would grow tired of working in a business if they didn't have a shot at the top slot, a chance at total control and an opportunity to buy stock at a discount. Some did such as Lester Pollack, once dubbed the "third Tisch brother" because of his close working and social relationship to brothers Preston and Laurence Tisch, who own Loews Corp. and CBS. Pollack left that fold for a chance to enter the private sector. He now works at Lazard Frères & Co., an investment house in New York.

Nevertheless, some professional managers haven't become restless and have relished supporting roles. E. Ray Kemp, vice chairman of Dillard Department Stores Inc., said that working for a well-known and successful family business for the last 25 years has offered challenges, extraordinary financial compensation, security and prestige in Little Rock, AR.

The correction of another misconception came as a shock: family businesses planned for their continuation. Most didn't because they said they were too busy, didn't know where to turn for help and didn't want to face mortality.

We also thought the issues affecting success and survival would be proportionate to the dollar volume of the company. As we interviewed our first few families, this idea seemed incorrect. They all seemed to have the same problems. But as we interviewed more families, we discovered that bigger companies faced bigger problems. The stakes were higher. They were more likely to be pressured to sell out, or to be overrun with relatives from different branches, or to need professional management and an outside board. And their fights undermining the success of the company were more likely to make for spicy reading. Judges in New York ruled last year against Paolo Gucci using his name in selling home furnishings. Gucci, grandson of leather goods chain founder Guccio Gucci, was ousted from the company in 1978. As a result of the turmoil, the company, which had been held tightly by male Guccis, is now half-owned by Arabs, run by a team of MBAs and headed by a woman.

We also didn't realize how much a family business is a product of its culture, which encompasses ethnic roots, religion and a value system. New York's multi-generational 7 Santini Brothers moving company has faced hard times, but was reluctant to alter its founding credo that family comes first before business. It was forced to sell in early January 1989, after several years of declining revenue, dwindling profits and increasingly bitter feuds among five family factions.

Our profiles are by no means all-inclusive or sociological, but they give a provocative human interest look into the subject. Why did families talk? Reasons varied. For the Smith farm family, it was a chance to be heard nationwide. They are in jeopardy of losing not just their family business, but their town, school, lifestyle and values. For Daniel and Ralph Elyachar, 60-year-old twin brothers who sued their 90-year-old father, Jehiel, their need to go public had to do with helping other families avoid the despair that has torn their three-generation family apart. For the William T. Dillard clan, with a cohesiveness rarely found in large and busy family dynasties, our portrait enabled its members to give outsiders a rare peek at how the healthiness of a family can carry over into the business, filter down to non-family employees and positively affect a service, in this case retailing.

No matter why families bared their souls, we discovered that almost all we interviewed cared deeply about their families, their businesses and their employees. Not one person said he or she regretted going into the family business, though some wished they had worked elsewhere first. We also found that while a family business has the same goals as other businesses—to offer a product or service and to make a profit—financial remuneration was not the key criterion that spurred entry, although E.W. Ingram 3rd, chairman of White Castle in Columbus, OH, may be our best exception. He bluntly admitted in a telephone interview, "Where else could I be president of a $282 million business at the age of 37?"

Our newfound insight has helped us conclude that there is no single way to run a family business. There are many different tacks a family can take. The C. Rallo Contracting Co. Inc. of St. Louis has an unwritten rule that no female family members are allowed to work in the business. Seven male third-generation family members run the $100-plus million business. Sons-in-law may work, but not as equity partners. The policy may gall some family business owners and observers, but it has worked for the C. Rallo firm by simplifying ownership.

Outsiders love dealing with a business person who carries the family name. Nobody else has that edge. A recent dinner conversation with French cognac mogul Maurice Hennessey, the eighth generation to run the business, sums it up. When asked his title, Hennessey wittily replied, "It's just Maurice Hennessey. Who needs a title?" Hennessey instantly turned to his dinner host, part of a third-generation family business, and asked, "And what's your title?" His host facetiously replied, "Son-in-law."

Who needs a title?

FAMILY BUSINESS: AN OVERVIEW

What is a family business?

It can be a small, private concern owned by one individual who intends to pass it on to successive generations. It can be a medium-sized private corporation in its third generation with several family members clearly in control. Or it can be a huge public conglomerate headed by family members who hold a sizable chunk of company stock. In general, the dollar volume of a family business and the number of family players are less significant in characterizing it than the input of the family—how it shapes the culture of its company, how it handles succession, how it uses non-family professional expertise.

Almost 90 percent of America's 15 million businesses come under one of these and related headings and are family controlled or have a major family involvement. They generate 60 percent of the country's gross national product and employ 40 to 50 million people, or about one-fifth of the population. These businesses range from tiny cottage industries operating out of basements and garages to gigantic multinational dynasties, including 175 of the Fortune 500 such as Anheuser-Busch Companies Inc., Seagram's Co., Mars Inc., Estee Lauder Inc., and Cargill, one of the largest and most secretive privately-held companies in the U.S. with estimated annual sales of $32 billion. The Newhouse, Walton and Bass families, all running family businesses, are reputed to be among the richest families in the country, according to *Fortune* magazine.

Most family businesses are started by independent entrepreneurs.

Through the centuries, they provided a birthright passed to eldest sons, who were expected to take up the mantle and follow in the tradition. Doing so offered heirs a viable option and held out the chance to get a quick leg-up in the work world, be one's own boss, start near or at the top, and have greater control. They also were a way to remain devoted to family and continue its name and legacy. Most important, family businesses gave the illusion of immortality—of surviving into successive generations.

In the 1950s, however, many Americans became disenchanted with family business. To call someone a family businessman or small businessman then was a pejorative label. The organization man became the ideal. Family business members were thought to be people who didn't have the schooling or couldn't make it in the corporate world. In the 1960s and 1970s, investment bankers, corporate attorneys and accountants commanded more prestige than most family business heirs.

The pendulum has swung back. Family business has suddenly become clic and a hot new topic in an era when juicier business subjects would seem to grab all the glory—billion-dollar mergers and acquisitions, investment bankers' staggering fees, insider-trading scams and the immense federal deficit. The reasons are varied.

An increasing number of primetime television soaps contain storylines in which rich and powerful fictional families vie against one another for control of family corporations. Some of the best known real-life firms in this country have been exposed in print as places that would make even the cast of "Falcon Crest" shake its head in collective disbelief. Who could have written a better scenario than this: the late patriarch Barry Bingham Sr.'s sale of his prestigious 70-year-old Louisville newspaper to squash sibling infighting over how it should be run and its dividends split? Or what about Canadian businessman Robert Campeau, who won a tough fight to acquire Federated Department Stores, but faces battles closer to the home front, with his adopted son, Jacques, waging a court battle over control of the voting rights on his $39 million block of stock in Campeau Corp. and a similiar suit against his daughter, Rachelle Archambault. The senior Campeau settled a similiar dispute with another son, Daniel, in 1987.

Something else has happened. More family businesses are up for grabs, vulnerable to being sold, merged, taken public or even shut down. Many were founded by men who used the GI Bill to start their companies after World War II. These family business founders, mostly men now in their 50s and 60s, are nearing retirement and many have no succession plans in place or no heirs.

Perhaps the predominant reason for America's heightened interest in family business is the emergence of a new wave of entrepreneurs. Every new entrepreneurial venture becomes a potential family business. One expert estimates that a new business in the U.S. starts up every 45 seconds. Entrepreneurship holds a strong attraction for several reasons:

—Corporate ranks have become swollen with middle managers, making it harder for new employees to climb to the top. Many workers are discouraged by hierarchial systems that stress office politics instead of meritocracy. Robert H. Brockhaus, director of the Institute of Entrepreneurial Studies at St. Louis University, says that 59 percent of all entrepreneurs start a business not because a light goes off in their head with a brilliant idea, but because they can't stand the kind of work they're doing, can't stand their co-workers or can't stand their bosses.

—Many new entrepreneurs are women who moved into the work place and also found themselves stuck in lower and middle echelons of corporations. Many left to start businesses. The Internal Revenue Service estimated the number at 2.8 million in 1985, a 43 percent leap from 1975. The number is now pegged at 3.5 million and is expected to hit 5 million next year. It is still rare to find women at the very top of America's biggest corporations and family businesses. Katharine Graham, publisher of the *Washington Post*, may be the most visible example. But she inherited her post upon her husband's death.

—The recent spate of mergers and acquisitions has wiped out companies and eliminated thousands of jobs, spurring people to form new businesses.

—More couples are going into business and more children are asking parents to go into business with them, a reversal of traditional succession. Children with good credentials are discovering that parents who are living longer and retiring earlier are a good source of funds, affordable labor and solid experience.

—Loyalty to an organization has become outmoded encouraging people to jump into new ventures.

—New magazines, new courses at the college and graduate levels, new family business institutes, workshops and support groups, new tools such as personal computers and cellular phones, a legion of family business consultants, and increased federal funding of new businesses have all fueled entrepreneurship.

At the same time, a small but strong undercurrent of anti-nepotism has surfaced among another new breed of entrepreneurs, who believe that family members should not be allowed entry into the business. Keeping them out, they feel, is the best way to attract and keep talented outside help and to prevent family feuds from undermining success. Instead, employees become "extended" family.

As a result of these changes, the old ways of operating and passing on a family business are under scrutiny and in the throes of change. Family businesses are professionalizing. Perdue Farms Inc. has a chief executive whose name isn't Perdue. Chairman Frank Perdue handed over the reins to Donald W. Mabe. James Perdue, Frank's son, sits on the company board and is learning the ropes. Said the father in an interview: "You go with the ability, not with the name." S.I. Newhouse, Jr., 61-year-old chairman of Conde Nast Publications Inc., says son Jonathan, 36-year-old publisher of *Details*, is his likely successor, "but it is not cast in stone," according to a *New York Times* story.

Max DePree, chairman of Herman Miller Inc., whose father founded the company 66 years ago in Zeeland, MI, decided he would be the last member of his family to head the firm. For the first time in the company's history, an outsider has been named head. DePree did so in order to encourage promising managers to stay with the firm and to keep the company as professional and competitive as possible.

Family businesses are calling on a new and expanding coterie of experts who are taking the pulse of the organization and treating both an ailing family and its business with an interdisciplinary approach of family therapy, management strategies, and tax and estate planning. In the past, each problem—legal, accounting, psychological—was treated by a different professional. Most were unfamiliar with the dynamics of families working together.

Family businesses are turning a corner in another way. Many are bringing in only qualified heirs, including women and younger siblings. Formerly, these members were discounted as legitimate leaders.

Family businesses are capitalizing on society's swing back to altruism and the family by playing up family traditions to connote quality, service and harmony. Nowhere was that more apparent than in the last Presidential election. Each candidate pitched family cohesiveness and values as a goal of their administration.

Perhaps the heightened interest makes the possible elimination of a family from its business seem so much more tragic, as in the case of the Campbell Soup Co. The late John T. Dorrance, Jr.'s children, the third generation, may have more interest in cashing in their stock than maintaining the company's independence, now that their father has died.

This family business book points out why some businesses thrive while others fail, and examines the common threads that hold surviving firms together and those that tear others apart. The book is for a wide audience—families in business, heirs apparent, non-family members in a family business, professionals counseling family businesses, and academicians studying them. The book also is designed to be read by a general public anxious for a glimpse into the often private world of family members working together to learn whether the many risks are worth the many rewards.

FAMILY BUSINESS PORTRAITS

Lazzara Optical
Villa Park, IL

Shirt unbuttoned. Sweat rolling down his face from unpacking cartons. Vincent A. Gioia has been busy since early morning. He imports hundreds of eyeglass frames for his company, V.A.L. International Co. He tracks new styles, colors, materials. He pays the bills.

He's also the right-hand man for his wife, Lucy. In a twist on the usual scenario of a wife helping her husband, Vinnie, as he's called by his spouse of 15 years, opened a wholesale eyeframe company after he learned the eyeglass business from Lucy and her father, Angelo Lazzara. Forty years ago, Angelo started Lazzara Optical, a retail optometry shop now run by his daughter.

The door of the shop that Vinnie and Lucy share opens. Vinnie looks up and shouts a cheerful, "Good morning, honey," as his wife steps into the professionally yet sparsely furnished quarters in a busy strip shopping center in suburban Villa Park, 20 miles west of Chicago. Arriving in her own car, Lucy is dressed simply in brown polyester pants and a white and brown polyester jacket on a perfect spring day in April 1988. As a way to separate their overlapping lives, the Gioias rarely come to work together.

Lucy takes over her post at the front of the family shop while Vinnie goes in back to balance the books. The retail business is showing the greatest profit since it was founded and more than a 25 percent jump since Angelo Lazzara retired in mid-1986. Annual sales recently hit $200,000. In less than three years, Vinnie's business has climbed to $300,000 in annual sales.

In this saga, a husband-and-wife partnership isn't the only storyline. For Lucy, who helped in the business doing menial administrative tasks from the time she was 14, the harder part was gaining control and ownership. It took patience on her part and a drastic change of mind-set for her traditional hot-blooded Sicilian father. He had babied and nurtured his business. He dreamed of passing it to his only son, Jack, Lucy's younger brother by two years. Angelo Lazzara did. Two years later, the father and founder's dream fell apart. Jack was not able to keep the business going.

Only when the business was failing and family ties were unraveling did the patriarch rethink his options and force his son to relinquish control to Lucy.

Is it possible for any parent in a family business to objectively assess the needs of the business and the qualifications of his heirs? Is it possible for an heir to know what a parent will be like to work with in spite of the older generation's promises of autonomy and ownership?

"Probably not," says John A. Davis, assistant professor at the Graduate School of Business Administration at the University of Southern California. "It's asking too much of a person you've always known to be able to see another person objectively. The best way to recognize a person's ability is to bring in an outside trusted party, someone who's not just going to mouth what you want to hear, but to determine what the business really needs and what each family member can bring to the table."

How did Angelo Lazzara choose the wrong heir?

In this case there was no one to guide him because of the small size of the operation. This wasn't a business that had outside members on its payroll or a board of directors. In addition, Lazzara was typical of a business founder of his generation. He always made the rules for his family. Eldest sons have been the traditional inheritors of family fortunes and Lazzara saw no reason to deviate from that rule. Only in a crisis was he forced to think differently.

For Angelo J. Lazzara and millions of other business founders who clawed and struggled to make it as immigrants or children of immigrants, to be knocked down and to get up again, passing on control of a family business is a visible sign of immortality and success. "I wanted to pass the tradition on to someone in my family. You hate to see something you built die. It's not for the money, but for the joy of carrying on the family name."

Lazzara never looked to his two daughters, Lucy and her younger sister, Lydia. A woman's role was to help out when needed, learn to type, get married, have kids and stay home. A son, however, was expected to take over. Lazzara considered his son particularly smart. "Anytime you tell him something, he learns it the first time," the father boasted.

When Jack was young, his father repeatedly told him, "Go and have fun. The business will be here for you, no strings attached, when you finish your education." Jack went to the University of Indiana, got married while in school and had a child at age 19. After graduation, Jack went to work in a relative's engineering firm. He returned to the family optical business several years later at a time when the eyeglass industry was changing. Small Mom-and-Pop operations, like Lazzara Optical, were being eaten alive by the chains that could stock more inventory, spend more on advertising and deliver quicker service and products.

The field had become wide open. Former Senator Charles Percy (Rep-IL) had worked to change Federal laws that forbade optometrists to advertise. Walk-in shops sprouted on every corner and in every mall and strip center. Pearle Health Services. Cole National. Royal Optical. D.O.C. Optical Centers. Sterling Optical. LensCrafters.

The industry became jammed with poorly trained technologists who were needed to fill the storefronts. Some observers questioned not only quality of workmanship in a number of these chains but also claims of lower prices. Telephone and mail order companies entered the crowded field.

Commercialism upset Lazzara, who had painstakingly built his business from scratch in 1944 and started over when he moved to the suburbs from Chicago in 1962. "The chains could make lots of money without offering the same type of quality service we did," said Lazzara.

All the changes in the industry didn't go unnoticed by Jack, who at age 27 wanted to jump on the bandwagon even though his only training had come from working alongside his father. Seeing his dad's business diminishing, Jack believed the only way to salvage it was to professionalize. To compete with the increasing number of one-hour chains moving into the market, Jack wanted to standardize prices. "Dad, you're charging different prices, whatever you feel like charging."

Lazzara shook his head. "You always wanted to run before you could crawl. All of a sudden, you want to do this and that. All those things take a lot of money. We've been in a sort of recession situation. We're both able to make a living, but we don't have the funds to capitalize this thing and I'm not about to go and borrow money. I always felt if you borrow you do so when you're going up, not when you're going down. You don't dig a bigger hole. As private optometrists, we need to try to keep to our ground, give quality service, which in the long run will be more substantial than reaching out for passes."

Jack wasn't convinced. "Dad, as long as you're here, we're never going to change this business. Why don't you turn the business over to me and let me run it? I'll hire a young doctor. We'll have a new approach and I'll make $1 million dollars."

Lazzara implored, "Jack, you're going too fast. You'll fall on your face."

"Dad, I know what I'm doing."

After haggling, Lazzara gave in to his son. Because Lazzara was just turning 60 and had a few more years before he could go on Social Security, he and Jack drafted an agreement that entitled Lazzara to get $800 a month out of the business. It wasn't much because Lazzara didn't want to overburden his son. At the same time, Lazzara believed he had worked too hard to hand over the business gratis. The agreement stipulated that if Jack couldn't meet his father's financial obligations each year for the next 10 years he would forfeit the business. Lazzara also insisted Lucy stay on.

Jack took over the business in February 1982. There was $15,000 in the checking account, a client roster of several thousand names, full inventory, one more year to run on the lease, plus a good name and reputation.

Lazzara and his wife, Marycarmen, left town. They went to Florida for a few months to relax and play golf. He felt uneasy about leaving, however. "Being productive all my life, it was difficult to give up the business so swiftly." But Lazzara felt that Jack, with three children to support, needed the business more than he did. But even more than that, Lazzara was afraid that if he didn't meet his son's demands, Jack might quit the business. Jack had left a previous job because he was dissatisfied with the traveling, insufficient pay and eventual sale of the business.

Jack quickly made changes. He upped the payroll by hiring a young doctor who Lazzara concluded "didn't know beans from bones."

Almost immediately there was tension between Jack and his older sister. Lucy couldn't believe how her sibling was making sweeping changes in search of millions in a business that had previously produced a comfortable but not overly affluent lifestyle—a nice house, new cars every few years, annual family vacations.

Lucy was afraid the company would go under as she watched the daily changes and saw costs mounting. She found herself saying more frequently, "Jack, why are you doing it this way? Dad always did it that way. It always worked for dad. Why do you say it's antiquated?" Lucy was increasingly disgusted with the way her brother treated their father. "Jack, don't shut him out. You took over a company he sweated and built up. Just because he's older doesn't mean his ideas are old."

Jack told Lucy to mind her own business.

When Lazzara returned from Florida, he dropped in occasionally. Soon his son was asking him to come into work Saturdays. "Mrs. Smith wants to see you," Jack would tell his father. Lazzara began to do more business on that one day than Jack did all week. Jack started resenting his father's help.

Lazzara told Jack to go back to school. "I'll help you. All you have to do is enroll at Illinois. You've got the college background. All you need to get are the optometry credits.".

"It's too late for me," said Jack.

Jack wanted to make money. He didn't want to sit in school. Lazzara blamed his son's greed and lack of ambition on his daughter-in-law, and tried to persuade Jack: "If you just wait a few years, I will have more income with my Social Security. I could then retire and you won't have to pay me the $800."

But Jack had to do everything in a hurry—"boom, boom, boom," according to his father.

Lazzara sensed the business was faltering. "His O.D. was sitting there never doing anything. And I'm getting a lot of complaints on Saturdays and doing a lot of work over again." One day he said, "Jack, how are you doing?"

"We're getting by," Jack said.

Lazzara knew his son would never admit if things were bad. Walking into the office one afternoon in May, Lazzara went to the back while Jack was up front helping a customer. Lazzara was looking for a prescription when he spotted the company's checkbook sitting on the desk. It was lying open. Lazzara peeked. He noticed outstanding bills like rent of $850. Overhead. Lighting. Salaries. There was no way his son could make ends meet with the balance down to $1,500.

Lazzara yelled to Jack, "What's up, what do you have here?"

Jack came to the back of the store. His father continued, "You've got to pay these bills the first of the month. How's your cash flow?"

Jack, not knowing that his father had seen the checkbook, answered, "It hasn't been that great."

Lazzara kept quizzing his son, "How are you operating? I left you about $15,000."

"I opened up a letter of credit," Jack said.

Lazzara didn't stop, "How are you going to pay your bills?"

"I'll just tell the bank to throw another $5,000 in my account," Jack said.

Lazzara began shouting. "What, are you crazy? You're digging a bigger hole for yourself. You've got to pay the money back plus all of the interest. If you don't, the bank will foreclose on you."

"Don't worry," Jack said. "I know what I'm doing."

"You don't" Lazzara screamed back. "Business is down more than 50 percent and overhead is higher because you just gave yourself a $600 raise."

A few weeks later in June their arguments surfaced again. Lazzara yelled at his son, "You're about a month away from bankruptcy. You can't make it. There's only one way we can pull this out. You've got to take a pay cut. Forget my $800. I'll come in and work full-time for nothing, I'm running this business now."

"I'm running it," Jack retorted.

"As of now, you're not running nothing," Lazzara bellowed. "I'm foreclosing on you because you can't pay me."

Jack became sullen and defiant.

Lazzara ordered him, "Now you're going to work for me. I'll give you so much a week."

"I'm not working for you. You can have the goddamned business," Jack yelled.

"You dug this hole and now you're going to leave me hanging with all this debt."

"I don't want to stay here any longer," Jack said and stormed out.

Lazzara didn't hear from Jack or see his son's three children for six months. Neither did anyone else in the family.

Lazzara called his accountant, furious that he hadn't warned him about the plummeting sales. "Get over here. Why if the business was so bad did you not tell me? Couldn't you pick up the phone and say, 'Dr. Lazzara, the business isn't doing very well?' "

"I thought you'd given him the business," the accountant calmly answered.

Lazzara shrieked into the phone, "You're fired!" Lazzara later rehired him.

Lazzara took control of the business. He went to the bank and found that Jack had mortgaged his home despite the father's warning, "Never, never, never, use your home as security." Lucy was still in the business. She and her father worked from June through December, morning to night, to pay off Jack's debts. "Never once did he thank me for saving his house or paying his bills," his father said.

Even today Lazzara tells Jack to his face, "You really screwed us. You're my son and I'll turn the other cheek. But never again. All these years I was waiting for you to take over and then you disappointed me." Jack, who went to work in the entertainment field, contends that the only way a business relationship between his father and him could have worked was if he had kept a lower profile and made changes slower.

Never once while Lucy and her father put the business back on its feet did Lazzara consider letting Lucy run Lazzara Optical. Instead, Lazzara called a broker and put the business up for sale. He asked $125,000. The broker brought people in. Lazzara kept telling the broker, "I don't want that kind of guy running it. It breaks my heart when strangers come in."

It tore Lucy apart that the business her father had worked so hard to build might be gone. She remembered how hard her parents had worked to make ends meet.

Angelo J. Lazzara successfully overcame the poverty of his youth. His father, a Sicilian immigrant, worked seven days a week. After working as a coal miner in Southern Illinois, Lazzara's father moved his family to an Italian ghetto on Chicago's East Side, near Racine and Taylor Streets, after his eighth child, Angelo, was born. Angelo's father went to work in a casket factory gluing wood together. He earned $15 a week.

Always ambitious, Angelo as a child worked hard. He wanted to be a doctor. While other kids took business courses, he took science classes. One day after his junior year in high school in 1939, he came home and told his dad, "I'm going to college and be a doctor."

"Who's going to pay for it? Son, I have nothing."

Lazzara was shocked that he couldn't go.

By the time he graduated from high school in 1940, his father had lost his job. There was no possibility of college. His father opened a small Italian grocery store and the family squeaked by, paying $15 a month in rent and 85 cents for gas.

Lazzara worked at his father's store during the day and enrolled in night classes at the University of Chicago until he was drafted in 1941. After the war—he served as a first lieutenant in the South Pacific—he got out of the Army in 1946 and took a job as a deli manager at an A & P supermarket. He was hired to run the counter with the help of six girls. Ending up with just one helper, he quit because the job was too hard to handle. He told his boss, "You keep your goddamned apron."

A friend convinced him to enroll at the Illinois College of Optometry. He had no intention of becoming an optometrist, but he was embittered. "When I came out of the service there were young men that had one or two years of college and the government gave them a free ride for the rest of their education provided they signed up for a three-year hitch. I felt like an old man. At least the government gave me $90 a week."

Lazzara graduated with a straight-A average and made the honor society. He lived at home. At a dance, he met and fell in love with a nice Italian girl and married her in May 1948.

Like most newlyweds, they had little. They split a flat with his parents on Chicago's West Side. Lazzara took a job as an office clerk at Helene Curtis Industries Inc., a cosmetic giant, and studied for his optometry boards. He kept working at Helene Curtis but opened a small optometry practice in his brother-in-law's medical office. Rent was free in exchange for odd jobs. Lazzara took medical histories, blood pressure, performed lab work. After two years, he had a falling out when his brother-in-law started resenting his growing practice.

Lazzara bought some secondhand equipment and set up shop in his father's basement. In 1952, he rented a broken-down store with Joe Traina, an optician. They worked day and night fixing it up. A year later Lazzara had enough clients to quit his assistant sales administrative job at Helene Curtis where he was earning more than $100 a week. "It was kind of scary financially, but my wife Carm wasn't afraid. I was the kind of guy who never wanted my wife to work. You get married, have a family and the wife takes care of the house and kids. It wasn't meant to be male chauvinism, but you felt emasculated if the wife worked." After saving some money, they bought a house at 5330

Congress Parkway on Chicago's West Side in 1956, a nice, middle-class neighborhood.

Three years later Lazzara's partner, Joe, was to move to the West Coast. Joe told Lazzara, "You've got to buy me out." 'We just got on our feet," Lazzara said. "I was 35 and forced to borrow $11,000 which was a fortune back then." Lazzara hired a young girl to help answer the phone after school. He worked seven days a week and in one year paid off the loan.

Lazzara felt good about the direction in which the business was going. He owned the building with five rental apartments at 4317 West Madison which was across from a nice shopping area. He was working hard and it was paying off.

Overnight, the neighborhood changed. In the fall of 1960 everything seemed peaceful. But by spring, 30 to 40 percent of the neighborhood had fled to the suburbs. People started selling in a panic. The clientele changed. Lazzara started working with a gun in his pocket. He thought, "This is crazy. I'm putting my house up for sale and moving with my parents out to the suburbs where many of my clients live."

In 1961 Lazzara's brother-in-law, Jim Esposito, found two corner lots in the suburbs. Lazzara bought one a year later by putting down $15,000. He opened an optometry business as well. He also kept the business in the rapidly decaying downtown section. It was about four blocks from where his home had been. He hired a doctor to work the downtown store and tried to sell the building. There were no takers.

One day, when Lazzara had enough, he closed the door and walked away. The bank took over the building.

Lazzara chose a new suburban office in Lombard in the Eastgate Shopping Center. He slowly built a new clientele. His former office was only 15 miles away, but without public transportation there was no way for his patients still living in the city to travel to the suburbs.

By the mid-1960s, the rebuilt business flourished with sales fluctuating between $25,000 and $30,000 a year, and he treated himself to a white Sedan de Ville Cadillac for $7,000.

Lucy came into the business as an extra pair of hands. She had been helping out as a part-time receptionist since age 14. She sat behind the front desk filing papers, making appointments, answering the phone, paying bills. Each year she took on more responsibility. Lucy's help was indispensable when her father couldn't afford to hire anyone else and when he wanted his wife at home.

Lucy, always the obedient soldier, accepted her position. "Nobody ever told me I was capable. Good grades didn't come easily to me. I'd burn the midnight oil and stay up till 4:00 A.M. to pull C's. I'd be happy. School was difficult for me. My brother, however, was naturally smart. Anytime you tell him something, he learned it the first time. He never had to study. He was the 'family prince' from the day he was born. He constantly was told by Dad that the business would be his someday."

Lucy went to a junior college in nearby Glen Ellyn and then to work for Zenith Corp. as a personal secretary. She came back into the business in the fall of 1974.

How did Lazzara, a man who lives by his pride, even when pride makes little sense, go from almost losing his business to asking his daughter to become the new owner? "I underestimated the qualities of my offspring. I didn't give Lucy an opportunity. When you raise kids you always look upon them just as kids; you still see them in diapers.

"One day this light bulb went off in my head. And I heard myself saying, 'Hey Lucy, how would you like to learn the optical business? I know you've worked a lot of years, and for other people as well as me, but all you know is the administrative side. I'm going to teach you in case anything happens to me. At least you could run it before I sell it.' "

Not quite sure what was going on, she responded, "Well, Dad, if you want me to. I've got to work anyway."

Lazzara wasted no time. He taught Lucy about frames, how to read prescriptions, how to put in drops. He taught her how to grind lenses, how to transpose the powers or alter formulations, how to fit and adjust bifocals, where to buy materials.

By 1986, patients had accepted Lucy as an equal owner. "We did it slowly. The only way it could be done," she said. Like the devoted student that her brother never was, Lucy consulted her father. They took care of each other. "Dad, why don't you go play golf," she'd say. He'd say a few days later, "Lucy, you want to do some shopping? I'll take care of the business."

Lazzara felt good about the relationship. In fact, he felt so good about Lucy running the business that one day he said to her, "Lucy, there's one thing I haven't taught you, the lab business, how to fabricate and make glasses. Guys like me are a dying breed, old dogs. I can make a pair of glasses for someone without machinery."

Within two weeks, Lucy mastered the simple aspects of the craft and Lazzara taught her more complicated tasks. By April, on a beautiful day he told Lucy, "I'm going to go home and do some yard work."

When Lazzara reached down to turn the lawnmower on, his back went out. He was in agony. The doctors discovered three ruptured discs. From his hospital bed he tried to conduct business and finally begged Lucy to sell. "No, Dad, I'll keep it going," she pleaded. Lucy called a retired optometry friend of her father's, Wally Lebetski, to pitch in. Just three days after her father returned home, his gall bladder became inflamed. Rushed to the hospital again, he had gall stone surgery. He lost 40 pounds and when he went home he could barely walk or eat. All the while Lucy ran the business, met expenses and kept patients satisfied.

By the end of 1986, Lucy and Lazzara were running the business together again. "I never realized her skills," Lazzara said. "Her determination. It was second to none. It wasn't because she's my daughter."

Feeling more confident as sales returned to $200,000 from a low of $85,000 at the beginning of 1986, one of their worst years, Lucy began to suggest changes. Her father agreed with them. A friend in the beauty business convinced Lucy to play up the company's father-daughter angle in ads.

Always a good writer, Lucy put together press releases and direct mail campaigns and tried to gain new clients. She hired a young O.D., Miki Kitahata, and kept Wally as a swing man to fill in when she or her father couldn't be there.

Lazzara, still recuperating, felt comfortable turning over the business to his daughter and called in his lawyer to draft a transfer of ownership. The one stipulation in the agreement was that Lucy's brother Jack never be allowed to work in the business, although the two men patched up their differences after one final confrontation.

Today Lucy and her father have forged a strong partnership. The black telephone on the desk rings. Lucy picks it up and listens. "Dad, get the phone," she commands in her role as owner rather than daughter. "Hi, Beth, how are you? How's the family?" Lazzara asks. He listens. Responds. "Those glasses will take about three days. Nice talking to you." He turns to Lucy and says, "That was a call from a long-standing customer? You know how our clients love us. Remember Lucy, we want them to feel warm and loved, like in a small supermarket. Everybody likes to be recognized."

It took years, however, and a crisis for Lazzara to learn his lesson and accept his logical heir, the family member most qualified and interested in running the business. Other family business owners need to remember the lesson: passing down a business to the eldest son may be traditional, but not always best for the business and family relationships.

Nevertheless, Paul Rosenblatt, a professor at the University of Minnesota, says that many family business owners still prefer to sell their businesses or have an outside male succeed them rather than pass the business on to a daughter. "Men are still men and they haven't changed their gender. It's women who are changing their minds about what they're capable of doing in business. In a crisis, a daughter may be able to gain control, but those cases are the exception." Yet by the year 2000, statistics from the U.S. Commerce Department and the Small Business Administration estimate that women will own 50 percent of all businesses with fewer than 1,000 employees. The figure today is 25 percent. Of the nation's 18 million business owners, 3.5 million are women, and by 1990, five million women will own businesses. Women are starting their own businesses at twice the rate of men.

At the same time, a look at father-son and father-daughter relationships points up that daughters often are better successors because they're less likely to compete with their fathers. "Girls are brought up to be collaborators while boys are taught to compete with their father and their peers, although a father-son relationship can work well if they're different enough, appreciate those differences and use them to the benefit of the company," says Deborah Menashi of the Family Business Resource Center, Melrose, MA.

Dan Bishop of the National Family Business Association in Los Angeles agrees that the father-daughter relationship offers distinctive advantages. "It's easier for a daughter in a family business because she's not in competition with dad, especially if she's in general management or serves as a vice president."

Marta Vago, a clinical and business therapist specializing in closely held firms, adds that daughters must also tread carefully with their mothers, who sometimes thwart their daughters' chances for success. "The mother's reaction may be jealousy if she's also very traditional and threatened that the father and daughter have a closer bond and she's left out. If the mother is in the business, she could get competitive with her daughter and put down her daughter's ideas or discredit them or undermine her daughter's relationship with other employees. Of course, mothers can also offer tremendous support to their daughters if they've had a positive relationship prior to the daughter going into the business. Patterns set by a mother and father at home usually continue and intensify in business."

Until recently, there were few support groups to help women in family business. The National Family Business Association started a group with a hotline. Surprisingly, most of the thousands of women who have called in have been the wives of the business owners or wives of the heirs rather than the female owners themselves, Bishop said. Why are more spouses than heirs calling in? Bishop believes it may be easier for women to run a family firm than to be a spectator on the sidelines watching corporate machinations.

Now in the second generation, Lucy and her father believe Lazzara Optical has more room to grow. Industry participants support that view. With additional schooling, Doctors of Optometry, O.D.'s, have been licensed in 20 states to diagnose eye infections and treat them. Within the next five years, O.D.'s will be treating some glaucoma cases and performing minor forms of laser surgery. Both once were the turf of an ophthalmologist, or medically licensed eye physician.

In addition, the country's aging population is increasing the potential client base for ophthalmologists, optometrists and opticians, who fit customers with glasses or lenses. Changes in the Federal Government's Medicare regulations also fuel growth. Since April 1987, optometrists have been reimbursed for treating patients over 65 years old.

All these factors have translated into a flood of new competitors. The American Optometric Association, the optometric group's main trade association based in suburban St. Louis, pegged the total number of practicing optometrists at 25,000 in 1980. The greatest number—18,200—were independent practioners. The second greatest number—4,250—were employed by optometric chains or department stores, with Pearle Health Centers of Dallas leading with more than 1,300 outlets in 45 states.

Lucy keeps expanding to compete. She moved the office down the street to a newer and more accessible shopping strip, Courtyard Shopping Center, right off Villa Park's main thoroughfare. She has gone from prescribing glasses and lenses and selling the frames and contact lenses to related eyecare products such as lens cleaner, eyeglass chains and eye makeup.

And she has added evening hours. She advertises in local newspapers and sends out mailers and reminders to more than 10,000 patients. Most recently, she's split the cost of the space with her husband, Vinnie, and his V.A.L. International optical venture. Vinnie, who had been an executive in a transportation business which took him all over the world, lost his job soon after he turned 40 in 1983 and had a hard time finding another job. His father-in-law convinced him to start a frame importing business. "Come on, we'll do it together, despite suppliers who keep telling us we need a fortune to do so," Lazzara said. With a small initial investment of $6,000, they began importing frames from the Orient, Canada and Europe. "It was slow at first," Lazzara recalled. "Those kids were like two chickens with their heads chopped off, running in different directions."

Lucy's store now stocks more than 1,000 frames, half of which are imported by V.A.L. Vinnie's frames are less expensive. Yet Lucy remarks that they have to carry the domestic designer ones from Chloe, Ralph Lauren and Anne Klein. In addition to tapping the Chicago market, Vinnie is developing regional clients and has four sales agents on the payroll. He plans to increase sales as he imports more contact lenses.

A big commitment to their jobs places strain on their marriage. Vinnie, an affable man with round face and flame blue eyes, bounces around the office in his faded blue lab coat, arranging inventory and showing off his parrot, Caesar. Vinnie's at home here and calls Lucy's parents Mom and Dad.

"Lucille is a great businesswoman. What she needs, and I think maybe she finally has it, is to become totally convinced that running the business is the right thing for her to do," he explains. "Then she'll be unstoppable."

Lucy says that it's hard for her to accept that she's good at what she does. "I've still got so much to learn. I don't see myself as having done anything miraculous. It was just something that had to be done. It sometimes floors me. The business came through it and so did I."

Grace's Marketplace
New York, NY

It is Thursday, January 21, 1988, 2½ years after the family fallout, when Grace Balducci Doria, 48, her husband Joseph, 52, and their six children abruptly left the family store, Balducci's. One of the pre-eminent specialty food shops in Manhattan, it was founded by Grace's parents 40 years before.

The Dorias sued Grace's brother, Andy Balducci, for their share of inventory and real estate.

The reason for the rift was a clash of personalities among the siblings and their spouses. The Dorias remain sad about the breakup between their side of the family and Andy's, which includes his wife, Nina, four daughters and two sons-in-law.

But most days the Dorias are too busy keeping tabs on their burgeoning enterprise. They opened a new store, Grace's Marketplace, on Nov. 4, 1985. It is the supreme corner family grocery and the corner happens to be one of the busiest in New York—at Third Avenue and 71st Street on the chic Upper East Side.

The Dorias are innovators and their groceries are among the most exotic. They seek out and serve the freshest foods they can purchase from 400 vendors. Pastas and cooling salads, dense and airy breads studded with raisins and garlic, homemade cheeses, delicate butter cookies, fruit tarts and pies, richly decadent cakes, imported olive oils and vinegars.

Not surprisingly, customers are among the most affluent and well-heeled in Manhattan and surrounding suburbs. Every day hundreds descend on Grace's. Some come in limousines that block traffic outside the store. Others come on foot. In winter they are wrapped in expensive furs and wool topcoats toting Louis Vuitton and Chanel purses, Gucci briefcases and designer shopping bags. They stop by to pick up a tasty morsel to add to breakfast, lunch or dinner or to carry out entire meals or party food.

It's hard to spot the many celebrities who blend in with the crowds at Grace's. Regulars include Elaine Stritch, Audrey Meadows, Diana Ross and Michelle Lee. Harrison Ford shopped on a recent day. "Should we get his autograph?" Grace debates. The family decides not to bother him.

Sales often translate into hundreds of dollars per customer, much higher than a typical customer spends elsewhere. On average, buyers purchase takeout food 1.5 times a week and spend a total of $16.50 on those purchases, according to the Food Marketing Institute, a trade association in Washington, DC. Altogether, consumers spend $1.2 billion a week on takeout food or $62.4 billion a year. The trend is expected to continue as more career people, more unmarried men and single-parent households find it easier to take out than prepare food themselves.

The 4,800-square-foot space, packed with more than $1 million in inventory, produces a healthy profit. It now rings up annual sales in excess of several million dollars, and posts an impressive 10 percent profit margin, almost double the standard of under five percent. The store's foray two years ago into wholesaling food to nearby restaurants and hotels adds to sales and profits.

Material success pleases the Dorias, a hard-working Italian couple, who have been married for 31 years. But rigorous schedules leave them little time to spend earnings.

Instead, what motivates this couple is providing a comfortable living not just for themselves, but for their six grown children, two of the children's spouses, two nephews, one niece and several long-time loyal employees, all under a single roof. "Money isn't important to us. We can make a lot more if we didn't care about quality. We're in this for the long term," Grace says.

What's more, the Dorias boast that they have been able to keep their family together long after the doors close at the end of the business day. The four unmarried Doria children still reside with them and Grace's parents, Louis, 89 and Maria Balducci, 88, in a six-bedroom rambling brick home in Flushing, NY. The Dorias' two married children live nearby and dine frequently with the rest of the clan. "We live, eat and drink the family and the business," says Pina, the couple's eldest daughter, who is in charge of accounts receivables and house-charge accounts.

Yet in creating such an enmeshed bond between their family and their business, the Dorias may be unwittingly repeating the mistakes of Grace's parents. The senior Balduccis also believed they had planted the seeds to produce a perfect family business, one that would allow *tutta la famiglia* to live and work together in order to pass on the legacy to future generations.

Like many tight-knit families, both generations believe that a strong bond between work and home, which shuts out the rest of the world, fosters family harmony. Instead, the Doria family has failed to look to itself and its family business to see the reasons why Grace and Andy had their falling out and why Grace and Joe's children could replay the same story.

"Accommodating growth is probably the biggest hurdle for a family-owned business," according to Pat B. Alcorn, author of *Success & Survival in the Family-Owned Business*. "Many businesses," she adds, "never quite find the key, either remaining disorganized and stagnant with relative-ridden management or going all the way to professional management and outside control as the family steps out of the picture. If the former is a tragedy, the latter is not necessarily desirable."

Whether Grace and Joe and their children will make changes in the business will be revealed in the second and third acts of this three-generational family drama. The Dorias must realize that to do so doesn't mean that they aren't good parents.

First Act

When Louis Balducci, at the age of 18 in 1917, rented a pushcart to sell fruit and vegetables in the Greenpoint section of Brooklyn, he had no grandiose plans to build the first of a series of well-known stores or a small family dynasty unmatched in the history of specialty food retailing. Rather, this native of Corato, Italy, who had arrived in this country penniless three years earlier, was merely trying to eke out a living for himself.

Louis Balducci knew farming. He knew how to grow the best crops and choose the finest. He was street-smart, with a background and business goals that destined him for success. "You got to offer quality and service above price," he told his workers. "If you don't offer the best, the people won't come. Don't ever fool the customer. If you fool the customer once, he'll never come back again. Don't try to make a big dollar the first sale. Take a nickel at a time. Gain their trust."

After the pushcart, Balducci bought a broken-down shack and a horse and wagon for $50 and became an American entrepreneur. By the end of the first day, he had turned the original investment twice. By the end of the first week, he had made $250. Polish people in the area were his customers. He went in the street and told people to try his foods.

Four years later, as business continued to flourish, he hired his older brother, Frank, to man the cash register while he went to market. He prospered. When he was 22 years old, his mother, who was still living in Italy, told Louis he needed a wife. "I got a nice girl for you," she wrote. She sent the girl's picture. He sold his store and returned to Italy to get married in 1921. But he came back six months later to avoid serving in the Italian Army. His wife followed him to America. They shuttled back and forth to Italy. They had three children, Charles, Andy and Grace.

Balducci tried various businesses in Brooklyn. One day when he was at market in the spring of 1947, a wealthy wholesaler took him aside. "Louie, I want to see you." Balducci thought he owed the wholesaler money. Instead, the wholesaler had big plans for him. "Hey, I got a good place for you at the corner of No. 1 Greenwich Avenue and 8th Street. The owner doesn't know how to handle what he's got. You're just the guy." Balducci took $3,000 from his pocket and said, "This is all I've got." The wholesaler rubbed the tips of his four fingers with his thumb—"A little more." Balducci said, "How about $5,000?" The wholesaler said, "Sounds reasonable." They signed a lease.

Balducci liked having a store in Manhattan and living nearby in Queens, a borough 12 miles from the store. He was at the store day and night. He rented a furnished room on 12th Street in Manhattan to be closer to the store.

Being in Manhattan made it easier to attract more upwardly mobile customers. Most who came were professors, artists and students who appreciated good food and scrimped and saved to pay for it. Louis brought his wife, Maria, and second son into the business.

The Balduccis waited for the crowds to come. None did. The store didn't make much money because it had a bad reputation from its previous owner. Louis fought to change the image. He quickly lowered prices, kept the store open 24 hours a day and moved the family to a nearby apartment on Christopher Street in order to be closer. He stuck to his original strategy. He told Andy, "Don't worry. Don't put anything in the bag you don't like. Otherwise you never get the people back." In the first few years, they threw so much produce out, they almost ran out of money.

Three years later, when Grace was 10, she started working in the store after school and on weekends. In 1952, Andy got married and went into the masonry business with his father-in-law. He begged his father to sell the store. The Balducci women cried, "Don't sell." But Louis found a buyer, a distant relative. Grace fought back. "Let's just tell Andy you couldn't come up with the money, Pop. I'll leave school. I'll help you." That's what she did. Grace finished high school and went into the store. Her father finagled around Andy.

Business started rolling in the mid-1950s. "Nonno," as Italian children affectionately call a grandfather, went to market, opened crates, tore them up to check produce and sent merchandise back if it was less than perfect. It got to the point where people said, "Don't send that to Balducci. He'll just send it back." Louis became a legend in his industry for his quality and product, items customers couldn't find anywhere else.

Joe Doria joined the business in 1955 and was put in charge of produce. He had been a friendly neighborhood boy, who had immigrated from Italy at 14. Lean, fit and muscular with a heavy shock of dark hair, Joe had a reputation for his hard work at a grocery store on First Avenue. He brought along his two brothers. Louis taught the three of them all he knew. They made a good team and made good profits.

Together, they unpacked the fruit, the vegetables. They cleaned everything. They served customers. They calculated sales in their heads. They kept the business going. Joe became the son in the business Louis didn't have. Joe met Grace and soon told Andy. "I'm going to marry that girl some day." In 1957, when he was 21 and Grace 17, Joe kept his word.

In 1971, Andy came back to work at Balducci's. He asked his father if it was okay. "Of course, there's a place for you," Louis said.

A year later, the store's rent escalated and the landlord tried to evict the Balduccis and Dorias because he wanted a tenant from whom he could get more rent. In March 1972, the Balducci clan made a major decision. They moved across the street to 9th Street and the Avenue of the Americas. They rented the middle part of a store that measured 3,500 square feet.

The eviction caused commotion among Balducci's loyal customers. There was much free newspaper and television publicity. They had a ready-made audience.

Even so, the Balduccis lost money the first 18 months. They knew a good salami, but didn't know how to price it. They knew about fruits and cheese but not how to cut and sell them. They had never operated a complete food business.

Andy and Joe were an odd match. Joe was affable and gregarious. Andy, businesslike and analytical. The Dorias were uneasy with Andy back. Louis reasoned with them. "What are you going to do?" he asked. Andy had four daughters. "He's got to eat. The store is wide open. What Joe takes, you take," he told his son.

Louis saw that Andy was trying to run a family store in a more professional way. Andy told his Pop, "We got to buy a truck." They bought a truck. "We got to buy an air conditioner." They bought an air conditioner. Louis always said, "Yes."

But Louis was more interested in what Balducci's could offer the customer than in the other amenities. He thought they had to improve departments. He learned about cheese. They hired a good man to run the department. "Jewish people like fish," he reasoned. They opened a fish department. "Now we need a good butcher," he thought. Janis Carr, the current chef at Grace's Marketplace, came in as the salad and prep person. Andy said, "We don't know anything about doing these things." His father replied, "We'll learn."

There was trial and error. The Balduccis put in a self-service counter for the meat. But they found that people wanted to be waited on. Out came the self-service counter. They added groceries—Entenmann's doughnuts, soda, salt and milk, but then changed their minds. "A & P has it so why should we have it?" Joe wondered. "You can't make money on salt and sugar. You can't compete with the price in grocery stores." Slowly the family got their formula right and added square footage. They took over a beauty shop on one side and a Japanese souvenir shop on the other side.

With more space and more work, responsibilities had to be divided. Louis bought. Joe opened and closed the store. Maria cooked and built up the catering department. Grace helped out when she wasn't busy at home with six children. Pop Balducci was the figurehead of the business. "You have to have one boss and a team working," Louis kept telling his family. Andy and Joe delegated responsibilities.

The store became well known throughout Manhattan and a tourist mecca beginning in the early 1970s, concurrent with the exploding interest in ethnic foods and the increased number of two-career couples, who had less time to cook and less interest.

But family trouble developed. The partnership became strained. Andy assumed more control, according to Joe. Andy decided what to buy, whom to recruit, how to expand sales and profits, and how to divide earnings. He rarely consulted his father, his brother-in-law and his sister, Joe said.

Joe, a mild-mannered man 12 years younger than Andy, wasn't the type to argue. He focused on what he did best—buying produce and dealing with customers. Nevertheless, he felt tension at work and decided he needed a place of his own. Andy told him, Joe recalled, "You'll never make it." Joe thought to himself, "Fine, just you see."

Every day on his lunch hour, Joe climbed into his car and circled the city seeking a location for a new store. He talked with everyone he knew. Food suppliers. Real estate agents. Customers. He knew he shouldn't open an outlet on the West Side near 80th Street and Broadway where Zabar's has reigned as the king of delicatessens for more than 50 years. Joe wanted to avoid opening a store too close to some of the better-known gourmet take-out shops on the East Side.

Problems at Balducci's became exacerbated when the third generation came into the business. Although there previously had been enough of a larder and enough jobs to spread among everyone, now there were too many people in quarters too close.

The Dorias' oldest son, Frank, a solid, broad-shouldered man, was brought in as a floor and personnel manager. His desk was next to his Uncle Andy's, his godfather, making him privy to his uncle's transactions. He didn't hesitate to tell his parents what he saw and what he thought was unfair. He thought Nina bossed his mother around in the kitchen. He thought Andy got all the credit.

June 15, 1985, seemed like an ordinary day. Frank described it as otherwise. Joe Doria Jr. was loading a truck in the street with fruit and vegetables. Andy walked up and said, "Hi." Joe didn't hear him. Andy went up to Joe and said, "What's your problem, son? Don't you know how to say hello any more?" Joe's cousin Louis ran downstairs to tell Frank that Andy was picking on Joe. Frank ran out in the street. It was 11:00 A.M. "Andy, I'll meet you downstairs in your office," Frank said. They had a terrible confrontation, according to Frank.

The entire Doria family left the downtown store. Grace later related in an article in *The New York Times* that the relationship between the two sides had been rocky. "We were the ones who were willing to do the hard work without complaining. We made the store what it is. We were always there, but no one knew we existed." Nina Balducci said in the *Times*, "We'd like to think the split is amicable, and there isn't any acrimony. I wish them luck."

(Andy Balducci refused to return several phone calls placed to him by the authors of this book.)

In an attempt to start his venture, Joe approached Allen Allen, owner of Fay & Allen's Food Halls on Manhattan's Upper East Side, which he had heard was having problems because employees and customers were robbing him blind. "I have a problem, too," Joe said. "I need a new shop." They made a deal. Allen gave Joe a 20-year lease on the property. Joe considered the area a great neighborhood. "The people are always working. They like to eat and they've got the money to spend."

Pop Balducci was supportive of Joe and Grace's dream. Louis told his son-in-law, "Go for it. I know you can do it. If you need me I'll be with you," Pina recalled.

A problem developed over the choice of a name for the new store. In the *Times* article, Grace said she planned to call her store "Balducci's." "That's my name. If my brother gives me trouble on this, I don't know how we are going to handle it."

How she handled the trouble that developed was to initiate a State Supreme Court lawsuit to determine respective ownership of the Greenwich Village store and its real estate. Trademark litigation was commenced in Federal District Court for the Southern District of New York over the use of the name, "Grace Balducci's Marketplace," for the new store. All parties settled and the Dorias changed the name of their store to "Grace's Marketplace" and agreed upon a just settlement.

Today, the two stores operate independently. They have different names, logos and different colored canopies. "Balducci's" has a dark green canopy with white lettering; "Grace's Marketplace" has a white canopy with the name in maroon.

Within the stores the layout and inventory are remarkably similar in spite of their different clientele and locations at opposite ends of Manhattan—similar produce, prepared salads, bakery goods and private-label items. The most obvious differences are the absence of fish and meat departments in the uptown store.

The syncopation and rhythm of each store also are identical and the tone changes as customers come and go. Food arrives daily from hundreds of vendors. Fresh food is cooked on the premises. Floors and cases are scrubbed clean. Customers crowd the shops. Leftover food is packed away by early evening. The doors are locked. Buying for the next day continues throughout the night behind closed doors.

Second Act

It's 6:00 A.M. and Joe Doria is at the Hunt's Point Market in the Bronx squeezing melons and checking crates for bad produce. He's had about three hours of sleep the night before, barely enough time to take off and put on his white smock. Joe's keen eye for detail is at work. He must set the stage to make his displays, equivalent to a gustatory theater, the best show in town.

The curtain will rise for the day on Grace's Marketplace in one hour. Fluorescent lights are flipped on. Props are in place. The key is to make everything look so dazzling and smell so irresistible that customers fill their small shopping carts or orange plastic baskets to overflowing.

Fresh hot loaves of pumpernickel studded with raisins and skinny loaves of sourdough French bread are propped up in wicker baskets. Cheese is cut, dusted with fresh dill or chives, and wrapped in Saran for display. Fruit and produce are colorfully and artfully arranged to attract attention. Pastries are set out on paper doilies. Prepared food cases are wiped and lined with crisp white paper in order to be filled from the basement kitchen by 10:30 A.M. At center stage, they are the star attraction.

Joe bolts to the back room where the phone rings with orders from nearby restaurants and hotels, who order wholesale from the Dorias. Back on the set, he turns left at the salad bar where the lunch time customers will congregate and stops to check his prize produce section, featuring raspberries at $5.95 a half pint and radicchio, fragile morels, Japanese Daikon radishes and live snails, which he has just purchased at the Hunt's Point Market. He heads across the narrow aisle from the cheese counter, which is next to the vast assortment of olives, caviar, smoked salmon and other pricey deli items.

Employees prepare to play to their audience. They arrive at staggered intervals and don their white costumes embroidered with the company's burgundy and white cornucopia logo. They set up their booths almost like carnival barkers, who beckon crowds with eye-popping prizes. This sales staff is not a rowdy bunch. They make time for polite chit-chat in spite of high-pressure roles. Big sales must be made daily or food spoils.

Joe and Grace set the tone. Joe graciously ferries customers from one department to another. He fills in for an employee who didn't show up in the appetizer department that morning. He runs down to the basement to bring up more freshly prepared pasta and chicken salads. "We cook 200 pounds of pasta a day, 800 chicken breasts a week, 500 pounds of tuna salad and 500 pounds of crab supreme salad," interjects Grace. "We give them the best and it pays off."

"Good morning. How are you?" shouts Lina Prillo, to the bread delivery man. "I'm okay. How's things here?" Hilary Waleson, in charge of pastries, greets one of her vendors cordially. "We'll need another cheesecake today. We had a lot of orders yesterday."

Wagner's Spice vendor, John Mazola, who also sells to Balducci's downtown, agrees that there is an unusual sense of camaraderie among the staff and suppliers. "I didn't expect this here. I grew up in upstate New York where people are this way, but not usually in New York City. It's a little bit of home in the middle of the Big Apple."

Customers begin to drift in, though the pace won't quicken until lunch time. Most who frequent the store several times a week know the routine well and are known by the Dorias, who greet them by name.

The store begins ringing with the welcome sound of cash registers as the five checkout lines grow deeper. There are occasional grumbles about prices, but the number of repeat customers proves they are happy to pay when they taste the food. The Dorias consider any comparison to supermarket prices unfair because of the quality and personal service they offer. Produce is the most profitable department, more than 30 percent of gross sales. Of the profit generated in this division, 20 percent comes from retail sales and 10 percent from wholesale. Buying is done a day ahead, with merchandise called in from around the world. Need mushrooms? Oyster mushrooms come from Pennsylvania. Oranges? Jaffa are shipped in from Israel and Sunkist from California. Raspberries? About 240 cases, which equals 2,880 half pints, arrives from Chile. All is stored in a large refrigerated room kept at 40 degrees. The room is packed floor to ceiling with more than 600 produce boxes. Eighty percent of the produce is replenished nightly.

The Dorias have perfected selling produce by hiring a food broker. Each night at 8:00, the Dorias phone in their orders. The broker peruses the Hunt's Point Market, starting at 11:00 and working until 7:00 in the morning. He lets Joe Faraci, Grace's produce manager and Joe Doria's godson, know what's available and what looks best. Decisions are made on the spot.

Joe Doria charts fluctuations in produce prices on a large white board in his basement office. Every imaginable fruit and vegetable is listed with its current price crayoned alongside. If the wholesale price goes up or down more than $2 a carton, he changes the store's retail price. On a recent day, a half-pint of raspberries sold for $3.98.

Prepared foods and catering bring in 18 percent of profits but eat up a big chunk of the store's labor costs, which average 20 to 25 percent of gross sales. Janis and his staff of 13 work in a cramped but clean white kitchen with stainless steel appliances, counters and baker's racks jammed with mixing bowls, utensils and ingredients. Each employee has his specialty. There is little conversation. The staff works in unison to the rhythm of loud, piped-in rock music.

Mario Barile, the pasta cook, who has since left Grace's, goes back and forth between the two six-burner Vulcan ranges, where he boils gallons of water into which he pours differently shaped and colored pastas, and the counter where he concocts sauces. Today, the menu calls for three meat and vegetable lasagnes.

Three brothers from Portugal, Manuel, Luis and Ricky d'Matos, act out their parts making salads and marinating chicken breasts. Other members of the kitchen staff help. Each day a pot roast must be braised, two fresh turkey breasts roasted and a few whole fresh fish baked. Shrimp fried rice and chicken livers for chopped liver are stir-fried in a giant wok. There are 175 dishes in the repertoire. Recipes are simple but tasty. Grace oversees the kitchen staff. She samples new dishes, offers suggestions.

Janis doesn't stray from his station. He has given himself a long list of daily assignments. He mixes the soup, today a tasty, fragrant minestrone. He stirs the walnut oil before deftly pouring it over stuffed rock cornish game hens. He explains what a few handfuls of fresh tarragon can do to improve the taste of a steaming dish of veal shanks. "Our customers are people who don't want to cook," Janis explains. "They go to work, come back home and want to have everything prepared for them. I've heard customers gloat, 'Now my wife can use the kitchen as another closet for her clothing.' "

Work becomes repetitive, he explains, but only tedious at holiday time when the crowds circle the block and the orders exceed the manpower. "I had to come in by 2:00 A.M. this past Thanksgiving, roast 90 turkeys, and I decided at the end of the day if I saw another turkey, I'd throw it through the window," Janis said. Frank recalls the throngs of people. "We had to lock the doors and let only two people in at a time. But we gave the waiting customers candy and samples of food."

Business slackens during summer when many customers vacation at weekend homes in the chic nearby Hamptons on Long Island.

The most challenging part of the kitchen staff's day is to get food sold before it spoils and recycle leftovers, Janis explains. He turns stale bread into bread crumbs for the meat loaf and meatballs. He estimates he throws away only five percent of the food on any given day.

Even though the Dorias and Janis think they're clever about not wasting food, Allen Greenberg, manager, points out that there's still room to improve portion control in the kitchen in the way that McDonald's employees are trained never to use more or less than a certain amount of food per order. Greenberg believes that the store can gain more lucrative sales and profits if the family beefs up its catering and wholesale divisions. "It's not profitable to go much beyond a certain geographic area with our delivery vans."

Grace and Joe try to position themselves near the front door several hours a day to answer questions and welcome customers. Joe answers a typical query, "Any lentils here?" "Yes, ma'am, they're right around the corner," he says shepherding her to the package.

The Dorias also try to be on the floor in order to guard against shoplifting by employees and customers, a major problem of any retail operation and one which they discuss with great hesitation. "It's easy to lift a loaf of bread or a jar of jam and stuff it in your raincoat or a shopping bag," Joe explains. On a busy Friday, money is missing from the cash register. Detectives have been called in to administer polygraph tests to employees who handled the cash. Dominic Diasparra, a nephew in charge of personnel, stresses that "finding good honest employees who are diligent and show up for work is the biggest hassle."

Also this day, Rusty Pacheco, the husband of the Dorias' daughter Maria, is doing the work of two in the cheese department. Rusty's assistant failed to come in and never called in sick. "This happens all the time," chimes in Joe Faraci, who can't understand disloyalty in a company that bends over backwards to treat its employees fairly and enforces only minimal rules.

There is no sampling of food. "This isn't a restaurant," Joe Doria explains. "Employees can have anything they want at a 20 percent discount. Of course, the receipts often get lost or never turned in." Everywhere signs are posted about keeping hands clean. Janis stations himself at the kitchen sink and makes his staff scrub, much like surgeons.

Keeping good employees who are willing to follow these guidelines is another problem. Turnover is rapid. The average employee stays four months. Pay starts at $4 an hour, though it can climb much higher for department managers.

After the crowd of lunchtime customers has dispersed, the kitchen checks to see what has sold well and what odds and ends are left. They begin preparing food for the next day—cooking two hams studded with whole cloves and baking 120 pounds of chicken cutlets for salads.

While all this is going on upstairs, Pina, the Dorias' daughter who arrives daily with her father at 7:00 A.M., has settled into her desk in her small downstairs office, which she shares with four others. It's filled with typewriters, adding machines, phones.

Reams of paper are stacked on the surrounding desks and stick out from file cabinets where perfect records of what she's done are kept. House-charge applications wait to be approved. Checking requires time. Pina must also act as a credit manager hounding customers slow to pay. Today she's having a better day. "I'm not drowning in as much paperwork and the phone is not ringing off the hook."

Pina is self-taught. The business is in her blood. Every day after school when she was a teenager, her grandfather waited outside her school to pick her up at 3:00 P.M. and take her to the downtown Balducci store. She was expected to be there and never considered doing anything else after she graduated from high school. Unlike their brothers, Pina and Maria never went to college. The store came first.

Pina started in catering but when the manager got sick during one Christmas holiday, she pitched in and eventually ran the department with her mother and Maria.

When the family moved uptown, Pina switched from catering to accounting as a way to establish her own base. She's become protective of her turf. When her siblings or cousins criticize her, she shouts back in defense, "You do what you know and I'll do what I know. They end up leaving me alone," she says smiling broadly.

Pina doesn't budge until her work is done except sometimes to stick her nose into the kitchen. She sees her parents or her siblings during the day in passing. "My parents pretty much leave me alone." So do manager Greenberg and her immediate superior, Bennie Diasparra, her cousin and her father's nephew, who is among the most professionally trained members of this family. Bennie earned an accounting degree from C.W. Post College on Long Island and worked two years for a public accounting firm. Bennie recently computerized payroll, inventory and accounts receivable and payable.

Pina's sister, Maria, who had a baby daughter at the end of January 1988, was expected back to work shortly, though Pina says it's most likely to be on a part-time basis. "That's the way my mother did it so I don't expect her to do any differently."

Louis, known as Louie, a dark, handsome 27-year-old, is only 18 months younger than his brother Frank. His voice carries a kind of tough-guy New York savvy. Louie arrives for work at 6:00 A.M. and leaves between 3:00 and 4:00 in the afternoon. He dispatches whole-sale goods to hotels and restaurants and routes delivery vans and pickup trucks.

The routine isn't complex, Louie says, now that he has got three vans and help. "Also, our radius is limited. We deliver midtown, to the Upper East Side and uptown to between 90th and 92nd Streets. We will go to 23rd Street on the East River where we deal with a yacht club. We don't go down to Wall Street, however. It doesn't pay for me. We could lose a truck for two hours in traffic."

Deliveries stop at 3:30 P.M. "I will tell Dominic Diasparra we can't handle any more. 'Tell the girls,' I'll say, 'No more deliveries.' Most customers will say 'Okay' and hang up the phone. If they squawk, I tell the girls to have them talk to me. Eighty percent of all retail orders are delivered in the end. It's one more service Grace's Marketplace prides itself on. It's always been done and it's something we'll always have to do."

Louie has plans to capture all the business at Kennedy Airport. "We have another 21-foot-long truck we intend to send to the hotels and restaurants out there. It will go from Hunt's Point Market to Kennedy and back each day," he explains.

In addition to expanding the wholesale business, Louie would like to take over Greenberg's job. "Someone has to be able to jump into his shoes. I can see me doing that. He's training me for it."

Louis Balducci, patriarch of the clan, arrives at the store. He and his wife shuttle between their children's stores. He's greeted fondly as he walks past the bread department. Everybody recognizes him, including many customers. His features are distinctive—animated eyes, jowls flanking prominent teeth and a full head of wavy white hair.

He slowly walks down the stairs and settles into a simple wooden chair in a basement-level office. His grandchildren and long-time employees come in to say hello and kiss him as he holds court. He chats about the old days, intermittently mumbling, growling and coughing. Grace stops by to ask about her mother, shaking her mane of black curly hair.

The youngest Doria children, Dino and Joe Jr., show up at the store like their older siblings did, after they finish school in the afternoon. They've come to help. They saunter into the office where their grandfather waits.

Frank shows up too, checking on everyone and the action. He seems the heir apparent because he is the eldest son. But Frank's ties to the family are not so strong as those of his siblings. He was the first child to move out of the house. "I could not deal with the store 24 hours a day," he said. "Too many heated and intense discussions. I love my grandparents a ton. After all, they helped raise me when my folks were at the store, which was tough since there were six of us so close in age."

Frank seems sure of himself. He was the last to join the business. He never intended to go into it. He wanted to coach football, though never seriously, especially after he got sidetracked because of a serious football injury during his college days at Purdue University. He views himself as the outsider looking in. He studied business and management and glibly says, "Not one thing I learned applies to really operating a business like this." Because Frank closes the store, he sets his own schedule.

In the beginning, Frank became the "odds and ends man," according to his wife Katia, French Canadian by birth, whom he met at the downtown store when she was trying to earn extra money to put herself through New York University where she studied ballet. "I was a little nervous at first about going out with the boss's son. But the real change was marrying into such a large family. I had like maybe three family members to invite to the wedding; Frank had more than 200."

When the new store opened, Katia started in catering. She soon took over the locked "Money Room," another of the small closet-sized cubicles on the store's lower level where money has to be counted daily. Frank and Katia's paths rarely cross during the day. "She's downstairs usually and I'm upstairs."

Although Frank took over managing the floor, which involves answering queries and being sure there's enough food in every department, he's decided that he should be the troubleshooter. "It's up to me not to close my eyes to anything. If there's a shortage of people in a department, I'll jump right in behind the counter. If a truck needs to be loaded and we're short staffed, I'll do it rather than see my dad out in the cold."

Joe and Grace pack up to go home. It's Friday, the beginning of another weekend. Grace carries a wicker hamper bulging with dinner for that night—two red snappers, clam sauce, broccoli di rabe, dry cavatelli, roasted red peppers and fresh fruit. All the family will again dine together, except for Frank and Katia who head out for a movie and Chinese food. Even Maria, who's expecting a baby, will be there.

Traffic at the corner of Third Avenue and 71st Street has waned except for a few last-minute customers coming home late from work and those wanting food after seeing a movie at the Loews Tower East across the street.

The curtain is about to fall for the evening on "Grace's Marketplace." Doors are locked at 8:30 P.M. Frank wraps leftover food, sweeps the floor and checks the registers. Caesar Linares, the floor manager, switches out the lights at 10:00 P.M., turning off life in the store which a few hours ago was alive with the glitz, noise and energy of a major production.

Outside, the moon grows brighter illuminating the shop, now shrouded in silence and darkness. The kitchen, which had been cleaned and hosed down in the late afternoon, is eerily quiet, a lifeless, dark echo chamber.

Tomorrow the curtain will rise again on the same production. Players will return to their positions. The store will come alive.

Joe and Grace Doria and their children are now rehearsing their lines for the third act of this three-generation family drama, which will center around the younger generation taking over. To succeed, however, they must have the right script.

Third Act

Togetherness, especially in a physically grueling business that operates from early morning until late at night seven days a week, has created a tough family business for the Dorias. Family members have little time to pursue other interests. Most conversation focuses on the day's goings-on.

Says Pina, "If Dad has something to say, he'll either tell one of us or maybe gather us together if he can find us. Sunday is the day we all get together, but then we try not to talk about business. At Christmas, which is another time we try not to talk shop, we talked about all the flaws that we hadn't had time to talk about the rest of the year. Unfortunately, problems aren't easily ironed out this way."

But perhaps the most important and underlying reasons for a potential second rift is that Grace and Joe don't realize that while they may pass on their business to their children, they cannot bequeath the love, feeling and hard work needed to keep it going.

Joe, Grace and their scions are determined to keep this family business a long-running hit.

Epilogue

On Thursday, August 11, 1988, Louis Balducci Sr. died of leukemia at the age of 89. The funeral, a mass of Christian Burial, was held at St. Andrew Avellino R.C. Church the following Tuesday at 9:30 A.M. Internment followed at Mt. Saint Mary's Cemetery. He is survived by his wife, Maria, and two sons—Charles and Andrew—a daughter, Grace Doria, 17 grandchildren and six great-grandchildren. The funeral did not bring the siblings together, according to one close observer who attended. "Everything is the same. There was no reconciliation."

On monday, April 3, 1989, Maria Balducci died of complications from a stroke at her home in Queens. She was 89. Her funeral also did not reunite the siblings, said an observer.

Dillard Department Stores Inc.
Little Rock, AR

Four miles from the tree-lined suburbs of Little Rock, long after big black Cadillacs and fancy country clubs give way to an odd collage of pickups and trailer parks, historic landmarks and sleek skyscrapers, is the headquarters of Dillard Department Stores Inc., the nation's largest family-run, publicly owned department store chain, smack in the center of downtown.

The four-story office building on West Capitol Avenue, six blocks from the state capitol, is as plain as William T. Dillard, 73, founder, chairman and chief executive of Dillard's. The boxy, beige-colored brick building blends into the barren landscape on a dreary day in May of 1988. Only a three-foot-high sign on the front indicates that these are the executive offices. The building abuts an asphalt parking lot enclosed by a chain link fence and faces a cheap diner.

"I don't think success has to change people. Look at Sam Walton, the head of Wal-Mart Stores. He still drives a red pickup truck. I'm no different from the way I've always been," explains Dillard in his soft-spoken twang. A large and portly man whose face is broad and fleshy with dark-ringed powerful eyes that stare out from tortoise shell-rimmed glasses, he is frequently spotted in his company's parking lot on Saturday mornings, dressed in suit and tie, hosing dirt and dust off his car.

But don't let appearances or Dillard's grandfatherly smile and slow gait fool you. He is no starry-eyed country boy. Dillard's an unlikely combination of bluegrass and blueblood, with a flair for retailing and making money. He's made millions by transforming his original one-man, one-store Dillard's into one of the country's fastest growing retail chains and into a public company with a staff of 21,000 and annual sales of $2.6 billion. Growth has been among the best in retailing between 1982 and 1987, averaging 25.4 percent in sales and 33.7 percent in gross income. Dillard has upped his salary to a hefty $1.1 million. He and other family members hold 98.7 percent of the outstanding voting stock of W.D. Co. Inc. The shares control two-thirds of the votes for company directors, which guarantees family control.

Dillard loves every minute of his success. He's chauffeured around town in a 560 SEL Mercedes-Benz. His home, known around town as the "Dillard Mansion" and estimated to be worth $1 million, is a three-story white colonial on one of the city's best streets, less than one mile from the Little Rock Country Club where the Dillards belong. Come summer, Dillard and his wife, the former Alexa Latimer, weekend at their Hot Springs house. Formerly, they vacationed at a home in Mexico that they sold. Dillard loves to travel for pleasure throughout the world and possesses an encyclopedic knowledge of geography.

Into the lobby of Dillard's executive headquarters and the contrasts of the owner's fantastic success versus the unpretentiousness of his surroundings become more pronounced. Walls of rough white plaster, crude wooden trim, painted iron railings. Past a security guard and up an uncarpeted institutional looking flight of stairs that appears to lead nowhere. Down a dark and dank narrow hallway lined with drawings of many of the Dillard stores.

Then, as if on cue, wide double glass doors swing open to a large and brightly colored corporate suite. Here two secretaries screen visitors and phone calls. But this is only a prelude. To the right is Dillard's office, an enormous expanse of antique rugs and deep-cushioned leather couches and wing chairs, richly paneled walls covered with plaques, framed newspaper and magazine articles, maps and travel books offering an almost chronological vignette of his 50 years as a retailer during which he became part of a power clique of the country's most elite retail and shopping center giants: Edward J. DeBartolo from Youngstown, Ohio; Melvin and Herbert Simon from Indianapolis; David Farrell from St. Louis.

Acclaim has come only recently to Dillard for several reasons. He remains an Ozark country boy at heart, the son of small-town Southern shopkeepers. He's a man who was content to keep a low profile and shun the limelight. His 150-store empire in 13 states didn't emanate from the typical epicenter of a major East or West Coast metropolis. Instead, the chain grew up slowly in the quiet fringes of the Central and Southwestern states and from competitors' failing or lackluster stores. Few retail observers could have predicted how big Dillard Department Stores' reach would become.

Then almost overnight Dillard's success became too dazzling to ignore. In the fiscal year ending January 28, 1989, the chain posted net income after taxes of $113.8 million. It has been ranked among the top five chains in square footage and sales dollars percentage gains, and become a darling of Wall Street analysts. Dillard's stock, listed on the American Stock Exchange, is frequently recommended by analysts as "a buy."

The chain's meteoric rise and Dillard's financial wizardry have pushed him to move on a faster track. He's hitting bigger cities like Cleveland and acquiring better known and healthier chains such as Higbee Co., all with the tenacity of a shopper on the trail of a hot bargain. Most recently, Dillard has set his sights again on Nebraska because of the good demographics. The company bought two Miller & Paine stores in Lincoln and one in Grand Island. By the end of 1988, three Dillard stores debuted in shopping centers in Omaha, Council Bluffs, and El Paso.

Dillard hasn't become successful alone, however. He's had major input from his wife, Alexa, whose father owned a combination hardware-furniture-funeral business. From the late '40s through the '70s, she advised and helped her husband in his business and operated it while he served in the Navy during World War II. Also providing input are his five children, aged 30 to 42, all considered highly qualified by industry observers. The five have assumed management positions and three are on the company's board, a rarity in the retail industry where many of the founding families of today's big chains have sold out because of poor succession plans, fierce competition or a golden opportunity to make millions. Gone are the Mays from May Department Stores Co. in St. Louis, the Fields from Marshall Field's in Chicago, the Gimbels from Gimbel's in New York, and the Rosenwalds from Sears, Roebuck & Co. in Chicago.

But much of the credit for Dillard's success should go to E. Ray Kemp, his professional manager during the last 25 years, now vice chairman of the board and chief administrative officer.

In the early years, while Dillard was out scouting the field, attending a whirlwind series of private meetings with retailers and developers, perusing his sizable holdings and relying on his instincts to expand, Kemp quietly stayed back at corporate headquarters and crunched numbers, analyzed acquisitions and lined up capital at private meetings to be sure that potential deals were smart and feasible.

A tall, ruddy-faced, warm and congenial man, Kemp at 63 long has relished his role as the boss's spokesman and loyal lieutenant. "William sometimes takes my advice," Kemp chuckles. "And then again, sometimes he doesn't. He's constantly coming up with new ideas and seeing new angles. He goes by his instincts and makes decisions based on a good deal of information. He talks to people. He observes. He acts quickly. He doesn't dilly-dally."

Kemp is an anomaly among professional managers in small and large family businesses. Most are brought in to produce short-term profits, maintain much of the status quo and rubber-stamp the boss's decision. They are well compensated in order to be snared and retained, but their salaries don't come close to that of their boss or that of his heirs. Many managers leave out of frustration. Often they don't have enough power or are excluded from succession plans. In fact, two-thirds of all family businesses have no written strategic plans and 63 percent have no annual budget according to a study by the American Management Association and Laventhol & Horwath, the accounting firm.

Kemp was brought in to introduce new accounting systems and was later allowed to make changes without the pressure of producing short-term results. "When you're working for a business that has to make figures every quarter, you sometimes make foolish decisions," Kemp explains. "You have to show stockholders you're making money. But a new store isn't always going to make money right away. It is going to be a drag for one or two years. A lot of corporate managers can't do that because they don't want the setback. Our people know that we're going to do what's best for the business long-range."

Kemp remained content in a supporting role, unthreatened by a legion of Dillard children moving into front ranks. He's been rewarded handsomely. His 1988 salary was $727,000, the third highest in the company after Dillard and Dillard's eldest son, William II, according to the company annual report. Kemp has bought 90,374 shares of Dillard's stock. "I've done very well financially and by virtue of my position with Dillard's, I certainly have received a lot of identity and respect in the community. I'm vice chairman of a hospital and I'm going to be making an address at a dinner for its 100th anniversary. It's all kind of nice," he says smiling.

Despite public perception that Dillard and Kemp are inseparable because they frequently travel together to attend store openings and check out possible acquisitions or new locations, they've never stepped beyond a professional relationship. Kemp's also sharp enough to keep his distance socially from the family. He knows that crossing the line could destroy the synergism.

Kemp's office is about 15 feet down the hall from Dillard's and is a comfortable jumble of the essential furnishings: a desk and chair, two pull-up visitors' seats and credenzas that hold reams of paper. His desk is an important nerve center with computer screens, printouts and telephones. Kemp marches in about 8:30 A.M. and immediately flips on his computer to monitor what every Dillard store sold the day before. Every sale made is fed instantaneously into a central computer and information is compiled hourly in the back of headquarters to give a readout on sales per square foot. Sales currently average $119. The information helps Kemp and Dillard make machine-gun decisions. Other data are also centralized at headquarters—accounting, finance, credit, system development, new store planning and construction, catalog and television advertising.

Little did anyone in the retailing field know how much Kemp would be ahead of his time when Dillard hired him to set up an accounting center at the company's first headquarters in Tulsa as the boss was getting ready to buy more stores. Kemp then was a formidable and well-respected certified public accountant in Texarkana, a town that straddles the Arkansas and Texas borders.

Kemp set up the accounting center in the mid-1960s. "Dillard knew he was going to build a bigger chain, though I'm sure back then he had no idea it would mushroom beyond 150 units." Dillard was impressed with Kemp's work and Kemp was impressed with Dillard's savvy. "He liked me and I liked the operations," Kemp recalls. It was a good marriage of complementary talents.

Kemp made some gutsy, courageous moves. He didn't just bring in adding machines and calculators. Computers were coming on line. They were big, clunky, complex and had little power. Few companies were buying. But Kemp's interest was piqued. He did research by attending IBM demonstrations that were geared for introducing computers rather than for selling them. He was awed by their potential and could see the long-term benefits of giving up tedious and inefficient manual record keeping.

He bought IBM 1401 computers that had a memory capacity of 2,000 bytes and took 12 hours to gather information. "Computers were the only obvious way to keep up and be able to handle vast amounts of information without tremendous and expensive clerical help." He wrote his own programs from the beginning. Today Kemp says the capacity of Dillard computers is "unfathomable."

The computers proved to be a boon, initially keeping track of customers' accounts and merchandise statistics and later analyzing inventory, sales, price changes, markups, markdowns, profits and losses. Customers' bills got sent out much quicker and money was in the Dillard stores' hands sooner.

When Dillard Department Stores moved into Little Rock in fall 1963 and bought first Pfeifer's two stores and then six months later the competing two-store Blass operation, Kemp updated the chain's computer programs to handle additional data. His foresightedness and drive caught the attention of Dillard, who rewarded him with a promotion and put him in charge of all four stores.

Dillard gave Kemp more leeway to introduce technological changes so the company could expand—not rapidly but slowly and carefully. Technologically, Kemp put Dillard's light years ahead of the competition. In 1970, when Dillard's was up to 20 stores, it outdid every other retailer electronically by adding point-of-sale cash registers which tracked sales and fed them to headquarters in a split second.

When Dillard's acquires new stores or chains, it immediately folds them into one of its five divisions and hooks them into the centralized system. Stores are restyled to reflect their new corporate culture and the name is changed to "Dillard's." The name change is done more quickly than in the past. The Stix, Baer & Fuller Co. name in St. Louis took 18 months to be phased out. The dozen R.H. Macy & Co. stores in Missouri and Kansas had their names changed in a week. Other companies have tried to copy Dillard's centralized computer system, but couldn't afford the massive changes, Kemp said. "Macy's in New

York tried to switch to our system two years ago and it's still having a lot of trouble."

Beginning in 1978, Kemp helped open distribution centers to gather merchandise from various manufacturers and then ship it quickly to individual stores. It was a way to reduce errors. "We didn't want merchandise in a warehouse long because it meant it wasn't for sale and that we were paying for goods to sit idle," he explained.

Merchandise remained in a single store rather than being moved around if it didn't sell, as most retailers did. "We thought taking the goods off the floor was a waste of money," Kemp said. "If goods didn't sell in one store, they weren't likely to sell in another. There's not much difference in buying habits of different regions in spite of what customers and some retailers say."

If merchandise sat on a floor, Dillard's buyers and supervisors had autonomy to mark it down to get rid of it. Stock options and cash bonuses as hefty as 25 percent of annual salaries became powerful sales incentives.

The same philosophy of centralizing operations pertained to the company's top management, which was given latitude but had to work within the Dillard framework. If one of the chains' five operating division heads or a corporate vice president left, in a couple of days someone else could easily assume command. Kemp believes this system would have eliminated some of the major problems Stix, based in St. Louis, had incurred. Stix's parent company, Associated Dry Goods Corp. of New York, kept changing store presidents, and each time a new leader stepped in, he restructured operations. Like Kemp, Dillard's top managers and presidents have been rewarded with generous salaries and stock options and the knowledge that promotions would occur from within.

Centralized operations also allowed for a lean operation that saved time, paperwork, labor and money. Just a handful of executives sit in Dillard's corporate suite—Dillard, Kemp and Dillard's two oldest sons, William Dillard II, nicknamed Bill, and Alex.

Today, Kemp continues to wield power even though the five Dillard children have stepped into high-level positions. Kemp knows he has the trust of his boss because he helped lead the once small proprietorship into a giant chain. He knows he has been the bridge between the first and second generations of a successful family business.

If Kemp is the unsung hero in this rags to riches saga, Dillard is the public persona who spins the dreams and who was smart enough to professionalize operations long before it was fashionable and despite his humble roots. Why was Dillard so smart? "I never had a plan. Things just happened," he modestly claims. But Dillard, now 73, was intuitive enough to know his limitations.

Dillard was the grandson and only child of the owners of a dry goods store in Mineral Springs, a one-blink junction 97 miles south of Little Rock. The population of his hometown was 777 when Dillard was born in 1915. He worked in his parents' store after school and on weekends from the time he was 12, selling everything from hardware to apparel and groceries. He knew he would pursue a career in retailing full time. "I had been born into it. My grandfather, who died when I was 10, had a country store in Center Point, AR."

Dillard's parents didn't push him into retailing, however. They encouraged him to continue his education. He became the only one of six seniors in his high school class to go on to college—the University of Arkansas, where he majored in business and accounting. The following year he received a scholarship to Columbia University's Graduate School of Business in New York where he majored in retailing.

Instead of heading home, Dillard went into a training program at Sears in Tulsa. He stayed nine months, mastered some of the nuances of retailing in a big operation, then returned to Arkansas to open his first store.

Although department stores had sprung up long before in the years between 1840 and 1860, most were in major metropolises. Marshall Field's in Chicago. Jordan Marsh in Boston. A.T. Stewart and R.H. Macy in New York. Wanamaker's in Philadelphia. Retailing in the Southwest hadn't changed much from the time Dillard left. It still was just slightly more sophisticated than selling from a country store like his parents did.

With $8,000 from his parents and the use of their good name, Dillard took the best building on Main Street in Nashville in 1938. He paid $35 a month for a 120-by-25-foot space. He knew the location was worth the price. He and three employees sold men's, women's, boys' and girls' apparel and shoes and learned to sell from a limited inventory. "You looked at the customers, determined what size they were and showed them something that you had in their size. If I'd had a big inventory then, I couldn't have turned it. I didn't have the customers."

Dillard's tactics worked and appealed to the masses. He rang up sales of $42,000 the first year. Profits hit an impressive $3,000.

Ten years later, Dillard became frustrated. He had locked up all the business. "There was a limited amount of business I could round up in a small town market." Dillard wasn't about to be left behind. He moved on to another challenge, selling the store, moving to the larger town of Texarkana, with a population of 50,000, and forming a partnership with a wealthy retailer, Tom Wooten. Six months later, Dillard bought out Wooten. "He wanted to spend more money than I thought we could afford," Dillard explained. Customers flocked.

Eight years later, in 1956, Dillard bought Tyler, Mayer & Schmidt, the leading department store in Tyler, TX. When sales materialized, he used the profits to buy the leading store in Tulsa, known as Brown-Dunkin. "It was losing money. Four banks stood to lose their investment. I got them their money back and they became my principal bankers."

Dillard slowly laid the groundwork for his basic retail strategy, though he dismisses any notion of a grandiose plan. From his new base in Tulsa, he sniffed out ailing stores in small towns and cities that other, and often bigger, retailers passed up, and he breathed life back into them with nicer displays, deeper and better inventories, more employees and greater service. He concentrated on the South and Southeast.

To generate additional capital, he sold his store in Texarkana in 1960 to Alden's in Chicago, a mail-order merchant, which would sell it back to Dillard's in 1978.

As Dillard opened more stores, he knew he should again play around with his original strategies. He quit buying stores with problems and built stores in new suburban shopping malls, which were beginning to turn up throughout the country. He believed that many downtown cities would witness a "big deterioration" and that their stores would suffer. Suburban stores were the wave of the future with free parking lots, easy access over good new roadways, pristine interiors and proximity to residential neighborhoods.

With Kemp at his side, he opened his first new store in the Hancock metropolitan suburban mall in Austin in February 1964, where Sears was the major tenant. Sears and Dillard's were ahead of their time. People talked. People came. Few bought much the first year. Then the store took off. "We knew we were on target; that we had a good leg up on our competition which wasn't ready to leave their metropolitan markets," Kemp said.

Dillard and Kemp didn't immediately rush headlong into dozens of suburban markets. They moved slowly. They opened two suburban stores in Little Rock and Tulsa in 1965. A year later, another one followed. Five years after that they were ready to step up the pace by opening several stores a year. The company went public in 1969 and used the money to fund greater expansion.

In the late 1970s as interest rates soared, Dillard wanted to slow expansion, but he and Kemp had committed to build. They didn't want to leverage the company up to its eyeballs. They decided the best tack was to find an outside investor. They talked to a number of sources and struck a deal in 1978 with Vendamerica B.V., the largest retail concern in the Netherlands with sales today of about $10 billion. The Dutch concern invested $24 million to expand Dillard's. Later, Vendamerica bought an additional $66 million of stock in Dillard and today that stake has swelled to an estimated $570 million or 41 percent. Although Dillard management has made no formal approach to buy the Vendamerica interest, there is talk that William Dillard wants to repurchase the Class A shares that Vendamerica owns. Should this happen, it would be the first major buyback of a foreign investment by an American retailer. Dr. Anton C.R. Dreesmann, former head of Vendamerica, promised Dillard that Vendamerica would remain a passive investor and agreed not to vote his stock for a takeover or sale without the Dillard family's go-ahead. But with Dr. Dreesmann's retirement in the summer of 1988, sources say that Dillard was unsettled by the news.

With money in hand from Vendamerica, a solid debt-to-equity ratio on the books and a successful network of stores, Dillard and Kemp were ready for a bigger and gutsier move. They would once again go after languishing chains rather than grab or build a store or two and they would find them in bigger cities. Opportunities cropped up in unconventional ways. In planes. Through public announcements. Through calls from anxious suitors.

In 1981, Dillard learned that the Stix chain in St. Louis was for sale when one of his seven company jets was parked at Newark Airport in New Jersey next to that of shopping center magnate Ed DeBartolo, from whom Dillard had leased shopping center space. An aircraft controllers' strike was in force and planes were backed up waiting to take off.

He knocked on the door of DeBartolo's plane. He went inside and was surprised to see Bill Arnold, the chairman of Associated Dry Goods. They chatted and less than 30 minutes later Dillard was asked if he wanted to buy Stix's 12 stores, which had been consistent money losers. The idea appealed to Dillard because of the possibility of a great price and the stores' good locations in well-respected shopping centers.

"I'll buy Stix if you throw in your Denver Dry Goods division in Colorado," Dillard said.

Bill Arnold answered "No" without hesitating.

Dillard dropped the idea of an offer until three years later, in 1984. Sales at Stix had fallen further and Associated was having a hard time keeping a chief executive on board. Dillard and Kemp took note of the patterns and Dillard's desire to expand out of the Southeast. The men phoned DeBartolo, asked him to rekindle a sale and Associated agreed on a price of $93 million. The deal was sealed in late January 1984. "If word had leaked out, we might have lost it or had to pay more. A lot of competitors' deals haven't gone through because the parties involved procrastinated," Kemp says.

The Stix transaction whetted Dillard and Kemp's appetite for more chains in more cities. By fall, they were ready to grab five John A. Brown stores in Oklahoma and 12 Diamond's in Phoenix and Las Vegas from Dayton-Hudson after reading a press release. The price was $143 million. Dillard's acquired 12 floundering Macy's stores in Missouri and Kansas in 1986 for $140 million after learning that Macy's needed cash to go private. In 1988, they bought two more chains for $255 million in cash: Joske's 27 stores in Dallas and Houston and Cain-Sloan's four stores in Nashville, both from Allied Stores. Campeau out of Toronto had bought Allied and wanted to sell some of Allied's divisions to raise capital to fund the takeover.

Once acquired, some stores were sold or liquidated. Dillard's unloaded 13 of Joske's weakest properties and a sluggish downtown Cain-Sloan unit. It liquidated the former Stix store in Jennings, MO, after struggling for years to keep it going by cutting square footage. Now Dillard's also is unloading a store in downtown Wichita. Its downtown St. Louis unit isn't doing well because of a dearth of evening traffic. But Dillard's has made a long-term commitment to keep the store open.

Some deals have been thwarted. Ten years ago, Dillard passed up the chance to buy Marshall Field's because he thought it wasn't financially prudent. He considered buying B. Altman in Manhattan, but declined because he decided its site at 34th Street was considered too far south on Fifth Avenue. In discussing Altman's, Dillard throws in one of his favorite retail truisms: Location, location, location. In the spring of 1988, he and Kemp were in New York looking to buy Federated Department Store's Lazarus and Goldsmith's chains from

Macy's if the New York retailer had outbid rival Campeau for control of Federated. Campeau won and Dillard and Kemp went home empty-handed. But they didn't sit still long. They were ready to pounce on a former Sakowitz store in Midland, TX, that became theirs in August 1988. They had previously acquired Sakowitz units and successfully transformed them into Dillard's. More recently, Dillard's reneged on the 17-store Horne's deal in Pittsburgh. The purchase price plus the dollars Dillard would have had to sink into the chain to rehab it made it financially unsound.

Dillard still would love to enter the Chicago market. "There are only two retailers of any consequence there—Field's and Carson, Pirie, Scott—and it's far from an overstored market," he says. "Neiman-Marcus and Bloomingdale's aren't a significant presence there." He's not interested, however, in the more cutthroat Northeast, Southern California and Pacific Northwest markets—unless a great opportunity materializes.

Dillard isn't enamored with specialty stores such as the Limited, Henri Bendel and Banana Republic, which promote one fad and are easy to start. "If it's a business that's easy to enter, it soon gets crowded. It takes a lot of money to go into department store retailing—between $150 and $200 a square foot. A typical 200,000-square-foot store costs between $3.5 and $4 million," Dillard estimates, calculating the costs on yellow legal pads.

With stores in place, Dillard puts other retail axioms to work: "There's enough business for everyone in a market." "You can't sell apples from an empty wagon."

When Dillard's moved into St. Louis to take over Stix, Dillard said there was no reason why his competitor, May Co.'s Famous-Barr, should have a corner on the market. Four years after the acquisition, Dillard's has gained a larger market share. "Famous has felt our presence because we're much more aggressive than Stix. Famous is still the dominant retailer—and it will be for the foreseeable future. But we've gotten to be a healthier No. 2," Dillard says.

When he took over Stix, Dillard stuffed the empty counters and aisles with brand-name merchandise. "Associated was a good operator, but it ran its stores light on goods," Kemp said. The area's Galleria store in Richmond Heights, he feels, has been the top performing unit in the entire Dillard's chain since it was salvaged and remodeled at a cost of about $8 million. "The Zorensky family bought the mall from us, made a major overhaul and we decided to bring our store up to their standards. We thought the Galleria could be the pacesetter for St. Louis." The Galleria has also brought a new image to the chain, which used to be described as a Plain Jane. The Galleria store's atmosphere is instant luxe—acres of beige aggregate marble, gigantic chrome mirrors reflecting bright lights and ornate wooden display cases.

Like Macy's, one of the few retail chains he admires, Dillard has emphasized giving customers their money's worth. "More than anything else that motivates people to shop one store over another is having confidence in that business and believing that what they're buying is worth what they're paying." Dillard's caters to consumers making average- and above-average incomes. It's in the middle-to-high-middle merchandise category. "I don't think the consumer gets value or a broad selection at a store like Neiman-Marcus," Dillard says.

Other bait Dillard has used to lure customers includes good service. He doesn't think his chain is in the same league as Nordstrom's of Seattle, another family retail chain, although Dillard's has put more sales help on its floors than most other department store competitors. William has been overheard telling his troops, "We aim to give good service and it's not much worse than anybody else's." He's also been known to say, "At Sears you really have to make an appointment to get a sales person to take your money. If you do a reasonably good job of offering service, you'll increase your sales a lot."

These days Dillard spends half his time in his office. He ambles in about 9:00 A.M. in a perfectly tailored dark suit, starched white shirt and tie. He carries himself tall and proud.

The rest of his time he visits his stores. Kemp used to accompany the boss, but now stays back in company headquarters so that Dillard's two eldest sons can travel with their father, learn the ropes and become known to employees out in the field. From Thanksgiving through Christmas, the Dillards trek through every store. Last year, they missed only one store, the unit in Flagstaff, because a company jet couldn't land in bad weather. Dillard never pops into stores unannounced. "Employees recognize me. I don't want to surprise them. I don't think that's fair," he says speaking slowly and revealing his polite Southern roots. "But, I don't give them much notice, maybe 24 hours," he adds.

In spite of Dillard's down-home demeanor, he craves public adulation. A few years ago his hometown organized a country-wide day for him. "It was thrilling," he said, eyes twinkling. "One girl and one boy from my highschool class were there. The whole town turned out."

Five years ago, Dillard again was the center of attention at the University of Arkansas, his alma mater. He endowed a chair. The school awarded him an honorary doctorate at graduation. Dillard beams as he relates the details and slowly walks over to a bookshelf in his office and pulls out the certificate encased in a red folder. "Look at this. Isn't it wonderful? This is what working hard is all about."

The president of Columbia University in New York and the dean of its business school, where Dillard completed graduate school, heard about the endowed chair at Arkansas and paid Dillard a visit. "They came looking for money," he chortles. "I knew exactly why they were here." But Dillard is too shrewd a shopkeeper to give something away for nothing. "So I showed them my honorary Arkansas degree. Wouldn't you know it, both of the Columbia heads smiled, looked at me and one turned to the other and said, 'We get the message.'

"Anybody who gets in my position likes recognition from the right sources," Dillard explains unabashedly.

When it came to understanding the business, the five Dillard children learned from an early age by watching their father and Kemp in action. The training had to be handled right. Dillard had just built an empire. He wanted to protect it and pass it on. Under Kemp's tutelage, Dillard knew his children would be viewed objectively. "There wasn't a thing they could learn from anyone else. I believe everyone of them could have gotten to the same point even if their names had been something other than Dillard. I made it possible for them to get the experience but they're all capable."

While many professional managers have a tough go working with young scions, Kemp's job was simplified by heirs who had a deep interest in the family business, who had forged a strong relationship with their parents and each other, and who were as healthy and uncomplicated as a 100 percent markup. Dillard and sons Bill and Alex and their families live on the same street. Dillard's other son, Mike, and daughters, Drue Corbusier and Denise, come to visit frequently. They spend Christmas as a family, fishing and vacationing. The siblings frequently take trips together.

The Dillards rally for family crises. On a recent weekday, Dillard rushed to finish his work so he could leave the next day for Columbia Presbyterian Medical Center in New York where Alexa would undergo surgery for a broken shoulder. Drue and Denise would accompany him and "the boys" would follow. Kemp would remain in Little Rock to keep the business humming and pinch-hit where needed. He would fend off queries from Dillard's division presidents, store managers, manufacturers, buyers, bankers and stock analysts, and colleagues and friends anxious to learn how Mrs. Dillard was faring.

To insure family harmony, Dillard and Kemp have given each scion a specific bailiwick so that they avoid competition. They rarely have to meet as a group. They are in constant touch when they need to discuss major issues. The boys refer to Dillard as "William" and the girls calling him "Daddy."

Bill, 42, president and chief operating officer and a member of the board, runs the operations end of the business and earns $797,000 annually. He has solid credentials: a B.A. from the University of Arkansas in business and accounting and an MBA from Harvard. He developed an intense interest in the business when he was young. Dillard brought him to the office and he learned by walking around the corridors and into the various offices with his dad and Kemp. The men took Bill on business trips. He heard his father and mother talk shop at home. Bill never considered working elsewhere.

He started as his father's administrative assistant and worked his way up to his current position because he's the oldest. He makes short-term policy decisions such as deciding whether to put in a Polo shop department or to build an entire store, even if the tab runs to $5 million. He'd go to his father, however, to get approval on a major decision like spending $40 million to buy several stores. Like his father, Bill makes decisions quickly.

Unlike his father, he quickly moved into a public role and has become a good front man as the company attracts more attention. He's forged deep roots in Little Rock, the state's largest city, which had its reputation deeply wounded when the late Gov. Orval E. Faubus block-ed desegregation of the city's Central High School in 1957, shortly after the Dillards moved to town. Bill likes going out with community leaders and entertaining visiting vendors. He also enjoys traveling with important clients. Recently Bill and his wife, Mandy, took a European vacation with personal friends John and Laura Pomerantz, heads of Leslie Fay, a large apparel manufacturer.

Alex, 38, executive vice president and a board member, thinks Bill is a carbon copy of their father. "He's a gambler like Dad. I'm much more cautious. I might be a little slower in pushing growth. I'd like to make the stores as profitable as possible."

Alex prefers to remain in the background, often tagging along with his father and Kemp for lunch and chauffeuring them around.

On a recent weekday, the triumvirate is off to a favorite downtown fast-food sandwich shop, driving past the state capitol building, the Razorback football stadium and the Park Plaza shopping mall, where they pull in to check out construction where Dillard's is the anchor at both ends, a fitting symbol of the family's prominence in the community.

"I'm surprised that your family stayed in Little Rock. I expected you to relocate to Dallas 10 years ago, after we opened stores in 1979," Kemp says. "I was ready to bet on that pretty strongly, but now I don't think so. You all seem real entrenched in the community."

Alex agrees and says that he's glad to be back in Little Rock after spending nine years in Texas where he received his law degree and worked for Dillard's as a vice president. Shortly after Alex entered the family business, he was moved back to Texas when the chain acquired six stores from Tandy and opened some new units. To handle the workload, Dillard decided somebody had to move to Texas and pull together the division. Alex replays the scenario:

"William said, 'I'm too important in Little Rock. I can't go.' "

"My brother Bill said, 'I'm married. I can't move.' "

"Kemp said, 'I'm pretty important here. It wouldn't make sense to move me.' "

"My father came back to me and said, 'Oh, you,' referring to me, 'You're not married. You're the one who can move.' He wanted me to work there two to three days a week, but it's impossible. You can't live in two places. William told me, 'You'll get the merger straightened out in six to 12 weeks.' I did it for six weeks, but that's not the way it works. It's like a battleship. You can't turn around a big operation like that in one movement. I stayed nine years and I'm glad in retrospect. When I went down there were 12 stores, then 14. When I left, we had between 36 and 40. I got a chance to do it myself. The incentive was enormous to prove myself."

Alex came back and now earns $720,000. As he sits in his small office, he is dwarfed by an enormous desk and a four-screen computer terminal with simultaneous sessions. A contingent from the Levi Strauss manufacturing company in San Francisco walks by. They're in town to meet with Bill to try to improve their firm's marketing position.

Alex admits working with family can be "challenging" at times. "There's a lot of rivalry between Bill and me and the rest of the family." Kemp helps arbitrate.

"We all think we've got the right idea and we have a lot of battles. It's really the subtlety of the way each of us wants to do a deal rather than a big difference of opinion. We get mad, but I consider my brothers reasonably intelligent and able at working through these problems," he laughs.

Alex recalls the time he wanted to change a store manager. Bill didn't want to. Alex knew it would be hard to pull rank on his older sibling, but he decided to try.

"Bill, I'm in charge. It's in my territory, and I think I should be able to make the change."

"I'm the merchandise manager of all the stores. It's my decision. That's final. The end," Bill shot back.

What happened?

"We settled," Alex said, "by changing the manager."

Mike, 37, is an executive vice president in charge of the company's most profitable Little Rock operating division and a board member. He earns $607,000. Drue, 41, a vice president of merchandising in the Fort Worth division, is considered the company's best merchandise manager by her father. Denise, 30, is a divisional merchandise manager in Little Rock. Neither of the girls sits on the board. When questioned why they've been excluded, Dillard says, "I probably should put them on the board, but I haven't. No claims have been made yet."

Alex thinks somewhere down the line Drue might serve on the board, but for now she's more involved in rearing a family and lives too far away. Denise, Alex says, is too young and inexperienced.

Jim G. Farmer, Alex's fraternity brother and now an executive with Mark Twain Bank Shares in St. Louis, says it delights him to see two generations of Dillards working together. "It's a family that should be in business together. Each Dillard shares a common goal: to build a family dynasty and not let anything get in its way. The parents have done an exemplary job with their children. Many families when they reach the financial level of the Dillards get into power struggles and family factions form. Oh, sure, I've seen them have disagreements. But they have healthy debates. They get it out and make a healthy decision."

Although the family doesn't always agree, they always march to-gether.

The Dillard family and Kemp, their professional manager, envision the chain becoming even larger by sticking to its current strategy. Dillard and Kemp acknowledge that the company will have to put on the brakes in order to maintain a good balance between equity and debt. The company's balance sheet is considered relatively conserva-tive with long-term debt at 34 percent of total capital at the end of 1987. A recent way to reduce debt has been to join forces with DeBartolo's shopping center company. Together, they bought the Higbee chain.

Such partnerships, the unity, strength and healthiness of qualified family members and its solid long-term relationship with a non-family manager who professionalized operations and trained the heirs have given this family business the leverage to wait out downturns in the industry and maintain family control.

"We've had offers from May and Macy's but turned them down," Dillard explains to a group of shopping center developers gathered in one of two of the company's board rooms. "We're in this for long term. I've been thrilled working with Ray. I'm also pleased with my family and their contributions to the business. I've had no reason to be disappointed. There are no scandals. No drugs. No alcoholism. All have been good students. What can I say? The only reason I'm still in the business is because of my children. If you don't grow, you wither away. You can't stand still."

The gradual transfer of power in this dynastic succession has been smooth, similar to the growth of the company. Its division of power and stock ownership should prevent any internecine wars in the coming generations as long as the next generation follows the same succession formula that its father adhered to.

Kemp takes it all in. He's helped get the company on a firm footing. He's confident about the next generation and he's financially secure. He's considering retiring when he turns 65 in two years.

But Ray Kemp won't sit idle. Ironically, he plans to go to work for his eldest son, Bill, 37, also a certified public accountant, who opened his own firm. "It worked well for the Dillards. At least when I get into this family business, I'll know what I'm getting into."

Bixler's
Easton, PA

It is a far, far better thing that I do than I have ever done; it is a far, far better rest that I go to than I have ever known.

—*A Tale of Two Cities*
CHARLES DICKENS

On October 2, 1727, young Christian Bixler set sail for America aboard *The Adventure*. He emigrated from his native Bern, Switzerland, via Rotterdam to Philadelphia in order to seek his fortune. When Bixler landed in America, he faced the landscape of a new country and the challenge of making his way. But Bixler brought with him his craft as a silversmith and clockmaker.

Today, more than 260 years later, his descendants, Philip Mitman, 43, and Philip's sister, Joyce Welken, 40, run Bixler's, the business started by their great-great-great-great-great grandfather. The company is in its eighth generation and is reputed to be the oldest jewelry firm in the country. It is now based in Easton, PA, a small, slow-paced college town of 26,000 with a rich history. Phil describes Easton and other small towns as places to treasure as carefully as you treasure family and friends.

Easton is the first city across the Pennsylvania line from New Jersey.

78

Even Easton's most vocal supporters play up the city's proximity to attractions beyond its borders. The Pocono Mountains 40 miles away. New York's Broadway 90 minutes door to door. Wall Street only slightly farther, making Easton an attractive bedroom community for up-and-comers seeking cheaper housing and lower taxes than in New Jersey suburbs. The fast-growing Newark International Airport can be reached in one hour from interstate highways.

On the surface, Bixler's hasn't changed much since Christian I set up the initial family business in Reading, PA, because of that city's burgeoning community of silversmiths, clockmakers and jewelers. He opened a shop stocked with handcrafted wares and fabric.

But the company's internal organization has been altered drastically in the current generation by a young sandy-haired, blue-eyed, charismatic president who is outspoken in his conviction to keep his family business downtown and thriving. His ideas flow nonstop. He recruits young, aggressive employees. He sells fashion jewelry. He provides old-fashioned service and offers employees merchandise discounts, profit sharing and the chance to earn national jewelry accreditation licenses as a way to become part of an extended family. His strategies are working. Bixler's has become a $3 million-a-year, three-store chain.

Phil and his sister, a vice president, made a clean break from the prior generation. They have also adopted a formal plan to ensure family control. Spouses have no say in business decisions. They hold no equity. Successive generations will be required to follow the same pattern.

"Healthy firms are notable for their humane treatment of relatives and employees, ability to cope with day-to-day projects and their strong ties to the community," says Ivan S. Lansberg, assistant professor of organizational behavior at the Yale School of Organization and Management and editor-in-chief of *The Family Business Review*, a journal published by the Family Firm Institute in Johnstown, NY, and Jossey-Bass Publishers of San Francisco.

A healthy workplace usually reflects healthy family relationships. On the other hand, many unhealthy families do not break the cycle of unhappiness and pass it on to the next generation, says Florence Kaslow, clinical psychologist and director of the Florida Couples and Family Institute in West Palm Beach. "Frequently, parents will lure their children into the business by overpaying them and starting them at the top. It's a way of keeping offspring on a tight leash. The children find it difficult to break away because they become used to a certain income and lifestyle which they may not be able to duplicate on the open market."

That wasn't the case with the Bixler clan and Bixler's, which developed a way of separating family and business systems so that some boundaries were established while communications also were kept open. The culture of the business evolved with each new generation—appropriate to the times, the people and the market.

Companies are not born great. They grow great and so it is with Bixler's. The tradition started in 1785 when the business was in its second generation. Changes had to be made to keep the family trade prospering, as the Bixler tribe increased. After returning from the Revolutionary War, Christian III moved his family to Easton, a booming economic center at the confluence of the Delaware and Lehigh rivers, founded just 33 years before, in 1792 by John Penn, son of William Penn.

Christian III, newly married, eased into the family trade. He served as an apprentice under John Keim, a master clockmaker. He supported his family by making and repairing clocks and silver in his small home at the northeast corner of Northampton and Bank Streets.

Christian III crafted 465 clocks between 1784 and 1812, according to an original ledger. Tallcase clocks were in demand and cost 38 pounds, six shillings and eight pence and a "quit rent of one barley corn, payable on the 5th day of March, each year, forever thereafter, if demanded," according to a fragmentary family history.

Soon the Bixler clocks fell out of favor. Cheaper Yankee clocks made with wood instead of brass movements became the rage. Christian III made more coin silver pieces. Business picked up and he became an active member of the community—a founder of its library, a fire fighter, the mayor. He died in 1811 and is buried in the basement crypt of St. John's Lutheran Church on Ferry Street in downtown Easton.

Sons followed fathers into business. Using basically the same approach as their father, Christian III's sons William and Daniel L. Bixler joined forces to form W. & D.L. Bixler, but after a few years parted ways. Both learned two important lessons in running a family business—it must change and grow with each new generation and too much family in a business may cause friction.

Daniel took control of his father's shop. Daniel's sons, Rush and C.

Willis Bixler, ran what became known as W.W. Bixler & Co. It was reputed to be a fine shop and the sons added popular Victorian jewelry styles of the day such as pocket watches and enameled pieces.

William formed a new shop, Bixler and Fox, which closed after his son's death.

Arthur Brookfield Bixler, the gentle, dour and apathetic grandfather of the current owners, took control about 1908 when his father, C. Willis Bixler, died. He named the store A.B. Bixler Co. The town was thriving. By the early 1920s, five major railroads brought passengers and cargo into the city daily. Early industrialists from Alpha Portland Cement built imposing stone, brick and clapboard Victorian homes and mansions in a neighborhood called College Hill, which overlooked Easton's shops and restaurants. In 1923, the city had one of the country's highest per-capita incomes. Almost a decade later, Easton became home to Lafayette College, a liberal arts and engineering school that dominated the Hill.

Arthur knew the Hill's residents who became his customers. He had the reputation of being a gentleman and a well respected craftsman. But Arthur slowly lost interest in running the store. His lethargy became legendary. He became seriously ill and more withdrawn. Also the onslaught of the Depression meant fewer people had money to buy fancy jewelry and silverware. Customers rarely stopped by. Arthur could be seen through the shop window sitting in a chair, getting up and ambling across the room to turn the lights on only when a customer came in. He instituted few changes. The business almost died with him in 1945.

Arthur Bixler's heirs, a wife, two daughters and their husbands, expressed no interest in running the store. One son-in-law, Charles T. Murphy, was a college professor at Oberlin in Ohio. The other, Kenneth Mitman, worked in the defense department of Western Electric in New Jersey. The business would have to be sold.

At Arthur's funeral, Aunt Clara, a senior member of the clan, took Kenneth Mitman aside and begged him to salvage the business. "There's no one else to carry on," she lamented. "I don't know anything about the business," Ken replied. Nevertheless, he and Kathryn "Kitty" Bixler, his wife, went home to debate the job. After several days, Ken made his decision. They were young enough to accept the gamble.

Both Ken and Kitty liked going back home to Easton and to their families. Ken was attracted by the prospect of having control of a business. The odds of succeeding were hardly in their favor. There was just $2,800 in the store's checking account. Bills totaled $3,200. They had little inventory and no cash to add to it. Ken knew nothing about selling jewelry. His wife knew less. Her father never discussed business at home.

The early years were tough. Ken and Kitty skimped and saved, sold their second-hand Ford and borrowed Ken's father's 1948 Buick. Ken took a pay cut to $100 a week. The jewelry business couldn't support that salary. He cut his pay to $75.

Yet Ken loved a challenge. Trained as an engineer, he was a man of systems and discipline who brought order to the store. He made a plan. He made lists. He did calculations in his head and on paper. No relatives interfered. He cleaned up the store and filled the cases with the best affordable merchandise. Main Line Easton customers, who had been shopping at Freeman and Appel in nearby Allentown, talked about the new look and service at Bixler's. They bought. More sales meant Ken could add inventory, open new departments such as a bridal registry and hire help.

Ken professionalized the business by becoming a member of the American Gem Society and expected his buyers to become registered gemologists. Company sales grew steadily from $92,000 in 1946 to $212,000 in 1956. The Mitmans put money aside to build a house and help support Kitty's mother.

As business improved, Ken carried on the family tradition of civic involvement as President of the Merchants' Association, President of the Chamber of Commerce, President of the United Fund and Vice President of the American Gem Society.

In the late 1950s, Ken generated enough profits to remodel the store—drop the ceiling and build a new front—and to borrow to buy new inventory. In 1966, he acquired an adjoining shoe store, doubling Bixler's square footage to 4,500.

Bixler's became Easton's downtown gift center, the epitome of a full-service jewelry store. The store was redesigned to keep traffic flowing. Jewelry shined in its own section in the store and was aligned in glass cases by rows on velvet fabric like candy in a gourmet chocolate shop. Up front were the diamond engagement rings, wedding bands and pearls. To the left watch cases were crammed full of expensive Swiss timepieces. The addition became the gift gallery. All together there were 10 departments.

Kitty began working in the business after Joyce, her younger child, graduated from high school. Ken and Kitty talked about the business at home. It was fun for Phil and Joyce to sit around the dinner table with their parents hearing the day's anecdotes. They couldn't wait to help in the store. Phil was initiated into the business in high school. He unpacked merchandise in the basement, learned to engrave jewelry and made deliveries. But the senior Mitmans never pressured their children to enter the business full-time. "It's no fun to work at something if you don't like it," Kitty constantly told her children. Ken wisely advised, "Try life outside the family firm before you come into it."

When Phil went off to nearby Gettysburg College at 18, he was cocky and unsure about life and his future. He was a good student and excelled at sports whether playing football or soccer. Going into the family business seemed the furthest thing from his mind.

After graduating in 1965, Phil took a $6,000 job in Sears, Roebuck & Co.'s management training program in Allentown, a larger city of 115,000. At Sears, he learned about personnel and what motivates employees. He learned you can't run a department or a business by yourself. He worked with many types of people.

It was a glistening time of big malls in which Sears and other retailers built stores. The malls attracted shoppers and sightseers in droves. The attractions were ample parking, dozens of shops under one roof and daily entertainment. Phil was intrigued but found himself caught between the responsibility of working for someone else and the freedom of working for himself and his family in a small town.

After three years with Sears, Phil came home, lured by a chance to work with his father, have a greater say in a business, continue a family tradition and get involved in Easton's civic life. His experiences at college and training at Sears had given him a new perspective. Phil was also now married to the former Antonia Barriga, nicknamed Toni, and they were ready to settle down.

Bixler's, too, was undergoing change. The store was housed at a far corner of the city's Centre Square in a three-story 150-year-old green and white Victorian building with an Italianate carved cornice and spires rising like hats in the air. The company name was inscribed boldly across the front in gold script. It was one block from its original site and right behind a bronze statue of General Marquis De Lafayette, the French Revolutionary war hero who fought for American independence. The statue loomed large as a symbol of downtown Easton.

Phil's father was impressed by his son's retail training and paid him well. Ken handled finances while Phil took charge of merchandising, promotion and advertising. He liked the work. His father liked having him there. Both liked the town and became adamant about not seeing it destroyed. But downtown Easton was turning into a ghost town of empty storefronts. Bixler's became an anachronism as most of its competitors exited their quaint downtown locations to resettle in suburban centers.

It was a vicious circle and there were fewer reasons for the city's affluent residents to venture downtown, except to make a specific purchase at Bixler's or visit one of the handful of remaining stores and restaurants. Phil questioned staying, but his father was vehemently opposed to moving into a mall. "What's the point of having developers dictate your hours, take a percent of your sales and send your hard-earned tax dollars to an owner in another state?" Ken rhetorically asked his son.

Easton further deteriorated into a small hamlet jammed with charred and abandoned homes and businesses. The Mitmans kept their business alive, though it proved hard. By the end of the 1970s, Easton sank deeper into a scene of smashed windows, dangling doors and caved-in roofs. The city's main department store, Pomeroy's, closed. Easton was headed for the national scrap heap.

Phil became outraged with all the talk about saving the town. Nothing was done. A Republican, he decided to run for mayor against the incumbent Democrat in 1979. His parents were torn. Ken worried about the effect on the business with Phil away. But at the same time Ken told Phil he wouldn't stop him. Although Ken wanted to retire, he agreed to stay in the business if Phil won the election. The family let Phil draw a retainer from the business, if he won to help supplement the mayor's modest $25,000 salary.

Phil's wife Toni was his biggest booster. She had grown up in the historic city of Gettysburg, 140 miles away, and her parents had restored the family's 1840 "Wildwood" home, which had been destroyed during the Civil War.

Phil proved to be a skilled ringmaster at gathering people into his circle. He knew how to work a room. He piled up good deeds like a banker piles up valued deposits. Family. Friends. Neighbors. He pumped men's hands. Kissed women's cheeks. Held babies. He spent $10,000 on the campaign, the most ever spent. When the meager 6,400 votes were cast and counted on the November night in 1979, Phil won by a slim margin of 392.

With Phil away, Ken turned to Joyce, his daughter, to take on more responsibility. Joyce had come into the business after working as a bank teller. But she never earned her father's total confidence. He kept telling her the business was too much for one person, especially a woman, to handle. Ken began to rely more on Mike Snoke, the young cocksure manager he had hired in 1972 from Hess's, then a two-store department operation in Allentown.

In the meantime, Mayor Mitman and his backers worked long and hard to reverse Easton's downfall. Phil crusaded to rebuild the city and keep the family firm downtown. "We weren't about to sit around Easton and watch the gates rust off their hinges and houses fall into the road," said Phil.

Phil took the city to court to halt demolition. He had 35 square blocks downtown declared an historic district. He helped save more than 35 of Easton's old buildings from the wrecking ball. Clapboard facades were replaced; windows and trim painted; bricks tuckpointed. With Toni at the helm, the Mitmans founded Historic Easton, a not-for-profit organization.

Toni and Phil invested $75,000 of their own savings in five downtown buildings, including an 18th-century home built for Daniel Bixler when he married Catharona Opp on April 26, 1789. In recent years, it had fallen into the hands of a slum landlord. Of the six couples who formed the nucleus of the preservation group, only Phil and Toni remained married. Cold coffee. Last minute plans. Calls made and unanswered. All the pushing, the hard work, the compromises, the late-night meetings, daily lunches and dinners took their toll. "The stress just tore people apart," Toni said.

When Phil's mayoral term was up, he returned to Bixler's. But with a surge in downtown restoration, he had a better base from which to build his business. Joyce, who had been an ardent supporter of her brother both in and out of the political rink, was glad to have her brother back. The business, which had been put on hold while Phil was mayor, needed his strength, energy and ideas. Having Phil and Snoke running Bixler's allowed Ken to step out of the family business at last in 1983.

Phil devised a way to allow his father to exit the business gracefully, retain the title of chairman, have some input, though not on major issues, and be taken care of financially for the rest of his life. No sooner was the ink dry on the plan, than Phil and Joyce made changes to get Bixler's moving faster.

Welcome to Bixler's today. It is a company that boasts about its history and displays detailed records. As you enter the main store in

Easton, a handsome 1810 Sheraton-style cherry tallcase clock made and signed by Christian III stands on the left. Phil knows where about 100 of the 465 clocks Christian III handcrafted are today, and he eagerly hunts them down to bring them back into the family. A glass case next to the clock is filled with Christian III's handforged signed silver, correspondence and frayed ledger book which has notes at the top of the page, fastidiously written in small pale black script. An ancestor portrait of Christian III hangs above the case, surrounded by a rogue's gallery of photographic portraits of the current heads of the Bixler clan and business.

Phil pulls out an old book of 170 pages in which family history was recorded in 1930 by a cousin, Floyd Smith Bixler, president of the Northampton Genealogical Society. It is filled with family trees and rambling flowery descriptions of family members and their commitment to good workmanship even in an age when mass production was unheard of.

In spite of all reminders of the company's history, Phil wasn't about to let this business live in the past. He had two good models of how to move it forward—his years of working with his father and his stint with Sears. Furthermore, he was a bit of a gambler. He was young and figured he had the time to wait. "We weren't wild. We looked at the downside and figured out how good it could be and then if it wasn't so bad, we'd do it."

Plugging forward was made easier by the fact that many of Ken's recruits, now also in their 60s, retired. The store's former diamond specialist, Robert Aretz, felt displaced after training Phil and seeing him take over. He left in 1971 after Phil was named president. "He may have felt there wasn't enough room for both of us. But I think that was an error. We were growing and there would have been room eventually," said Phil.

Phil and Joyce opened two other downtown stores in small cities similar to Easton: in Bethlehem, touted more now for its Christmas decorations and Moravian stone buildings than for its steel mills and Mack Trucks, and in Lebanon, a still slower-paced rural Pennsylvania German community. In Lebanon, the Bixler store still is called Thomas Clark Jewelers for its previous owners. All three stores retain the flavor of Mom-and-Pop operations and employ a total of 24 full-time workers and 15 part-timers.

To stay abreast of industry trends, Phil and Joyce joined a management group that works with small businesses in different fields. Members attend bi-annual meetings and receive monthly inventory and sales reports of members in the same field, a barometer of how well a company performs.

One of the biggest problems Phil faced was attracting customers downtown, not only because of the dearth of stores and people, but also because of Bixler's reputation for expensive merchandise. "We've always had a lot of threshold resistance. We didn't just want to be the Tiffany's of the area," he said, referring to the New York-based jewelry and gift store. "But we also knew that we weren't going to get the bulk of the mall traffic, which is aged 16 to 23. So we decided to carry a little of the $20 gifts, such as our silver Hershey kiss necklaces for $19, as well as more of the higher-priced lines. We also knew that we couldn't serve everyone," he added.

Bixler's put together expensive and eye-catching window displays. The store retailed a wider variety of merchandise for customers, aged 25 and up. Today, the bulk of sales are still in jewelry, which remains the most profitable department. About 15 percent of sales are in gifts including flatware and china, which takes up a disproportionate share of square footage, Phil, Joyce and Mike agree. The remaining 10 percent of sales comes from engraving and repairing merchandise.

Joyce, a broad-shouldered woman with short hair and small hazel eyes, quietly slips into a seat next to Phil in his windowless office at the back of the store. The telephone on his cluttered desk rings. Phil picks up the phone. While he appeases a customer, Joyce describes her job. She works closely with her brother, never steps on his toes and makes a point of talking business only at work. She stays on the selling floor and mingles with customers. "A lot of customers want to know a Bixler is out there," she says. She doesn't mind the long hours because her husband, Lloyd, is away frequently as a flight engineer for Pan American Airlines. Employees know Phil's the boss, Joyce explains, but his open-door policy makes them feel comfortable about offering their point of view.

"I sometimes get on Phil about running a democracy around here," says Mike as he steps into Phil's office. He's been working in his cramped cubicle a few steps away. He remains as crucial to the business under the new generation as he did with the old. He is also as dedicated as the owners to making fatter profits and to increasing earning power of all employees.

Mike and the Mitmans rely heavily on their staff. Phil views a strong staff as one more way to be sure the business will survive him. The stores' three buyers, all women, have divided up the work according to their expertise.

Michele Nadeau, who's been with the company 11 years, buys the fashion jewelry for all three stores at the industry's two major trade shows in New York in February and July and at the annual craft show in Baltimore in February. She has a budget that Mike has calculated, based on the inventory of all the stores, each store's prior sales, the country's economy and trends.

For spring 1988, she had $175,000 to spend on the three stores and planned to use it primarily for porcelain earrings and face pins, silver bracelets and necklaces. She also buys daily as need demands. Michele is typical of the Bixler employees. She's low-key but can be tough when necessary. "If we get someone in buying one item, I try to persuade them to buy something else. That's where your real salesmanship comes in," Michele says. She also knows that trends in her jewelry lines can be ephemeral—popular today and gone tomorrow. Alys Happel buys the more expensive and classic diamonds and colored stones.

Adds Mike, 45, who buys Mikkimoto pearls and Rolex watches for the store, "You try to get a customer to switch over to such purchases, or something gold or with diamonds. You try for a tie-in such as getting an engaged couple to buy their wedding bands with us and register for gifts. A typical wedding today means sales of $14,000."

Snoke and the others are spurred by the motivational seminars the Mitmans organize, by the courses they encourage them to take to become registered gemologists and diamond experts, and by the discounts and incentives the company offers. A trip to Atlantic City. A Broadway show. Holiday parties at the boss's house. Sales translate into Bixler points, equivalent to airline frequent flyer programs, and which the Bixler employees use toward free merchandise.

Yvonne Zulick, the manager of the Bethlehem store who's been with Bixler's 14 years, eagerly shows off the Rolex watch she earned. She's now saving for a sapphire and diamond tennis bracelet. "It's going to take me a while. It's important for us to encourage employees and not to dictate to them," says Phil. "You also have to give them credit for what goes right."

Many of the employees have been with the company for more than 12 years and, as a result, have worked for both senior and junior Mitmans. Giving employees autonomy is made easier by the fact that most get along. Many went through high school together and live a block or two apart. They are able to share in each other's successes without feeling jealous or intimidated.

On a Friday afternoon in February 1988, Carol squeals with excitement and her colleagues share in her enthusiasm. She has just sold a $10,000 sapphire and diamond bracelet to one of her steady customers. It is her biggest sale in three years at Bixler's. She had been working with the customer for weeks, trying to find just the right bracelet through one of Phil's wholesale contacts. When the customer viewed the one Carol finally settled on, she liked it, bought it and walked out wearing it.

Most large dollar sales are made in the November-December season, not February. In December 1988, sales exceeded six percent over last year, which was higher than the average increase for most retailers. Christmas sales account for 40 percent of annual volume. (The Easton and Bethlehem stores rang up a combined total of $623,000 in December 1988.) A champagne reception and 20-percent-off prices on the Sunday before Christmas bring in the crowds—343 customers in the Easton store last year. Traffic has historically doubled in December.

Advertising, a minimal six percent of the Easton and Bethlehem stores' sales, is used to keep the company's name before the customers and to promote monthly jewelry specials. The company uses some print, some radio. "Hi, I'm Phil Mitman," says a deep strong voice in radio ads. The company has tripled the advertising of its newest store in Lebanon, acquired in December 1986. Recently, Phil spent $5,000 to improve the front of the Easton store. "We upgraded the area behind the diamond cases putting in dark green velvet. We also removed the glass doors and put in new lighting to create a more dramatic look."

Merchandise that doesn't sell is moved, or "creatively transferred," among the three stores. A "killer whale" mid-winter sale is a final attempt to move unsold merchandise by dropping prices 40 to 50 percent. After that, it's donated to a charity. "Too many jewelry stores hold on to their merchandise too long," Phil reflects. "If it's two years and you've got the same merchandise you're in trouble."

Phil, Joyce and their employees toss around ideas to bring in more business and beat the chains. The two largest, Zales and Gordon Jewelry, now account for about 3,300 of the country's 20,000 to 21,000 stores, according to the Jewelers of America trade association. The U.S. jewelry industry has been undergoing more consolidation, with many of the buyers swooping down on chains and stores from overseas. By attracting more traffic, the mall stores are able to turn merchandise over more times than a small shop. But mall stores, Phil counters, can't offer the same quality of service and product. "We routinely receive letters from clients," he says pulling out a thank-you note touting the store's service in repairing an engagement ring.

Phil and Joyce now mull over an idea suggested by Mike and Yvonne that would involve replacing part of the gift departments in the Easton and Bethlehem stores with private salons for showing customers jewelry. "There would be some good art, sleek couches and good wine," says Yvonne. Phil says he's considering it, but doesn't want to tie up capital.

Phil and Joyce get ready to leave the store. Employees put the jewelry into a safe and lock up. Phil heads for home on College Hill.

Like downtown Easton and Bixler's, College Hill also is being revived. Affluent residents' children left the neighborhood in the 1960s after going to prestigious colleges and universities. The Hill resembled a monopoly board of rows of empty estates, churches, schools and a few scattered businesses.

But all has changed. Charming Victorian homes have been restored. Their gingerbread trims colorfully painted, front porches festooned with wicker chairs. The streets are jammed with kids on bikes. Houses line well-manicured streets in an area dominated by Lafayette College, now a co-ed school of 2,000 students that has one of the largest endowments in the country and that has benefited recently from the financial largesse of alumnus William E. Simon, former Secretary of the Treasury and now chairman of a private investment firm.

The Mitmans were pioneers in the neighborhood. At the time they moved in, they were only one of the few young couples in the area.

Sitting in their cozy home, Phil and Toni talk about their recent efforts to revive downtown Easton and restore it to its full potential. Phil wants to see the empty upper floors of the company's shop become artists' lofts. He knows he'll have to wait until real estate prices downtown bounce back. "Owning real estate and being in downtown Easton isn't so bad. We are increasing our transactions. And as more people from New York and New Jersey opt to live in Easton, we will have to continue to upgrade our downtown area. It will come."

Phil's need to keep Bixler's going and downtown Easton alive has little to do with material gain, status and power. "We're not a greedy family. Our ancestors were never wealthy, just good hardworking, well respected folk, an Easton tradition," Phil says. "A lot of what I do I've done for posterity."

Many family business successions are marked by conflict or worked out hastily during a crisis. Not Bixler's. The current owners fashioned a clean and orderly break when they took over. Their father willingly agreed.

The family called in a coterie of attorneys, accountants and financial aces to draft a long-term plan. It provided a comfortable lifestyle for the senior Mitmans by giving them rental income on the Easton store and a nice pool of money. Mitman and his sister each received 45 percent of the company stock. Their parents retained the remaining 10 percent with the stipulation that they would gift shares to their children to reduce estate taxes. The plan also provided a buy-sell agreement so that neither Phil nor Joyce could sell out to one of the large jewelry chains looking to increase their empire.

Once in control, the eighth generation didn't hesitate to extract the best of the former generations' culture and add new timely elements.

Phil and Joyce also were determined to separate family and business in order for both systems to survive, a strategy Paul C. Rosenblatt, a family business expert and author, and psychologist Florence Kaslow both think preserves family relationships and the business. Phil and Toni have never discussed business at home. Toni wasn't interested in the business and company transactions needed to be kept confidential. Joyce, too, tried not to take home shop stories to her husband.

Now Phil is rethinking his strategy. As other experts advise, Lansberg, for instance, thinks it's impossible to totally separate family business and suggests playing up the advantages, such as hirinig only qualified relatives, and downplaying the disadvantages, like never putting outsiders on the board of directors. By not discussing the business at home, Phil thinks he may have diminished his children's interest.

His eldest daughter Brooke, 20, a sophomore at Pennsylvania State University, proves him wrong. She hangs on every word while her father in a rare moment openly discusses Bixler's specific successes and failures. Most are anecdotes she's never heard. In a conversation away from her parents she confesses, "I love the business and I could see working with my younger brother, Christian." Her father is told of the remark and is pleased. "Did she really say that? I had no idea. That's great," he says with a grin.

In this family, a strong love of the business continues to filter down through the generations and ensures that Bixler's will survive.

The 7 Santini Brothers
Bronx, NY

Now far since then the ocean streams
Have swept us from the land of dreams,
That land of fiction and of truth,
The lost Atlantis of our youth

Ultima Thule! Utmost Isle!
Here in thy harbors for awhile
We lower our sails, awhile we rest
From the unending endless quest.

HENRY WADSWORTH LONGFELLOW
—Ultima Thule

In the early hours of a hot, steamy day in 1927, the Santini family celebrated. Their headquarters in the High Bridge section of the Central Bronx in New York, then an upwardly mobile neighborhood, was complete and would be open for business the next day. Feelings soared. They had accomplished in 22 years what thousands of immigrants before and after them had dreamed America could offer.

The ten-story brick headquarters, with its steel-gray water tower dominating the neighborhood's squat all-purpose shops, small apartment houses and elevated subway line, became a symbol of strength

92

and hope. Here, in this choice, self-contained community at the corner of Jerome Avenue and 170th Street, the Santini brothers, their spouses and children began prospering together.

Little did they know that the Santini name would go on to become a legend in the moving and storage business.

The interior of the 110,000-square-foot building was luxurious with the pristine look of a bank. The 18-foot-high lobby was a spacious formal entranceway, a grand and glorious glass and Carrara marble chamber clad with speckled marble floors, ornate iron grillwork around finely-arched windows and carefully placed palms in decorator jardinieres. A large black marble counter dominated the lobby where business was transacted. A wrought-iron gate divided the reception area from the offices. Furniture was large and elegant, reflecting a time and place that more than 50 years later would be dramatically different.

Many of those early company images are now just a blur for the second generation. A daughter of one of the founders, Dorothea Santini, who still comes to work daily though she is past 70, is hard pressed to describe in detail the original lobby. For the successive two generations, the memories are little more than family chronologies.

Santini's well-known name and reputation for service had gently lulled the company and its employees into a false sense of security. All is now in a state of upheaval. Along with obvious external changes, little about the company, or the Santini family, which founded its business in 1905, remains status quo.

The company's president, third-generation Tino Santini, 36, son of Martin L. and grandson of founding brother Martin, can't afford to mourn change. Santini Brothers, along with hundreds of other moving companies nationwide, hit hard times. Revenue has declined and the company hasn't made a profit in two years. In 1988, it posted a loss of $1 million on revenue of $30 million. The reasons are extensive: Partial government deregulation of the trucking industry, high insurance rates, an oil glut in the Middle East, a lower dollar, the resulting trade deficit and a recession between 1980 and 1982. Then, too, there's the change in how goods are packed and loaded in containers by the International Longshoremen's Union, which now has the right to handle goods within a 50-mile radius of the New York ports. That used to be the moving company's job. Tonnage has dropped. Discounts on rates, based on the weight of the cargo and the mileage, are offered. In addition, not only is there a shortage of drivers, but companies like Santini have to keep buying longer and wider trailers needed for long distance moves and that cost an average of $27,000 and the smaller local trucks that are 24 feet long and which cost $45,000 each.

The external factors are painful. The key to making money requires a mixture of difficult options: cutting costs, lowering rates, picking up more profitable routes and busting the unions. But Santini's internal philosophy may be the most difficult to change. It states that family comes first, even before the success of the company, which is the antithesis of all non-family businesses.

Yet there now are too many mouths to feed for the amount of business transacted and too many Santinis, some not qualified, taking pieces of the shrinking pie. There are 24 family members active in the business and a total of 70 family shareholders with common voting stock, who try to call shots from the sidelines.

Tino, many of his relatives and most long-time, non-family employees know they have to make changes fast. If not, the business faces continued stagnation or, worse, being sold or closed. In just one year, in 1985, 1,533 domestic carriers went out of business, according to Dun & Bradstreet data.

The weakest companies have been eliminated. Tino says that those surviving have become sharper operators. "You now have to review every job more carefully. That's good in the long run, but it's tougher and tougher for us to do as the problems unravel the family's togetherness."

Tino's style is slow, deliberate. He fixes attention on details to grasp the larger picture. But he hasn't been able to build a new infrastructure to include everyone and make profits return. To do so would require eliminating family from the business. Company by-laws offer little help. The only guide is a shareholders' buy-sell agreement executed in July 1970 that states that in the event a shareholder wants to sell his shares he must first offer them to the corporation or to family members. The largest block of stock, about 10 percent, is held by the late Zachary Santini's branch of the family. The next largest block, about seven percent, is held by Dorothea, a lifetime board member and daughter of Godfrey E. Santini, one of the seven founders.

Like atoms exploding, the number of shareholders will continue to expand as family members give and bequeath stock to sons, daughters and grandchildren. The situation creates a built-in conflict with more relatives, who hold stock but don't draw salaries and don't receive perks asking, "What are we getting out of this company?" Furthermore, many of these relatives have few memories of the founders, little love for the business and, in some instances, barely know one another.

Part of the reason for the Santinis' dilemma is that stock originally was divided equally among the founders, who passed it on to their children and grandchildren, whether they were active in the business or not.

"It's a hell of a choice for Tino to decide between the business and his family, but it's needed if Tino is going to get the firm moving forward again," exclaims Vinnie Petrillo, a vice president and non-family member. Petrillo has been with the company 29 years. "Tino's in a real quandary because he stands in such awe of his family."

Adds Richard Shawn Farrell, the only fourth-generation relative on the board of the 7 Santini Brothers, "He's going to have to treat the business as a business. I'm probably one of the few, if not the last person, who believes the company can make it through the fourth and into the fifth generation. But it's going to take some gut-wrenching and a lot of people looking in the mirror." Farrell is operations manager of the company's Chicago branch.

Tino isn't alone in facing this family business dilemma. The leaders of thousands of family-owned companies feel compelled to keep their legacies going for emotional rather than sound financial reasons.

Italian families traditionally have made room for everyone in any generation to join their family businesses. When a company was young and short on capital, the strategy proved beneficial. Family worked longer hours and for lower salaries. They were drawn by love of family and common religion, a ritual and tradition. As business grew, additional family meant more manpower and new skills.

"There is a whole Italian family phenomenon," says Luigi G. Barzini, an Italian writer living in Rome and author of *The Italians*. "It is therefore not surprising that the Italians, living as they have always done, in the insecurities and dangers of an unruly and unpredictable society, are among those who found their main refuge behind the walls of their houses, among their blood relatives." The family was the one institution they could rely on.

The Santini story reflects a struggle between continuity of a family culture and forces of change, especially problems in transferring ownership from generation to generation. Each generation follows a different philosophy. The founders were entrepreneurs. Most of the second generation followed in the footsteps of the first generation and has been stubborn about stepping aside. The third and fourth generations are trying to institute professional management skills to keep business viable.

The saga of the Santinis began more than 80 years ago. The seven Santini brothers, all deceased, had been pushed by their mother, Albina, to leave Lucca in northern Italy. Farming the hilly terrain in Tuscany was futile.

"Go to America," she advised them affectionately, as she watched her husband, Zaccaria, farm to support her, their seven sons and three daughters. A stern taskmaster, he pushed his sons into working for him day and night.

Over the next few years, the sons left one by one. They had little money and spoke no English. Pasquale, the eldest, was the first to depart in the 1890s. Zaccaria opposed emigrating. He feared that the family would split apart. But his wife won out.

In America, they joined their cousin, Annuccio Santini. The fledgling business began to thrive once Annuccio capitalized on an important trend.

Every summer, hard-working Jewish families, who had settled in the Bronx in the late 1880s after moving from the slums of Manhattan's lower East Side and the Brownsville section of Brooklyn, packed and changed apartments as their yearly leases expired. A Yiddish journalist found the Bronx "a beautiful area—a suburb that could have sun, and air and cheaper rents," when he visited in 1903, according to Irving Howe in *World of Our Fathers*.

By about 1929, the Jewish population in the Bronx had climbed to 420,000, double what it had been at the start of the decade. What began as a lower-middle class settlement, gradually evolved into a respectable hub. The families turned to the Santini Brothers to move them, choosing them because of their competitive prices and quality service. They also used the Santinis to store their valuables during long vacations.

The area bustled with energy. Sepia-tinted photographs of that era show children playing in the streets, families parading up and down the boulevard in their best attire on the Sabbath, and shopkeepers peddling wares. The families, mostly professionals, turned the Grand Concourse, the area's 4½-mile thoroughfare from East 138th Street to the Mosholu Parkway, into a thriving showcase of the latest apartment houses, shops and eateries. For a person to live in an Art Deco apartment building with a fashionable sunken living room on the Grand Concourse in the 1920s, was equivalent to being a member of high society, according to *Guide to Jewish New York City* by Oscar Israelowitz. The Grand Concourse became known as the Champs Elysées of the Bronx.

The opening of the Jerome Avenue and Concourse subway lines in the 1930s further spurred the area's growth. The Jewish population reached its peak of 585,000 and accounted for 48 percent of all Jews in New York City, according to *American Jewish Landmarks* by Bernard Postal and Lionel Koppman.

To cater to this clientele, five of the Santini brothers started a household moving company. Headquarters were modest at first, inside one of two horse-drawn moving vans at the corner of Trinity and Westchester avenues. Eventually, the two remaining Santini brothers joined their siblings in America. All seven set up shop in a shanty on a vacant lot. They shared not just a business culture but a common culture, a real heritage, as well. They lived near one another; they socialized frequently.

On a typical morning, the brothers loaded trucks at the docks and delivered cargo. Their name and reputation brought in more offers to move offices and goods overseas. The brothers were a capable lot. Martin was considered "a kind, humanitarian person who cared deeply about the entire family and how it transacted business." Although second to the youngest, Godfrey E. Santini, the most charismatic of the brothers and the one who assimilated ideas the fastest, was named president at the age of 29 in 1919. He was a self-educated businessman who became a mentor to the next generation.

In spite of the brothers' closeness, disagreements over how to run the business crept in, causing August, the eldest, and Pietro, known as Pete, to sell their shares to their five brothers. As those brothers dispersed from the Bronx to other neighborhoods, the seven Santinis got together less frequently.

More changes occurred after World War II when Jewish residents began scattering to Manhattan and to the just-built sprawling suburbs on Long Island and New York's Westchester County and New Jersey. Decline continued into the 1970s when there were only 143,000 Jews in the Bronx or slightly less than 12 percent of the total New York City Jewish population. According to Philip Freedman, director of the budget for the United Jewish Appeal/Federation of Jewish Philanthropies of New York, a not-for-profit, fund-raising organization, the Jewish population in the area now numbers less than 5,000. In their place, large Hispanic and black families gradually moved in to the unrenovated low-rent brick apartment houses. They came from Harlem and Puerto Rico, seeking cheap housing and jobs in nearby Manhattan.

Abandoned buildings decayed. Some blocks contained so many burned and empty shells that they resembled miniature bombed-out cities. In the midst of this squalor, the new residents became stuck for good. Instead of a constant stream of fast-paced people with places to go, slow-moving types with time to kill crowded the sidewalks. Most residents still have little reason to go faster or to budge at all. This neighborhood and even more the adjacent 30 blocks known as the South Bronx have become the quintessential symbols of urban decay. The Santini family stubbornly kept its headquarters there, the tall tower dominating its corner now surrounded by littered streets, crowded with transient grocery stores and discount clothing shops. Members were convinced the neighborhood would rejuvenate.

Santini Brothers had to look to other markets to pick up slack. Years before, to make room for everyone in the second generation and for immigrants coming over from Italy who needed work, the family opened branches. An office and warehouse was opened at 49th Street in Manhattan in 1949. Zachary, a cousin, opened one of the three Florida branches in 1955. Lou, another cousin, opened the fine arts branch at 22nd Street in New York in 1958.

Three years later, Leo, Lou's brother, took control of domestic operations and opened an office in Chicago. Tino's father opened the new international division in Maspeth, Queens, in 1963 to export goods and equipment abroad.

To reach into the suburbs, Santini Brothers opened in 1969 a branch in Larchmont, a suburb in Westchester County. Additional hubs were opened to pack, load and move goods domestically and internationally, one in Texas in 1976, and another in Norfolk, VA, in 1979, which was closed in 1982.

To man these new divisions, strangers were taken in and treated like family, though they were not given an equity position. This worked well when business thrived.

By the late 1970s, Santini Brothers was among the largest moving agents in the country with a staff of 1,000 and 50 company trucks. Revenue was $55 million and profits were $1 million.

But by 1980, partial deregulation, initiated by President Jimmy

Carter to encourage open price competition and free entry into the business, threw the moving and trucking industries a curve. The Motor Carrier Act of 1980 made it easier for small, non-union independent drivers to haul goods interstate. All they needed was a truck, a driver, a few business cards or a billboard and the open road. Whatever routes they wanted were theirs.

In contrast, the previous Motor Carrier Act of 1935 had frozen in place the trucking routes and industry rates assigned by the Interstate Commerce Commission (ICC). From 1935 until 1980, the only way for carriers to gain new routes was to acquire them from existing carriers or to take over another carrier, said Nicholas A. Glaskowsky in the "Effects of Deregulation on Motor Carriers," a study funded by the Eno Foundation for Transportation. Having fixed rates was supposed to keep the transportation industry profitable.

About 15,000 carriers jammed the highways after partial deregulation went into full swing around 1984. Almost 80 percent were small family owned operators, according to the National Moving and Storage Association in Washington, D.C.

Unlike the totally deregulated airline industry, truckers had to file for approval to change their rates and tariffs. They were subject to ICC guidelines.

Most of the moving companies were similar to Santini. They increased their volume, but became winded trying to match discounts of competitors who charged less than the published Tariff Bureau rates. The discounts climbed as high as 35 to 40 percent. Smaller moving companies, which numbered about 6,000 nationwide, were known as agents. Most affiliated with one of the country's four largest van lines—United Van Lines, North American, Allied and Mayflower—in order to gain a wider geographic reach and fill their trucks, especially on return trips. The average truck could hold up to 30,000 pounds or the contents of three households.

Santini Brothers became affiliated in 1935 with United Van Lines, headquartered in Fenton, MO, a suburb south of St. Louis. United is a private company, whose 130 agents, including Santini, hold all its stock. The board consists primarily of the agents, who are elected to represent their regions.

Deregulation became a boon for the $3 billion van line industry. Their agents forked over about 8.5 percent of the total cost of the line haul which varied among the van lines and sometimes included packing, labor and materials charges. Strong sales and profits in 1987 spurred United to divide a one percent sales bonus totaling $4 million among its agents.

In return, the agents got administrative help, liability insurance, training programs and claim settlements. The owner-operator driver, who owns the cab but not the trailer, received the largest compensation, 52 percent of the line haul plus 60 to 80 percent of the cost of packing depending on geographic locale. Santini gave United its cut, retained the remaining 39.5 percent of the line haul and received 100 percent of the cost of materials used.

Santini has given United an average of $5 million in business each year over the last four to five years. Santini's sales to United hit $8 million in 1987, making it the sixth largest domestic agent out of United's 575. Until the late 1970s, Santini was United's number one agent. James L. Wilson, United's Executive Vice President, said he expects Santini Brothers, which has used United primarily to handle domestic household moves, will soon give United its overseas business as well. This could give United $5 million more in revenue.

In spite of Santini Brothers' strong tie to United Van Lines, Santini struggled. Over the last seven years, revenue has plummeted to $30 million in 1988 from $35 million in 1986 and $55 million in 1980.

All the turmoil hasn't completely shaken Tino's or his relatives' confidence. They believe the company will survive this downswing just as it has survived other crises. Optimism varies. "It's just one more lesson in change," says Tino's uncle, Godfrey F. Santini, known as Fred, who is chairman and was president from 1963 to 1984. But Fred and others admit that this downturn may prove the most wrenching.

The Santini headquarters reflects the physical and emotional deterioration of the business and its family. The lobby of the building is a chopped-up maze of small monochromatic paneled cubicles. The once 45-foot-long shiny trucks that careened through the crowded streets to carry precious cargo in and out of the company's terminal, were replaced more than 15 years ago by enormous white trailers, 48 feet long, with bold black and blue lettering and a big number "7." They have even greater difficulty negotiating the busier traffic and crowd the warehouse.

Fred, who turned 70 in 1988, is chairman in name only and serves as a consultant. He comes to work daily shuffling through the lobby in a wrinkled sports jacket. He stoops over, often puffs on a cigarette. A small, stocky man, he works in a cramped first-floor corner office. He is surrounded by huge stacks of papers and Santini Brothers' memorabilia including faded newspaper clippings about how important the company used to be.

Dirty, dog-eared telephone books are stored amid the clutter. They contain lists of countless competitors who traded off the Santini name as a measure of credibility. "Just look at this," he says pointing to two open pages with the name Santini in every ad. "A lot of these aren't even related, but they liked to use the name Santini. Everybody got off the boat and thought that the name was synonymous with moving. We are a full-service mover," explains Fred.

Fred represents the past. He's incapable of accepting his company's fate, its outmoded way of operating and the fact that he's been asked to step down. He likes things the way they were, the finely-crafted and specialized cartons that the company used to pack possessions in rather than the standard crates used now. He also favors passing ownership strictly from generation to generation, though none of his three sons was qualified to take over.

Fred drags boxes from the shelves, looking for more family records and pulls out a sheet of paper on which is printed the company's motto, written by his father:

Unity of all. It was the pooling of our meager resources that first made our organization possible, and later its expansion by the combined efforts of the Seven Brothers, aided by its personnel in a spirit of cooperation, tolerance and understanding.

The credo is posted throughout the building. So is a family portrait of the seven brothers. The brothers were a handsome, imposing group all with their hands tightly fixed in the pockets of their three-piece suits, pocket watches dangling from their vests and shiny black wingtip shoes. Each had jet black, slicked-down hair and half-smiles. Their names revealed their Italian heritage—Rinaldo, Martin, Paride, August, Pasquale, Pietro, Godfrey.

Fred also applauds his company's philosophy that family has a larger meaning than a parent-child relationship. Employees in this company are treated like family with several generations of non-Santinis gaining jobs.

When Fred ran the company, many of his decisions were based on emotions rather than good business, Petrillo says. "He should have sold some of the properties his father bought, but there was no way he could force himself to get rid of them. Too often, when a company is tight-bound, too controlled, too enmeshed with family, you can kill it."

Just one floor above, reached by a steep, straight staircase, Tino, whose real name is Martin L. Santini, Jr., and who has been president of the firm since May 1984, sits tall in his brown leather executive chair. His thick shock of brown hair is peppered with gray. Tino is dressed the part of president in a gray pinstriped suit, white button-down shirt and paisley tie. He's refined and soft-spoken.

Tino represents the future and even his office reflects a more professional approach than his predecessors. He has stripped his brown desk clean, almost as smooth as the surface of a freshly-cleaned ice rink. From the windows of his second-floor office he has a clear view of the neighborhood.

Tino is quick to point out that in spite of his youth, he's been with the company more than 19 years. He worked his way up from the bottom, beginning at age 17 as a summer intern in the export division under the thumb of his father and Petrillo. He continued to work summers until he finished graduate school. He handled every type of moving within the export division. He wrapped furniture in paper pads, packed dish packs and loaded books into specially designed cartons. He helped design cases for heavy machinery. One summer, he oversaw the warehouse, dispatching and loading trucks, after the manager took ill.

His dad and Petrillo gave him no preferential treatment. "I got the hard jobs, and boy was it hot out in the yard," he said, laughing about how a friend, who also had a job with the company, got the inside, easy work. "I guess they wanted me to prove myself so that someday I could take over."

He graduated from St. Bonaventure University in Olean, NY, where he majored in math and then received a master's degree in math from Fordham University. He joined the business fulltime right out of graduate school.

Fred, Leo and Martin ran the company then as a triumvirate. All three had been close growing up. Martin and Fred roomed together in college. But gradually they pulled apart and championed different younger relatives. Fred trained Bobby Francesconi; Leo took Ralph Imperato, his nephew, under his wing; and Martin pushed for Tino. As a result, Fred, Leo and Martin set themselves up for a succession disaster, having failed to plan for one person to take over.

At the same time, company morale was sinking as revenue and profits declined. Fred and Martin didn't have the energy to deal with the problems. Staff was beginning to squirm. Managers became disenchanted. Employees looked for other jobs. Younger Santinis and many of the long-term non-family employees, whose vision wasn't clouded by family loyalties, decided the old ways had to go. This meant changing the guard.

Meetings of the 13-member board of directors, which included only one non-family member, the firm's general counsel, George Mutterperl, turned into heated debates, sometimes drowned out by boos and hisses.

At the March 4, 1984, board meeting, Tino's father, Martin, who was chairman of the management committee, stood up and calmly read the position of the company's eight managers, all vice presidents: "to find solutions to the corporate problems and to seek a turnaround of the corporation."

The management committee was particularly concerned at the report by a vice president of finance at Barclay's Bank, who told the committee that he was worried about the company's line of credit, which hadn't been called in, but needed to be increased. The management committee also decided the company's "current conditions" necessitated an immediate change in management. The specific changes would include Godfrey S. Santini and Martin L. Santini "retiring with honor, being retained as consultants in order that the company may have the benefits of their years of experience and expertise in company affairs and making room for new management."

After a two-hour grueling discussion, the elder Santinis retired. Tino was named president.

Tino thought he was the logical choice because of his education and years of working in the company. "It would have involved too much juggling to bring Imperato, vice president of the domestic operations at the Houston branch, up to New York and find a replacement for him." But Imperato's credentials were impressive. He had worked as a marketing representative for Shell Oil company for two years after receiving his MBA from Iona College in New Rochelle, NY. "Francesconi, a vice president of traffic, hadn't had enough experience handling financial matters," Tino said.

Right away, Tino wanted to use his mandate as president to eliminate the glut of family from the board. But his hands were tied because of the lack of non-family board members to back him up. All Tino was able to do was make token gestures. He switched members of the second generation from being full-fledged officers to consultants. They retained their titles and received the same financial remuneration—a combination of pension benefits and yearly consultation fees in lieu of previous salaries.

"Fred needs to retire," Tino says. "But I know we're going to have a battle royal on our hands this May when his contract is up for renewal. He can't afford not to be compensated because of his divorce."

Tino also wants to get Fred Ruther, a son-in-law of one of the founders and a vice president of warehousing, off the company payroll. "I've got allies on the board, but not enough to outnumber them. If I threaten to leave, I know there are people who would jump at the opportunity to fill in. A lot of the second generation has been hearing wolf cried for the last 10 years and unless their backs are up against the wall and we say, 'Guess what? Your paychecks aren't going out next week,' I don't think they'll listen."

Petrillo is among the most outspoken. "People are carried in a position where they shouldn't be. It's put a lot of pressure on them to perform though they're not always capable. Some of the third generation really doesn't want to be in the business, but they don't know what else to do. It also hurts non-Santinis who feel they should be moving up the ladder but aren't. It's draining the company. There's a family man in every spot and a back-up non-family member checking on him."

Farrell, who joined Santini Brothers after high school in 1973 and is a board member because of all the business he's brought in, believes that the second generation must retire. He doesn't mince words: "They've been paid for 50 years. If they didn't save, it's their problem now. When I'm their age, I'll step down. I don't think of myself as a family member any more. I think of myself as just another hard-working employee."

Remarks Landry, "Tino and his cousins are less tied to their roots. I'm often introducing cousins to one another at funerals and weddings. Tino should be able to pound on the table, lower the gavel and say, 'Damn it, I'm the boss.' That's awfully hard when you've got your uncle and father sitting two seats away from you. Tino's too polite."

Fred is a holdout for maintaining the status quo, typical of the second generation, blinded by tradition. "We've always said there would be work for family, or we'd do without amenities. We have to make room. We respect our family as we respect our clientele. The seven brothers faced the Depression and survived. We should put our noses a little more to the grindstone."

In contrast to dealing with family issues, Tino had the blessing of the board to act swiftly in making financial changes.

He cut overhead by closing three of the company's nine branches, which were scattered throughout a four-state region. Each branch handled a variety of moving tasks, but each also had its specialty. Chicago focused on moving electronics. New York catered to the office and art markets. Florida warehoused goods.

Through attrition and layoffs, Tino cut 200 employees. The company's total ranks have dropped more than 50 percent since 1980, when it employed 1,000. The 500 employees include 200 white-collar and 300 blue-collar workers, broken down into 12 vice presidents, 50 owner-operators under contract but not employees and 50 company drivers, 38 sales people, 25 coordinators who act as liaisons between the salesmen and the customers, 10 traffic managers who schedule the moves, 50 packers who calculate the tonnage, and the remaining 200 helpers who do a little bit of everything.

These cutbacks were mandatory. "I hated to do it," Tino said, "but we had mounting financial losses, a major $5 million accounting error at our Maspeth branch which had been buried over the last five years, plus problems with the Teamsters union. The union kept wanting concessions. We got them to agree to cut their lunch hour and work longer for the same amount of money—about $10 an hour, which is about $3 more than unionized truckers get elsewhere, outside New York."

Tino also decided that the company needed to capitalize on its commercial and office moving division, which brings in the most profits and highest volume. Companies continually move in New York, even in a recession. Here Santini Brothers shines. Its expertise in knowing the exact locations of entrances and elevators for thousands of buildings helped save clients hundreds or thousands of dollars. The company also offers efficiency by designing special cartons, nesting bins and file containers to hold anything a company needed to transport papers to another location.

Results were immediate. "Our revenue was up 50 percent in 1986 over 1985 for this end of the business," Tino said.

But continuing the upswing is hard. Tino explains that it's not easy to pick up new office business because of stiffer competition. The division's 10 sales representatives make daily cold calls on potential clients. When they see a building going up, they find out who's moving in and call. "By the time a move is mentioned in the newspaper, it's too late to grab that business. It's all in the timing."

Santini Brothers' office sales were hurt dramatically in early 1987 when Francesconi, a grandson of Rinaldo Santini, left the firm with two employees. He set up a competitive office moving firm in Maspeth when he wasn't named president, Tino says.

Francesconi disagrees with Tino over why he left. "I'm doing what I want to be doing and that's it. My lawyer has cautioned me not to talk to anyone about the situation," he said in a telephone call from his office, Central Moving and Storage Co. in Maspeth.

Tino shakes his head in disbelief when discussing Francesconi. "He's certainly made my year miserable. He's gone after the office business, which is the strongest and most lucrative part. He's definitely taken business away from us."

Fred, too, looks dismayed when he talks about Bobby because he was the family member Fred had groomed to take over. "There was this one side of the family, Rinaldo's side, which Bobby was part of . . . " His voice trails off and he doesn't finish his thought.

Even non-family employees think Francesconi hurt the company by leaving. "He's a fine young guy but he's not a workaholic. He enjoyed the good life," said Petrillo.

Petrillo is also concerned that other family and non-family members may abandon the firm if they don't receive raises or promotions. Even worse, they may try to cash in their stock by forcing the company to buy it back. Others disagree, pointing out that this isn't a greedy family. Members draw modest salaries and receive no perks. Tino is among the highest paid at $80,000. The company does not pay for cars, country club memberships or expensive houses.

To further slash expenses, Tino made his most gut-wrenching decision. He closed the company's Maspeth office at the end of 1987. It took two years to reach a verdict because at one time the 250,000-square-foot-plant spread over eight acres had produced 20 percent of the company's profits and revenue, more than any division. The trade deficit and falloff of business in oil-producing countries translated into little need for companies to ship goods overseas. "We used to do a lot of work for Aramco, which sent people and oil field equipment abroad, and Corning Glass, which shipped fiber opticals overseas," Tino said. "Now they send almost nothing."

Tino and a few of his colleagues tried to salvage the division because they believed business would turn around. "I was among the largest supporters, along with Petrillo, Robert Landry, a non-family senior vice president, and Martin Santini, of trying to keep Maspeth going and gain more concessions from the union. There's been a long ongoing argument in this family about export versus domestic operations," Tino said. "I figured, let's not drop $3 million in revenue. Let's figure out how to make a profit from it. It was especially difficult for Vinnie to close down a division he built up. Vinnie was made a consultant."

Tino is reminded that export trade has picked up as foreign countries use their pricing advantage to send for American-made goods. "I don't want to think about that," he says. But Tino is somewhat comforted by what experts have told him in the same breath—that the trade may never return to prior levels because of the necessary long negotiations to close a deal and the inability of foreign countries to afford American-made goods even at reduced prices.

Fred Santini, Imperato and Farrell thought closing Maspeth was unwise. Even Tino's brother, David, who is his only sibling in the business and had worked at that division, went looking for another job, but decided to move to Santini's New Jersey branch. The one immediate benefit of shutting down Maspeth was the $3.75 million in equity the company gained from selling the property, Tino said.

Now, Tino seems almost as torn between staying put or selling the company's landmark Jerome Avenue building and moving to New Jersey where union wages are lower. Property there is less costly and the company could build or buy a more modern facility to speed loading and unloading. Drivers would feel less anxious about leaving loads unattended.

"Property values are beginning to come back in the Bronx after hitting rock bottom a year or two ago," Tino says. Recently, developers bought land on speculation. Commercial activity is beginning to hum. The Red Apple grocery store chain plans to reopen a 12,000-square-foot store on the east side of Third Avenue, north of Tremont Avenue. New York City officials turned over the last five vacant apartment buildings on the Grand Concourse to private developers. Whether these changes will spill over and help transform the whole area remains to be seen.

Once Tino stabilizes operations, he plans to consider diversifying into new profitable niches such as moving more electronics equipment, setting up non-union subsidiaries and warehousing individual and corporate goods for self-storage.

One of the prime reasons this well-respected family business faces so many problems is its ties to tradition. This has been compounded by a failure to communicate, eliminate unproductive family members, and operate as a professional corporation with a strong outside board and long-range business and succession plans instead of an extension of the entrepreneurship founded by the original seven Santini brothers.

Part of the reason for the company's problems is the lack of a corporate directive. Dorothea Santini defends her company's loose structure and absence of a succession plan. "Succession isn't always something that can be planned. There's also the human factor. Everybody's different." Dorothea has devoted more than 50 years to the business.

Even Tino rationalizes the family's lack of professional planning. "Everybody's been too busy to plan beyond the next few months. I know we should sit down for four days and make some long-term decisions. But we just haven't been able to get everybody together long enough to do that," he says.

Tino's indecisiveness takes its toll as he struggles with sweeping the company clean of the excesses of its past and transforming a paternalistic culture into one that puts winning in the market above familial concerns. He feels guilty, re-running in his mind his many memories and frenetic schedule. "I'm always here early and always bring work home," he said. "I go in for half a day on Saturdays. Things may get easier. My wife sure hopes so. I know some of the second generation should go, but it's hard to cast people aside."

His wife Colleen comments. "He spends a lot more time by himself than he used to collecting his thoughts. His mind is off someplace else which has bothered me and our nine-year-old daughter, but we've gotten used to it. I don't want this to go on forever. I want to have more time as a family."

The next few years will tell whether Tino can make enough changes and make them fast enough. If he doesn't, Tino and his relatives may be left with a company that has only its reputation for service and prestigious name intact, or he may be forced to sell. But in this family business, the majority of the family is not ready for change. They still need Tino to serve as a buffer between the old and the new ways.

A typical work day ends. Tino stands in the lobby of his headquarters on a late November day in 1988. He stares at the small park across the street from his office as family members head home. Shabby steel subway cars rattle past, another reminder of the old days. Being at this spot is like looking backwards, not unlike the expectations of the family and its philosophy, which also belong to an earlier era.

Footnote

On January 6, 1989, the seemingly inevitable happened. The 7 Santini Brothers was sold to MacDonald Moving Services in Raynham, a suburb outside Boston, for $9.3 million. Francesconi tried to buy the company.

The Jerome Avenue headquarters and the 49th Street building in Manhattan were shuttered and put up for sale. The office moving division will operate out of the 22nd Street building and the interstate moving business will be transferred to New Jersey.

MacDonald's, a 70-year-old, three-generation United Van Line moving business headed by Bruce A. MacDonald, a member of the second generation, has changed its name to the 7 Santini Brothers.

Gone from the original Santini Brothers company are all the members of the second generation, fourth-generation Richard Farrell and many long-time employees such as Landry and Petrillo, a total of about 30 people. This has meant a savings in salaries of $350,000.

Tino Santini is no longer with the company. His brother, David, still manages the New Jersey office. Ralph Imperato, whom MacDonald knew from college days at Holy Cross and who interested MacDonald in buying Santini, has been named Vice President, Marketing, and manages the Houston office.

"We had no choice but to sell. There was no way we could agree on who would be cut from the firm to make it profitable," says Tino. "We kept losing money. Overall, most felt okay about the sale, but nobody's ever totally happy with money. I'm personally relieved in a sense. This is very, very sad and it's too bad we couldn't work out a deal ourselves. Fred holds me personally responsible. My dad wishes he could have done something. Right now, I'm out looking for a job. It's slow, based on what I want to do and earn. I've had several sales job offers, but I'm over-qualified. Francesconi offered me a sales job, but I turned it down.

"In retrospect," says Tino, "sometimes families are too large and there is too much animosity to keep the family working together, especially as it moves from the second to the third generation. The older generations need to step aside at some point. And families need to plan long in advance for a succession to take place."

The experience of the Santinis is not unlike that of many companies, such as Mars Inc., whose culture needs an overhaul to match a changing business climate.

MacDonald, 39, is making all decisions himself as the sole stockholder. He learned by observing his family's business that too many family members can't work well together. After his father passed away he gave his uncles, cousins, mother and sister an ultimatum: "Either I take over or I'm not coming in." He bought out the family. His business makes a solid $200,000 in profits on revenue of $6 million. He sees the Santini acquisition as a way to broaden his market share. "The name Santini is definitely 'the name' in the moving business."

MacDonald believes the Santini credo became a sham. "Each family member came first, not the family as a unit."

MacDonald, who has three sons, 11, 10 and 6, plans for only one to head the business, though all of them and any other relative who's willing to work hard can have a job.

The Firestone Vineyard
Los Olivos, CA

"Every useful occupation gives ample opportunity for service. The happiest men in the world are those who are making their jobs mean more than simply an endless routine of work and wages. The whole structure of business is based upon making useful things for others—this is service."

   Harvey S. Firestone, founder of Firestone Tire & Rubber Co.

The Leonard K. Firestone circle of friends didn't lack for celebrities. Dwight D. Eisenhower. Henry Ford II. Jimmy Stewart. Randolph Scott. Dick Powell and June Allyson. Laurence Rockefeller. All the Beautiful People congregated in Leonard's Beverly Hills mansion, a place that reeked of old money. They came to talk show business and politics, to glean nuggets of information and hear titillating scraps of gossip.

Leonard Firestone had panache of a different sort. He was rich. Respectable. He was an heir to the billion-dollar Firestone Tire & Rubber Co. that had been founded by his father, Harvey S. Firestone, in Akron, Ohio, in 1900. In the 1920s, when Southern California flourished as the movie capital of the world, Leonard, one of five sons, was moved 2,350 miles from Akron to become in 1933 vice president of Firestone's West Coast hub.

111

Leonard and his wife, the former Polly Curtis, three children, Kimball, Anthony Brooks and Lendy, led a privileged life. The best of Los Angeles society was open to the Firestones. They were an exciting and fascinating family. The household included servants, fancy cars and beautiful antiques. The children had the children of movie stars for friends. On a typical afternoon, Skip Montgomery and Brooks chased Elizabeth Montgomery around the house.

While other families spoke across dinner tables, went together to movies and to soda fountains and played ball in open fields, the Firestone scions were shipped to prestigious boarding schools and colleges. They gathered during vacations at chic resorts.

At age 18, Brooks was off to Princeton University, alma mater of his father, Leonard, and his four uncles and home to the Firestone Library, built by his grandfather. Leonard was the only one of four second-generation Firestones not to be voted "most likely to succeed" at Princeton. He lost out to Laurence Rockefeller.

Princeton didn't appeal to Brooks. He felt out of place in the eerily quiet almost confining environs of a college town. He craved the glitz, the noise and the energy of a big city and switched to the less conventional Columbia College in New York. He moved there with his young bride, Catherine Boulton, nicknamed Kate.

Kate Boulton, a dancer with the Royal Ballet, had led a sheltered life as the daughter of a clergyman with the Anglican church in Darjeerling, India, where she was born. One fall evening in early October, 1956, Kate was performing in New York at the Metropolitan Opera House when Brooks and a group of Princeton buddies came backstage to meet the dancers. He was smitten with Kate's bold and bright good looks, graceful demeanor, and most of all, her lack of interest in his family's money and status. Kate fell instantly in love with the 6-foot, 2-inch tall and skinny handsome man with boyish good looks who was fun, made her laugh and feel wanted. He exuded charm and a certain *je ne sais quoi* quality.

This was to be the beginning of a long-distance courtship of more than two years that gave Brooks time to grow up and Kate time to adjust to living in the States. They married in 1958. Three years later, Brooks graduated with a bachelor's degree in economics and immediately went into the family's tire business. Kate went along with the decision that Brooks should work for family and she too took a position in the company's public relations department, perceiving it as a good way to learn about the business and the family—like any good Firestone relative would do.

Brooks only had vague memories of his grandfather who founded Firestone Tire & Rubber Co., and died in 1939 when Brooks was three years old. Yet there was never any question that Brooks would step into the family business. He and four of his male cousins all did. It was expected, though it was also understood it wasn't a business for Firestone women. They were supposed to get married, stay home, have children and encourage their sons to follow in their fathers' footsteps. Martha Firestone, Brooks' cousin, married William Clay Ford, Sr., and years later would encourage their son, Billy, to go to work for his dad's company, Ford Motor Co., after graduating from Princeton. Today, Billy, 31, head of Ford's operations in Switzerland, who is returning to Detroit for a new assignment, and his cousin Edsel Ford II, 40, general sales manager of Lincoln-Mercury Division, are the only family members serving on the company's board. They are seeking a bigger say in strategic decisions. The Ford scions have been at odds with Ford chairman and professional manager Donald E. Peterson and have their sights set on running the company some day. This situation is similar to what Brooks encountered as a family member in a business controlled by non-family, though the Ford cousins have won slots on key committees after publicizing their problems.

Brooks joined Firestone Tire & Rubber Co. fresh out of college. He started in a training program, but never trained under his father and uncles. He was a student of non-family mentors. Leonard was too busy playing golf, dabbling in politics and supporting charities. A close friend remarked that Raymond C. (Leonard's older brother) was the only one who put in a full day's work.

Brooks' cousins and brother, Kimball, were put through similar hoops but had minimal contact with each other. Preferential treatment was given to family members in the business. They reported to the board rather than to immediate supervisors.

Brooks was a brilliant salesman, bright and quick. He was determined to be more than another family ornament. He first sold tires at a store in Salinas, CA. Shortly after, he took over sales for the entire territory. After nine months his success at hucksterism gained him a quick promotion to foreman of the Salinas plant to learn manufacturing. He made final inspections and supervised the thread tubing of tires.

Sometimes, Brooks felt overwhelmed. He didn't always know what he was doing. A department manager for thread tubing would have been in the company six to seven years, had some manufacturing or engineering background, and would have been physically and mentally tougher and harder than he was. Brooks worked like hell to keep up. Hard physical work. Twelve-hour days. He was always short of money, but never worried about it. He lived well, had a house in Pebble Beach. He had the stability of knowing if there was a disaster, a financial cushion was there.

Brooks continued to climb. After two years, he was moved to Akron where he became the Salinas liaison for the Zero-Defects program, an early forerunner of later quality control systems. Workers were encouraged to be safety and quality conscious. For their good workmanship they were rewarded financially. The program was Brooks' proudest accomplishment. It helped motivate many of the company's 12,000 to 15,000 employees.

Next, Brooks helped roll out Firestone's private label tire business. He liked the idea of dealing with companies other than Firestone and learned by observing their operations.

Three years later, corporate bigwigs deemed it time for Brooks to be promoted, but weren't quite sure what to do with him. In 1968, the executives sent him to Rome with his wife and three children to take over the International Seiberling Tire Co. that Firestone had bought out. Brooks began to question his career choice. This proved to be the beginning of the end for him at the family firm.

He took over a bad situation, but couldn't convince the company it was disastrous. He also came to disagree with the executive suite's decision to keep producing bias tires rather than switch early on to newer, longer-lasting radials. To make the change would have meant higher capital costs to outfit plants.

"It was extremely short-sighted and typical of such a large conservative company that had let non-family members dictate short-term profits," he says. "I knew we should do it, but what was the incentive? It was a better product. It lasted two to three times longer. And we had to tear our plants upside down to make it. With radials, we were in effect, cutting the market in half in one fell swoop. I wanted to go to the board and say, 'We ought to invest $250 million to obsolete all our plants and make a product that will last twice as long.' But it would have taken vision and strength on the part of the Firestone executives to do that. Not only were we totally behind in developing radials, but we made one that fell apart. I skipped a dividend for a year. I forced the company not to shut down the radial line and sell it to Amoco. The company didn't like me for that, either," he added.

Brooks had a communications problem with top management and

that included his family in the business. They didn't back him. It soured yet toughened him up.

Instead of quitting right away, however, Brooks accepted a transfer to England where he was determined to prove he could do a good job. He did.

But, almost unconsciously, he plotted his exit. When the chairman and chief executive of Firestone, Richard A. Riley, a non-family member, visited the London office, Brooks, a vice president, offered an ultimatum: He deserved a promotion. Brooks wanted to be deputy managing director, a board member of the European branch and head of the company's injected molded tire project. The company had nobody running that project, Brooks reasoned. He also wanted the company to view him as a big boy worthy of his position.

Firestone told Riley, knowing that he was being slightly pushy, "I've decided on my next job. And if you want to give it to me fine, and then you've got me. If not, I'm quitting. I know I have to produce. If I don't produce, you can fire me. I know I'm putting you in an awkward position. But it's nothing you can't deal with. I'm an up-and-coming executive."

"God damn it, Brooks. Don't do this. You don't do this in a company. That's crazy," Riley replied.

Firestone felt he could. "I'm sorry. I really apologize. But take it or leave it."

That night, Firestone president and Brooks' Uncle Raymond took Brooks to dinner to talk him out of his decision. Brooks was confident in what he was asking. He was disappointed that his uncle didn't compromise to get him to stay.

Days passed and nobody called to say, "Brooks, think about staying. Reconsider."

At the same time, Brooks tried to be magnanimous about the impasse. He and his uncle were good pals. Brooks understood that Raymond didn't want to butt heads with the company chairman.

He also understood that in family corporations, non-family members have a strong and selfish interest in getting the family members out of the business. "Sometimes the outsiders have a need to demean family members, especially if they are neophytes right out of college and are being pushed right to the top," Brooks said.

Brooks didn't leave Firestone bitter. He left to be on his own. He no longer bought into what the company espoused.

In the fall of 1976, Brooks' Uncle Raymond retired. The next year,

Brooks' brother, Kimball, left the tire company disillusioned with the family business, although he continued to serve on the board and as a member of the executive and audit committees. Kimball went to raise thoroughbreds in Maryland.

Their exits signaled the end of the Firestone family dynasty. And 11 years later, on May 6, 1988, the company would suffer the ultimate insult to a family business: It was taken over by a Japanese conglomerate, Bridgestone Corp., for a stunning $2.6 billion. The union of two disparate corporate cultures has posed its problems. Firestone's chairman has continued to focus on maximizing return to shareholders. On the other hand, Bridgestone, still 40 percent family owned, is committed to product quality and manufacturing efficiency at the expense of short-term profits.

Brooks knew he had to forge a new identity and career rather than recycle that of his father and grandfather. He had a special reason. Brooks was a product of an alcoholic family. His father, Leonard, would get drunk. It became Brooks' job to find him and bring his father home. One day, Brooks called Kimball and Lendy. As a group, they kidnapped their father and took him to the Menninger Foundation in Topeka. There was no such thing as intervention therapy then. Everything was hushed up. The subject was taboo. The kids devised their own treatment in 1965.

It was later recounted in Betty Ford's book, *Betty, A Glad Awakening*. Leonard woke up in a hospital and his three kids were standing at the foot of his bed. They said, "You have to do something."

Leonard responded, "Okay, I'll go to Los Angeles and join AA."

They said, "No." Lendy added, "Will you do something you don't want to do? Just for us?"

"Well, you know, I was so beat and hung over, and you have to be a real low-down not to respond to three loving kids when they're so concerned, so I said yes, I'd do whatever they wanted me to . . . In 10 minutes I was on my way to Topeka, Kansas."

Leonard recovered and went on to lecture about alcoholism for the Betty Ford Center in Rancho Mirage, CA.

Children in alcoholic families may harbor permanent scars, often in different ways depending on whether they suffered physical abuse, how old they were, how long the parents had been drinking and whether anyone outside the family offered any nurturing, says Kathleen Johnson, Executive Director of ONSITE, a Rapid City, SD center that specializes in treating families of alcoholics.

Brooks knew that alcoholism could cause instability, a lack of reality. It could be compounded by great family wealth and a family business. It could bring a whole mixed bag of background to the individual.

Kimball, a more introverted man than Brooks, also knew that alcoholism could take its toll on a family. But he felt it was lessened in his family's case because he and his siblings spent an inordinate amount of time in boarding schools.

Getting away from what at times was a troubled and an internationally prominent family business probably helped alleviate some of the stress for Brooks. So did gaining control of his life. Brooks broke the cycle of the poor little rich kid caught in an alcoholic web.

Out of a job at age 35 in 1972, Brooks went searching for work in the States while Kate and their three children remained in London close to her family.

Brooks' only work experience had been at Firestone. He didn't know what he wanted to do. He tapped his resources. He called up Justin Dart, founder of Dart Industries and a family friend. Dart took a long personal look at Brooks and his situation and decided he could give him a break. Dart wanted Brooks to go into real estate. That wasn't what Brooks wanted. He next considered a carbon fiber manufacturing company that was involved with pre-fab housing. The job didn't pan out. Brooks' father, who had been appointed ambassador to Belgium, came through with still another offer.

Leonard wanted to invest $500,000 in a parcel of property in California's Santa Ynez Valley, a lush green area 300 miles south of San Francisco on Highway 101 and 45 minutes north of Santa Barbara. Leonard needed someone to check out the site and possibly take care of it. Brooks would be a perfect choice.

The area was spectacular. Redwood trees and sagebrush blanked the coast. Shafts of sun hit the hilly terrain. Deep greens and browns glistened. Horses and cattle grazed on the hillsides.

Even though the particular site in question was inexpensive, it didn't seem a good investment to Brooks. What could be done with it? There were too many grapes in the northern Napa-Sonoma Valleys and the price of grapes was heading down. Then Brooks had an idea. Why not be the first in Santa Ynez to go the next step and turn the grapes into wine?

Brooks also decided he liked the village mentality. The Danes in nearby Solvang, a kind of Disneylike small town founded in 1911 by

Danish educators from the Midwest. The handful of ranchers. He knew he could never go back to the corporate life. He would stay here and farm the land for his father and family.

Going into farming was not quite so foreign to Firestone descendants. In the early 1700s, Nicholas Firestone, Brooks' great-great-great-grandfather, had been a prosperous farmer in Berg, Germany. He moved in 1752 to Eastern Pennsylvania where he also farmed.

Brooks' grandfather Harvey had been born in 1868 on a farm in Columbiana, Ohio. Because Harvey had plowed the ground on steel-rim wheels when he was young, he devised the idea to put America, including its farmers, on rubber tires after the bicycle craze hit. Harvey met Henry Ford at the time when Ford was building his first horseless carriage at the Edison Electric Co. in Detroit and was looking for a set of rubber tires. Harvey, who worked at the Columbus Buggy Company, had gone to Detroit as its salesman, bookkeeper and manager. He and Ford became good pals.

In 1900, Firestone introduced the first solid-rubber sidewire tire. Five years later, he introduced a straight-sided pneumatic auto tire. Sales hit $1 million one year later.

Farming grapes also was not totally new for the Santa Ynez Valley. Franciscan monks had planted vineyards in the 1780s. By the late 1800s, the area had more than 5,000 acres of vines. Prohibition temporarily eliminated the Valley's viticulture. Planting resumed in 1964 as settlers looked for a way to produce good crops from the land.

Nevertheless, a career in farming was a big financial risk for Brooks and his family. They had some income from his prior jobs, a small trust, the sale of a house and some investments. But it all wasn't sufficient to support Brooks' family in the manner to which they had been accustomed.

At the same time, Brooks was determined to try and make a go of what would become the first winery in the valley to grow its own grapes. He had the skills. He was organized, shrewd and able to envision the future. He was energetic and enthusiastic. He approached the task the way he tackled problems in the tire industry. If you don't know what to do, call in consultants. Talk. Listen. Learn.

He rang up Don Chappellet of the Chappellet Vineyard in Napa. He called Russ Green of Signal Oil, who had purchased the Simi Winery in Sonoma.

Brooks' initial plan was to invest about $7.5 million in the winery, or about $100 per case. In addition to his father's financial backing and his own heavy borrowing of one-third of the costs, he got capital from Japan-based Suntory Ltd. Co., one of the largest spirit and beverage houses in the world. His father knew the head, Keizo Saji. They played golf together. Brooks' dad phoned Saji and asked, "How about being partners?" Suntory sent some people over to check out the land and took a one-third limited partnership. The limited partners, however, let Brooks serve as general manager and run the show, much to his surprise and delight. He thought it somewhat peculiar that a company that size would not insist on managing its investment. But Brooks didn't complain.

Brooks hired Andre Tchelistcheff, the dean of California winemaking, to be a consultant. He went looking for a winemaker and found a plethora of candidates. Winemaking had become chic. Everyone wanted the job, especially with a winery connected to such an illustrious family. With Tchelistcheff's prodding, Brooks decided on a cellar master, Anthony Austin, a 22-year-old graduate of the University of California's famous School of Enology at Davis. Austin and Brooks worked side-by-side. Kate pitched in as well to help run the winery. She was never idle.

As owners of a fledgling winery, Kate and Brooks epitomized the American dream, a good-looking, hard-working couple determined to make a good product and to sell it themselves by dealing with distributorships. Brooks reasoned anyone who sold tires, a rough, tough and basic business, could sell anything. He figured his background was perfect. So many people in the wine business were either winemakers or farmers or hobbyists without a business background. Brooks also knew how to buy materials, make a product, deal with distributors and earn a profit.

As a business founder and owner, Brooks finally was able to put into action his highly detailed business ideas based on long- rather than short-term results. He drafted a 20-year plan. But it didn't include a professional manager who would demand a quick return on the dollar. In contrast, he reasoned, a family manager would be able to say, "This is going to happen. We are going to be the leader in this and that and it's going to take a while."

Brooks, Kate and their employees slid into a routine of growing, picking and harvesting grapes. Brooks brought in extra hands as he needed them. He wanted a lean operation so that he wouldn't lose control.

Brooks and his team built a crush pit and a fermentation room. They made plans to build an aging room the following year.

That spring they planted six varietals on 200 acres, wines made primarily from one specific grape listed on the label. Chardonnay, Johannisberg Riesling, Gewurztraminer, Pinot Noir, Merlot and Cabernet Sauvignon. The gravelly limestone soil was a perfect composition and offered great drainage. The structure of the soil made it better than in Napa where the floor of the valley doesn't dry out so well as it does further south, Brooks thought.

Full-scale production began. The Firestones bought a couple hundred French oak barrels at $200 to $250 a crack, expensive but necessary to produce fine complex wines that Brooks also planned to age in bottles. With everything in place, Brooks stood back knowing that he wouldn't see a profit for 10 years. "We had never planted grapes before, but nothing's hard if you want to do it. This wasn't going to be a frivolous pastime."

Brooks and Kate settled in. They bought a house in 1973 in Los Olivos, a tiny town of 200 named for the olives grown in the area. They bought a 120-acre place and a 2,300-acre cattle ranch. They were land poor, but the only mistake they made was not to buy every piece of property in the valley as prices skyrocketed. They became partial owners of the 1886 Mattei's Tavern in Los Olivos that Leonard had purchased, restored and turned over to his children. They helped build a church, St. Mark's in the Valley Episcopal, where Brooks became a lay reader.

As in any new business, there were glitches from the start. The year of the first harvest, the vineyard's assistant winemaker, Austin, left after two weeks. Brooks hired Alison Green, another graduate of the University of California at Davis' program. A conveyor that removed the pomace, the grape skins, seeds and stems, from the grapes, broke down. Brooks, Kate, Green and the other employees went to work around the clock. The Firestone kids, who had never formally worked for a winery, pitched in. Everybody picked grapes, checked labels, led tours and manned phones.

The first crush took place September 25, 1975, a day Brooks considered the best of his life. The first sales took place nine months later in June 1976, another benchmark.

The gamble paid off.

Brooks now looks the part of an experienced ranch hand in a pair of perfectly pressed Western pants, well-worn leather cowboy boots that add two inches to his height, two plaid flannel shirts and a gleaming silver engraved belt buckle with his initials, A.B.F. He's known by everyone as Brooks, the vintner, not Firestone, the tire mogul. In a voice that sounds like actor Lew Ayres' and with his big, conservative and still boyish looks that make him resemble Joel McCrea, both 1940s matinee idols, Brooks frequently comments about how overused the joke about his new-found celebrity has become. "I want to become known for my wines and not for my you-know-whats."

Brooks is also tired of the string of corny jokes that pair the two businesses:

"Firestone, the tireless wine producer."

"Firestone Vintner, a big wheel."

"Firestone—Riesling not radials."

Off Highway 101, the Firestone compound seems to embrace Brooks and Kate's new lifestyle. Simple. Rustic. Unadorned. Up a hill on the Firestones' cattle ranch sits the main house. It's a 1930s two-story, yellow-and-white frame farmhouse with a welcoming porch. Inside the combination living and dining rooms are done in flowered English chintzes. Furniture is placed in intimate groupings. Fresh flower arrangements are everywhere as are paintings and lithographs. The focal point of the living room is a large black lacquered grand piano balanced by a stone fireplace on the opposite side of the room. A cozy kitchen nearby oozes snug efficiency. Kate, who loves to cook, was featured in the Los Angeles County Art Museum and Art Museum Council's newest cookbook, *California Cooking: Parties, Picnics & Celebrations*.

About 100 yards down the hill is a bunkhouse with a vaulted redwood ceiling and a style that hints more forcibly at the Firestones' former, more grandiose lifestyle. Strong blues and greens with accents of peach predominate the rooms filled with comfortable antiques and reproductions of French and English pieces. A large hutch is jammed with pewter plates. There are deep couches upholstered tightly, corner chairs, coffee tables with fat piles of trendy magazines and copies of a book about polo that Brooks wrote and that he had a vanity press publish. It's a slim, 77-page, green-bound volume, titled *High Road, Low Goal*, about the three months he spent on the polo circuit in the summer of 1986.

Both houses have been featured in chic publications such as *W* and *Architectural Digest* and both serve as a retreat from a hectic physical plant. The cattle ranch includes 250 cow units, which Brooks explains means a cow and its calves. It also includes one thoroughbred. Foxhounds are kept at the Santa Ynez Valley Hunt Club from which he rides. A nearby sales office, close to the highway, is where Brooks and his neighbors auction off cattle a few times a year.

All is sandwiched in the middle of the green hills where wealthy Hollywood types have grabbed acreage. Mike Nichols. John and Bo Derek. Ray Stark. Hollywood producer Douglas S. Cramer of *Dynasty* lives in perhaps the most spectacular house in the valley—a one-story modern extravaganza filled with contemporary art by David Hockney, Ellsworth Kelly, Frank Stella and Roy Lichtenstein, and bordered by his Douglas Vineyards. The newest neighbor to be buzzed about is singer Michael Jackson.

As Brooks drives along Zaca Station Road, a dirt and gravel path that threads through the Sierra Madres, he points to his vineyard in the distance and boasts that it's among the largest and most successful of the valley's 30 vineyards and 24 wineries. He pulls up in the parking lot and jumps out of his four-door Chevrolet Malibu. The cavernous winery lies straight ahead, a striking four-story redwood structure designed by the prominent Santa Rosa architecture firm of Keith & Associates. He moves quickly toward a cluster of vines and grabs one in his enormous and calloused hands. His arms are tan from working outdoors. His face is flushed.

"What do you say when you look out the window and see this terrific natural territory and brilliant blue sky?" he says, sounding like an old master of ceremonies.

He quickly struts over to another clump of grapes. This is where he planted 12 acres of Pinot Noir but then took the grapes out because the winery's Merlot became its most sought-after wine. He put in a phylloxera-resistant grape plant and then grafted the Merlot on to it. It was a bad take. The vineyard lost 30 percent of its grapes. It embarrasses Brooks and his team that the vines are next to the winery and still quite visible.

Even with temporary setbacks, Brooks has no regrets. Firestone Vineyard has won countless awards for premium varietals, starting with first place for a Johannesberg Riesling at the Vintner Club's blind tasting in San Francisco in 1977. Awards aren't said to do much for sales, but they give a jolt to keep momentum and morale going.

An even better barometer to some are the vineyard's profits, which showed up ahead of schedule in 1981, the first year the vineyard had a full 12 months of wine sales. Brooks has now maximized his property's yield. The vineyard produces 75,000 to 80,000 cases a year, all of which are made with grapes grown on his property. Gross sales are about $4 million a year, though Brooks describes the margins as "thin."

Brooks walks inside the 35,000-square-foot winery where there are enormous sleek 9,000-gallon stainless steel fermenting vats, huge 3,500-gallon 12-foot high French oak tanks and 55-gallon fermenting barrels for aging such varieties as Chardonnay six to eight months. The equipment almost dwarfs the 50-foot-high winery, which boasts all the best—handsome wood floors, a nighttime venting system designed to keep the building at 56 degrees Fahrenheit and a moisturizing system that looks like a home humidifier designed to retain moisture in the wood barrels. Winemaker Green is testing different aging processes to get a better taste. One lot of a 1986 Sauvignon Blanc was barrel-fermented and allowed to remain in the barrel on the yeast where it underwent malo-lactic fermentation to change the malic acid into lactic acid. Green explains that a secondary fermentation gives the wines a softer flavor. She has fermented a second lot in stainless steel, then transferred it to French oak to rest on lees, the settling from the solids, for a month in order to add an oak flavor. She then aged both lots in French oak before master blending them in one big tank for four more months. Everything has been scientifically determined. Only an occasional spill of wine or beer mars the antiseptic cleanliness and orderly look.

Brooks moves on to the tasting room, used by small groups who come to visit the Firestone Vineyard. The tasting room is furnished in dark woods and red velvets. One of its doors is heavy oak that Kate found in a church in Europe, Firestone notes proudly. Brooks' corporate office is right above and reached by a handsome open stairway.

Brooks is his own best public relations man. In the evening and on weekends, he dons a suit and tie and traverses the state to meet the demands of a wine superstar. He speaks about Firestone wines at gatherings of aficionados and neophytes.

But even as Firestone Vineyard becomes better known, Brooks insists on limiting visitors. There are no signs on the highway giving directions to the winery. Brooks doesn't want people showing up who saw a sign. He wants to control the flow of traffic because Firestone wine is in limited supply and the winery is too small to accommodate large groups.

Brooks contends with other pressing problems. His property is landlocked. Yet he doesn't want to buy grapes from other farmers and lose control of quality. But he can diversify and recently made a champagne for one of his daughters' weddings. He's also perfecting the mold that attacks grapes, the Botrytis Cinerea, in order to make a Johannisberg Riesling dessert wine. He had success in 1986, and his Johannisberg Riesling Santa Ynez Valley Late Harvest Ambassador's Vineyard Selected Harvest earned an "89" rating in *The Wine Spectator*, a "very good wine with special qualities." Such challenges rev him up.

Perhaps more surprising may be Brooks' latest feat, a non-alcoholic beer. It contains less than 0.5 percent alcohol and has only 75 calories. He produced it in a joint venture with Hale Fletcher, a biochemistry graduate, and Michael Lewis, a professor of brewing at Davis. They packaged it in a dark green bottle with an eye-catching red and green label. The run will be just 1,000 cases of a yeasty, malty fresh-tasting product. Quality comes first, and on a recent weekday, Brooks told an employee to throw out a bad batch. The beer is brewed right next to the fermenting grapes on the ground floor of the winery. One wine expert is impressed that Firestone is moving into a field that has been dominated by the Europeans. "Firestone is among the first to offer a low-calorie premium domestic near beer. It's a fabulous idea," says Glennon Bardgett of the Wine Cellar in St. Louis.

The winery is also the hub for a satellite operation, J. Carey Cellars, another winery just four miles down the road.

Brooks bought J. Carey in January 1987 at the urging of two brothers, both surgeons, who as a hobby were making fine wine at their 25-acre vineyard, but weren't making money. It was a coup. The land alone made it a great business decision. Others had bid on the property, including Brooks' former winemaker, Austin. At first Brooks considered using J. Carey as a second label, a way to sell wines that he didn't want to bottle under the Firestone label.

He changed his mind. Brooks "resuscitated" the vineyard which now produces premium wines, 7,000 cases from Chardonnay, Sauvignon Blanc, Cabernet Blanc and Sauvignon grapes grown on the property. He named Kate its vintner here, and she adds a decided cachet with her clipped English accent. Kate is superb in her new role. Brooks considers himself a commercial sweat, but about her he says she's a thoroughbred.

Kate describes J. Carey as a small venture where wines are hand-crafted in small lots to make a statement of quality and individuality.

Although the two wineries both produce varietals from their own grapes and with distinct labels the operations overlap. J. Carey grapes are picked, stored and fermented on site but trucked over on flatbeds to the bigger winery to be bottled, distributed and tabulated.

Each Firestone vintner knows what the other is up to throughout the day. They talk on the phone. They visit. Their paths may cross two or three times a week, sometimes at lunch at J. Carey on a deck erected by Lorimar Productions for its television series, "Aaron's Way," which was filmed at J. Carey. They'll dine on redwood picnic benches set out under a cluster of live oak trees. Kate will break out a bottle of J. Carey, perhaps a 1985 Chardonnay or a 1984 Sauvignon Blanc. Brooks is likely to help himself to one of his beers.

The tranquillity and perfection of the newest Firestone endeavor stand out in a meadow rich in wildflowers. Kate is content. And Brooks' new-found confidence has enabled him not to dwell on how either winery is going to survive in the future without him and with non-family conglomerates gobbling up family-owned wineries. In some cases, the new non-family owners have hurt the quality of the wine as they have expanded output to improve bottom lines, says Brooks. Brooks thinks there's too much emphasis on a fast return on a dollar, what he terms the Harvard Business School mentality.

He says that a really strong and brilliant professional manager could never run a winery because he'd run it into the ground. "Many of our decisions are crazy, like aging wine in French oak. There has to be a pride and a longing and that's part of a family business. I'm building my business up for grandchildren. A professional manager has no incentive to do that. He's judged on what he does in the short term, the year's results, and so he manages accordingly."

Brooks likens what's happening in wineries to what is occurring in the world outside. He says it's all part of our disposable society, which leads to a modern Tower of Babel and which could spell the decline of Western civilization. Any trendy idea can get itself forced upon anybody.

Yet Brooks, an archconservative Republican and an unabashed patriot, isn't all talk. He ran for the California State Assembly in 1981 with $80,000 from his father and a total outlay of $494,000. He lost by 1,190 votes out of 102,550 cast. He lowers his voice when talking about the Democrats. "I'd never support the party of Jesse Jackson or McGovern. They're a bunch of well-intentioned half-wits and Jackson has no qualifications."

Brooks wasn't enamored with Reagan, who has a ranch in the

nearby Santa Barbara Hills and whose photographs and thank-you notes for wine are posted throughout Brooks' offices. "He's more form than substance." Brooks doesn't wax enthusiastically about Bush either, thinks he has "adequate credentials." Nevertheless, he was Santa Barbara Valley co-chairman of George Bush's campaign for President.

Brooks' time for leisure, his new successful career and the sale of most of his family's business doesn't make him feel vindicated. He seems shell-shocked that it happened. He says he didn't benefit from the sale because he didn't own any stock. Most family members had previously sold their shares because they felt they should diversify their holdings. Kimball was an exception. He is listed in the company's latest proxy as owning about 8,000 shares.

Brooks has continued to care about Firestone Tire & Rubber Co., even 16 years after he quit. "Companies like that helped make this country great."

Brooks is confident about the long-term prospects for Firestone Vineyard but would love to have a second generation come to work in it. Any of his children would be welcome. For now, his three older children are pursuing other careers. Hayley, 27, is a teacher; Adam, 25, is a lawyer; Polly, 23, is an actress. Andrew, 12, shows the most promise as he reels off names of Firestone labels as fast as he might list today's rock stars.

"I never had a sense of my own worth," Brooks says. "Kids shouldn't start out in the family business. They'll never have a sense of their ability, the confidence that comes from doing a good job. They're never treated normally in a family business and never taken seriously by family and non-family or by themselves. All in my family went directly into the tire business."

As Brooks and Kate sit on the hillside that overlooks the vineyards, Brooks talks about what he would do if all four of his children suddenly wanted to come to work in the winery.

He turns to face Kate. His eyes are large, clear and somber. His brow is furrowed. A wide smile spreads across his face.

"I guess I'll just have to find more J. Carey wineries," he says, no longer questioning his worth or that of his family. He knows that his grandfather, Harvey S. Firestone, would approve of the new family business, which produces a quality product and looks to the future.

Smith Farms
Chula, MO

I see young men, my townsmen, whose misfortune it is to have inherited farms, houses, barns, cattle and farming tools; for these are more easily acquired than got rid of. Better if they had been born in the open pasture and suckled by a wolf, that they might have seen with clearer eyes what field they were called to labor in. Who made them serfs of the soil?
—*Walden* by HENRY DAVID THOREAU

The letter announcing the closing of the John Deere dealership was buried in the dusty clutter of Bob Smith's mail. The mail had not been sorted for days, maybe weeks. Stacks of cancelled checks, bills and newspaper clippings with the latest farm statistics filled the scrubbed pine kitchen table, reaching almost as high as the grain inside the sleek steel silos that stood outside a few yards away. News of the closing meant Bob would have to drive his combine and tractors 60 miles farther to Princeton, MO, to buy parts and have them repaired.

On another day, the inconvenience and greater expense would matter more. But Bob has become immune as his family farm and community have been hard hit. Four months before, the only grocery store in his small town of Chula in North Central Missouri closed as the population dwindled to 150 from 230 during the last few months. A decade ago the town numbered 350. More recently, the town's tiny post office cut back its hours.

For seven generations, the Smith family farm had been a comfortable solitary retreat off blacktopped highway KV, 20 miles north of Chillicothe, the area's largest city. When Bob bought the farm from his parents in 1981, he increased his spread to 3,280 acres. With his wife, Patty, and a staff of two, they plowed, planted and harvested corn, milo, sorghum and beans.

Each day on the farm was different and a challenge that row croppers like Bob and Patty met with strength and optimism. "It's a complex juggling act to get everything done and to do it efficiently," says Smith.

Before work began, Bob checked the weather to gauge what needed to be done that day. Typically in winter, he spent most of his time in the shop repairing machinery or on the phone discussing business and arranging meetings.

In the summer the routine changed. Bob and Pat did the field work. Up and out by 7:00 A.M. Their children were too small to help, although Billy Bob, 9, started driving the tractor last year. They worked the ground, planting, hoeing and cultivating until after dark. Bob rarely left the fields to eat dinner Pat brought out to him. She then joined in planting and hoeing. If a machine broke down, the Smiths couldn't afford the down time of repairing machinery and bought new.

"No longer," Smith says sadly remembering better times. Just seven years before, he was one of the most successful farmers in Livingston County with a net worth of $650,000.

The picture has changed. Smith, 41, a 6'1" hulk of a man, sits hunched over the table looking out at his remaining 680 acres. They still represent a good-sized piece of land, though the once green and hilly acreage is pockmarked by eroding topsoil, much like the farmers' lives. The fields produce fewer crops to take to market and fewer products for their own table. They are dry and barren, mowed down as part of the Federal Government's program to encourage farmers not to plant until prices improve. Altogether the Federal Government paid farmers not to plant 71 million acres in 1987 as part of its Conservation Reserve Program. Bob is $1.6 million in debt to the Farmers Home Administration. He hasn't paid his real estate taxes of almost $1,000.

Bob and Patty are trying to come to grips with how this happened. They want to remain the close-knit, independent Missouri farm family they have been for 19 years and continue the legacy from the Smith ancestors, who settled the area more than 125 years ago from England and Ireland.

But farming has become almost insurmountable for the Smiths and thousands of others. Farmers have always struggled with external, unpredictable forces such as weather and crop disease. More recently, they've had to fight soaring interest rates, plunging land values, hungrier creditors, stiffer government regulations, overproduction of crops such as corn, soybeans and wheat, and the worst drought since the Depression. As exports fell, the money supply became tight and farmers lost their borrowing power. As a result, farmers, traditionally independent and private people, reluctantly became more dependent on government subsidies. Farm subsidies climbed as high as $22.4 billion in 1987. Those hit the hardest are the small- to medium-sized farms. The farm population fell 240,000 in 1987 to a record low.

Farmers also have lacked sophisticated managerial skills and knowledge of changing tax laws to cope well.

Added to this external crisis, farmers face a bigger nemesis. The eternal optimism that has always driven them to believe there would be another day and another time is now undermining their lives, tugging at them to stay longer on the land than they maybe should and plunging them deeper into debt.

Change for farmers is a foreign commodity. They have no opportunity to set prices or regulate costs. Inventory and property values, which escalate for most small business owners, have declined more than 60 percent for Missouri farmers since 1980.

In contrast, when most family business owners see danger signals, they revamp their strategies. They hire new management. They cut inventory and employees, and change product lines. Farmers cannot. When the problems in non-farm businesses are beyond repair, some owners consider selling out or merging.

Farmers, generally a private, conservative lot, think differently. Their businesses and their lives are tied to the land. Farming offers a long-term chance to pass on the same home, the same land and the same values to future generations. It offers a chance to remain rugged individualists. "Nobody's breathing down your neck. You know what you've got to do. You set your own pace," declare farmers again and again to explain why they can't let go, even if they've had little or no success and may be drowning in debt.

How does the farmer measure business success?

A profit is fairly insignificant. Financial perks are inconsequential. Instead of a company car, stock options and club memberships, the rewards are intangibles such as working the land as a family and seeing things grow. "Success for me means having a unit someday to pass on to my son. Something that is not necessarily debt free, but close to it. I'm not sure it can ever be attained. And for most guys, to be successful, is to be out of debt on the farm," Smith explains.

Computerized corporate farming, where farmers don't live on the land they farm but work it for large insurance companies and corporations, absentee ownership, sophisticated foreign-made equipment and five- and ten-year growth plans hold no appeal for Smith who believes all would rip apart the structure on which the family farm is built.

For the first time since the Depression, farmers who are parents question whether their children should follow them into farming or leave and make this way of making a living as extinct as other family businesses such as the corner druggist and grocery store owner. In a vulnerable moment, Bob says he hopes that Billy Bob will choose a different career. "It's really hard to come to that point. As a father, I'd love to see him follow me, but I question whether it makes sense." Patty quickly nods in agreement. Both sound convincing, but in the same breath, are proud that Billy and his older sister, Amy, 11, learned how to drive the family combine when they were just eight.

Bob is trying to balance what his life used to be against the realities of what it has become and what lies ahead.

"If it weren't for my parents, my kids and my wife, it would be a lot easier to forget the farm and turn to an outside full-time job," Bob rationalizes. Nothing remains the same. But his sense of duty has compelled him not only to try to keep the farm going, but to take on two part-time jobs to make ends meet. In doing so, he has almost lost his independence, one of the main attractions of farming.

Bob digs out his calendar. On it he has scribbled everything he must do that week. "There is no routine any more," he says as he spews forth his disjointed schedule. Every week he juggles three part-time jobs that easily can stretch into full-time work.

Three times a week, Marlen Owens, District Sales Manager for Funk Seeds International, a division of Ciba-Geigy Corp., arrives at the Smiths' door. Owens, a fourth-generation farmer, is a jovial man with a pleasant, lined face. He and his wife and two sons escaped bankruptcy. They could also foresee some of the looming problems, including a lack of money to afford replacing $100,000 tractors and other aging equipment.

"Net farm income will be up this year, but over 50 percent of the farm income this year will be from government subsidies," Owens says. He leans back with perfect ease, his hat slipping to one side. He crosses his legs, ready to tell good stories about his farming days. "I hope some day, we can go back to farming the land rather than farming the programs. I miss farming especially in the spring of the year when I can smell the soil and I don't have a tractor to crawl in. My job is as close to it as I can get, but without losing my shirt." His wife works four days a week as a nurse to supplement his earnings.

After a cup of coffee and much-craved conversation, Owens and Smith slowly make rounds to neighboring farms. It's hard work trying to convince farmers to pay $16 an acre of corn seed that will bring the equivalent of $130.50 an acre for the final product on the open market. That may seem like a good profit until the costs of growing the corn are added in—fertilizer at $60 to $85, insecticide at $8 and chemicals at $16 to $22 plus the cost of the land.

For Bob, this job means not only sales commissions but free seeds and a chance to show what a good farmer he's been. Owens enjoys working with Bob, his partner of 5½ years. "Bob's a real promoter. He likes to get out there first. He plants the best rows. It helps me look good."

On other days, Bob becomes the businessman, a rural employment specialist for the Green Hills Regional Planning Commission. He feels self-conscious in the *de rigueur* coat and tie, but he loves the thrill of finding jobs for farmers, who are losing or have already lost land and homes. The job is emotionally draining as he figures how to market skills for the outside world, teach them to interview and write a resume. Most have never held down an outside job or received a paycheck. For 40 hours a week, squeezed in between his farming chores, Bob earns $240.

In his precious spare time, always at the mercy of the weather and the season, Bob tends to his remaining acreage and does custom work for other farmers. They, too, are pressed for time, but can no longer afford full-time help. The work is taxing. Up at dawn. No break for lunch. Working past dark. Returning home exhausted.

The uncertainty of who will be next, eats away at the Smiths as they try to maintain their charade. It's become harder. Bob conducts most of his business within full view and earshot of his family, from a telephone sitting on the kitchen counter. He paces back and forth as he preaches survival tactics. The cord swings fiercely. He becomes excited and flushed, his face as red as his hair. A CB radio that is hooked up to his farm equipment and to other farms regularly brings more bad news. This is one way the farmers stay in touch.

The tension of everyday life is chiseled into Bob's fleshy face and body. With less farm work and more time to sit around the kitchen, Bob smokes compulsively, a habit he had given up before Amy was born. Patty shuffles around trying to dump the ashes as fast as Bob fills the ashtrays. He eats when he's not smoking and is 60 pounds heavier than he was five years ago. Patty tried to get him to diet by changing their meals. "Hell, we don't eat that way around here," was his reaction after a few of her low-calorie attempts.

Even with a $4 billion Federal boost to the Farm Credit System, from the farmer-owned bank lending network mired in debt and designed to keep the 287 Farm Credit Banks from closing, Smith sees little direct help for the farmer.

To salvage what little the Smiths have left, Bob leans on Patty more than ever, but she, too, has spread herself thin. Although they had vowed that Patty would never work outside the farm once they had children, they've broken that promise. Patty, a large, round woman with short brown hair streaked prematurely gray and bright blue eyes that look out at the world with an older woman's wisdom, fills in at the local post office several days a week.

That money wasn't sufficient, however. She now gets up in the frigid darkness shortly after 1:00 A.M. and drives down the narrow highways to a job in Chillicothe. She sorts mail until 5:30 A.M. three to four times a week and earns $5 an hour. Home by 6:00 A.M., she has one hour to crawl back into bed and catch some sleep before Bob and the children rise.

"Can you believe she has the 1:30 to 5:30 A.M. shift and she's excited and loves the job," Bob chuckles nervously. His tone of voice reveals his excitement that more dollars are coming in, though he has already spent the money for expenses that keep mounting like a pile of dirty dishes.

The rigorous routine means that Patty is often exhausted when the children get off the big yellow school bus that lumbers down their street with fewer riders. There is little reason for traffic to ramble past their home, a lonely outpost. Nobody lives in Bob's grandmother's 100-year-old decaying farm house down the road. "We could really make do with a car and driver for the kids," explains a neighbor. Patty's more frequent absences also mean that dinners, once a labor of love with staples from their fields, are now no different from meals prepared by busy two-career couples in large metropolises. Tonight, it's spaghetti with canned tomato sauce, salad with bottled dressing and store-bought bread.

The family farmhouse is a brick and clapboard six-room ranch that closely resembles the millions of postage-stamp-size houses dotting middle-class suburbs everywhere. Bob's Uncle Wade built the house in 1947. He went bankrupt in 1952 and his brother, Bill, Bob's father, bought the farm at the courthouse steps for $200 an acre. Bob bought the house and property from his father in 1981 for $1,500 an acre. Bob added a private master wing for his parents' retirement.

White paint peels off the clapboard. The concrete patio that Bob started to build off the master bedroom is on hold, unlandscaped and crumbling. The children's dipping pool has never been filled and is rusting from neglect. The richly-equipped metal tool shed a few yards away, which used to be Bob's winter retreat, has become a messy warehouse of uncompleted projects. Bob apologizes for the clutter. "I've always tried to keep things up to snuff. When you lose financially and you can't keep things up the way they were, it absolutely drives you over the brink. Those little things probably hurt me more than anything," he acknowledges.

Almost every day, what used to be a busy, noisy household is deafeningly silent. Few children come to play with the Smiths' three children. They romp most days with the Dalmatian puppies the Smiths raise to augment family income.

The family rarely escapes their farmstead except for support group meetings they attend. There are no extras, little to look forward to. A respite for Patty is to go every other month to the beauty parlor in town for a $6 shampoo, haircut and blow dry. She tries to take her girls along and treat them as well. She doesn't expect vacations. They have taken only two in 19 years. For her birthday, Patty gives herself a visit to the gynecologist because she can't afford to get sick. They have no health insurance.

Money is a bone of contention. The Smiths even quarrel about how to spend what they don't have. As Bob loses confidence, he turns begrudgingly to Patty for advice. He sends in a $250 registration fee for the Young Farmers' Annual Convention in Peoria. Patty disapproves. "How can we afford that when we can't even clothe our kids?" Bob pushes about why they must go. Patty relents as usual.

The children pick up the gist of the conversation, though their parents shoo them away when the talk turns to bankruptcies and foreclosures. "Now, get on," Bob says, often to Billy, who most resembles his dad and who tries hardest to get Bob's attention by clinging and interrupting.

A moment later, Bob admits that he's become tougher on the children, spending more time away, demanding perfect manners and giving in to fewer requests. He tries not to duplicate the same mistakes that his father made in raising him so strictly. "My parents were so damned strict. I never could take a vacation. My father would say, 'You can't leave livestock. Someone's got to stay.' I never took a date to barn warmings."

Yet Bob hasn't broken the cycle. He can't let go. He got so down on Amy at one point that she acted up at school, he said. "They had to call me down there," Bob said. Patty often acts as the silent mediator and quietly pulls the children away from their father when he starts to seethe. She knows they are insecure as she watches them eat junk food nonstop and drink bottles of cola. In their garage, 16-ounce glass soda bottles are stacked like books in a well-ordered library. Not once do Patty or Bob tell the children to stop eating.

The childrens' youth offers a cushion, as the Smiths see it. "Fortunately they were young enough when things were really bad so they weren't aware of everything going on. I'm glad we didn't have them when we were young and first married. They would be adults now and really aware of what's going on," Patty said.

Even the outside support many farm children have received from grandparents and extended families, who often live on the same farm, is minimal. The Smiths' relationship with Bob's parents, who were dairy farmers and now reside in an apartment in Chillicothe, has become distant from the time the younger Smiths declared bankruptcy. "They thought you just don't do that," Bob said. "They're not upset about the money and the fact that I can't pay them back, but about the disgrace I've caused the family. It's not like we were living high off the hog or anything."

Phone calls and dinner invitations from Grandma and Grandpa have become rare. Visits take place on holidays, more out of obligation than love, Bob says. Bob's mother, Gracie Ann, terms the relationship "a little strained. Maybe they'll come out okay, though the transition will be hard," she said.

Patty's family is the main source of unconditional support, even though they discouraged her from marrying a farmer. When Pat was in third grade, the Farmers Home Administration foreclosed on the family farm. Patty's father became an alcoholic and died in his burning farmhouse.

The town of Chula mirrors this deterioration in its 40 square miles. It has become a ghost of a town 102 years after it was founded. Many farmers are unable to pay their real estate, property and school taxes. Mansure Street, Chula's equivalent of a main street, is eerily quiet. There is little reason to come to town and little reason for other businesses to set up shop.

Both barbershops are gone. Only one of three gas stations remains open. There is a tiny post office with its squeaking screen door and two windows nearly opaque with dust from lack of attention. The community hall is rarely occupied. The only school, Livingston R-III elementary school, is $43,000 in debt, combining classes now that enrollment is down to 83 from 134, cutting its kitchen staff to one, begging teachers not to go to Chillicothe where salaries are higher.

Even the three remaining churches, Catholic, Presbyterian and Baptist, which have often been a haven during their congregants' individual and communal crises, draw smaller attendance. A decade ago the Presbyterian church couldn't hold everybody. On a typical Sunday, four cars are now parked in front. The Smiths quickly tick off names of active family members at their Catholic church.

The geometric neatness and snug neighborliness that once characterized the residential streets beyond the public strip is untended. Neat brick and clapboard farmhouses no longer define productive farm acres.

Some like the Smiths have been able to hang on to their farms and farm sporadically. Others reside in their homes, though they own none of the land around them. Those who haven't been able to pick up a mail route, drive a milk truck or school bus, or sell insurance have moved away. The Smiths have lost three of their four nearest neighbors since 1980. Some are forced to go on welfare, live in shelters for the homeless or eat in soup kitchens. Says a concerned Roger Allison, director of the Missouri Rural Crisis Center, a not-for-profit agency, "It's not unlike the Depression, when farmers were killing jack rabbits and making gravy to keep from starving." Allison is in danger of losing his 400-acre farm in north central Missouri. He owes $265,000 and has made no payments to the Farmers Home Administration since 1980.

In the dark of the night, neighbors, too proud to use the food stamps they've received, surreptitiously drive up to the Smiths' open garage, lift the trunk of their unlocked Jeep Cherokee and remove a loaf or two of days-old bread. Patty picks up the bread every Monday at a bread store, telling the employees there it's to be animal feed.

Chula never had a bank to tally the lost dollars in every farmers' accounting ledgers. But if you ask the Smiths or their neighbors, they can reel off which family filed for which type of bankruptcy and after how many generations. Although they bare their secrets to one another and a few selected strangers, they do so quietly.

The Smiths and their neighbors are far from alone in Livingston County, Smith says, as he jumps out of his chair to grab a local newspaper story citing the latest statistics. "Just look at this. Only 75 families work the area's 800 farms full time. Their gross production is less than $40,000 a year. Thirty-nine of those 75 have either filed for bankruptcy or quit." Every six farmers who go broke take one rural business with them.

But perhaps the biggest tragedy of Bob Smith's life is that he never wanted to follow his father and grandfather into farming.

For the senior Smiths, farming was a foregone conclusion. Bob's great-great-grandfather, Robert Smith, came from Ohio in the 1850s to farm land in Missouri. Bob's grandfather and father also farmed the land. Farming was simple then. All farmers needed were some horses and a plow. Neighbors helped out. It was a community effort.

Gracie Ann, Bob's mother, was raised in town. Her father drove a truck. Farming wasn't a family tradition. But soon after she and Bill Smith married in 1942, farming took hold of them. They liked the values that farming encouraged, the togetherness and working side-by-side. They started with 160 acres of rented land in Chula. "It was a way to get started. You bought a house and you rented some land," recalled Bill Smith. He went off to fight in World War II and when he returned, the Smiths bought 80 additional acres of land a half mile away. They planted soybeans, corn and wheat. When they couldn't make a living with row crops, they added a dairy herd. They made a better living. They next got into the hog business. They raised lots of pigs and paid off their mortgage. When they needed more land, they bought it. They never went into debt, though they were less conserva-tive than their parents, who lived through the Depression, had been.

Bob was born in 1947, the year his father returned from the War. By the age of five, he learned to dairy farm. He always tried to please his father and stuck to a rigid schedule. Up at 5:00 A.M. to milk 50 to 60 black and white Holsteins and back in the barn as soon as school ended. "That was all I ever did and I hated it," Bob recalled. "I was never allowed to date, go to dances or do anything with friends. I was held down. As the oldest, I was expected to do everything. My parents did the reverse on my younger sisters and let them run. There was no way I was going into farming even though my parents were living comfortably. I wanted to get away from the goddamned mess. I didn't want any part of it."

Farm work was backbreaking, Gracie Ann remembered. "We rarely went into town. We worked all the time. Hours were much longer. It took a lot more time to farm. Fortunately, we didn't have as many expenses then. We didn't have all the big modern machinery the young fellahs have today and we didn't have all the help. My husband and I did it all. Bob had to pitch in mornings and nights. We always worked as a family, each doing our assigned chores silently and automatically."

Bob went off to college in the mid-'60s to become an agricultural teacher. He decided he didn't want to deal with the daily grind of working the land. Convinced that his son wasn't going into farming, Bob's father sold the dairy operation the day after Bob left for college.

Bob spent an inordinate amount of time at school drinking beer, partying, playing cards and having a good time. But it was hard work trying to pay the bills which he did by taking out several student loans. "The only time my father ever paid for anything was a $55 book bill and two tanks of gasoline so I could get back to school."

By the spring of his junior year, he remet Patty whom he had known since high school. She had grown up in Brunswick, 70 miles away. By summer 1968, they married, disappointing Bob's parents who knew a wife could disrupt their son's plans to move beyond the family farm. His father thought there were better opportunities than farming.

Bob and Patty returned to school together where she got a job at a glove factory. The responsibilities became too difficult, especially with a $10,000 educational loan looming in their faces.

Bob wanted to make money even if it meant returning to farming. He left school without graduating. They moved into a trailer in Chillicothe that they sold to come up with money for a farm. A parish priest loaned them $1,000 to buy 120 acres. "We had asked him if he knew anybody who would lend a guy $1,000 to start out. And when he walked by me the next Sunday at church, he stuck a piece of paper in my pocket with a $1,000 check with his name on it. No papers were ever drawn up. No interest ever charged."

Patty wasn't upset by the decision to farm. "We were up at Bob's grandmother's all the time anyway, so we figured we might as well get paid for what we were doing. We both had outside jobs which helped bring in more money."

Bob and Patty slowly settled in like newlyweds. They covered walls of their home with photographs and needlepoints with sayings that reminded them daily that they were a farm family: "Farming is close to God's work." "Crime doesn't pay and neither does farming." They decorated the kitchen walls with china plates that sparkled like monuments to orderliness.

No sooner had the ink dried on one land contract, than they bought more land. Both found they like farming. They liked the gamble even more. "There's nothing like watching the wind rippling through rough waves of golden wheat, corn and milo. You just can't imagine the feeling of seeing that little seed going into the ground and coming up as a little plant, seeing two leaves on a soybean plant and that little sprig of corn just start up and turn into a whole field. There is something to all of it. Like a disease. It's lethal."

The booming economy in the 1970s made the addiction harder to break. Agriculture exports increased. Interest rates fell in the early 1970s. Land values shot up to $1,500 an acre from the $400 that the Smiths had paid when they got started and which had been considered exorbitant then. Banks encouraged borrowing with little or no collateral. Farmer after farmer grabbed as much equipment and land as he could, in spite of being averse to debt. Then, something changed. Farmers began to think it was more important to own their neighbor's land than to have a neighbor.

The Smiths were no exception. They bought two combines, three tractors. They had machinery worth more than $1 million. The trappings made Bob appear successful. His parents warned him not to borrow so heavily. "No, no, no," his mother said. Bob shouted back, "I've been to college. I know what's best. Don't tell me what to do."

Bob loved the empire he was creating and the long days that stretched into long nights. "Boy, were we on a high. Better than any pills. We tried to be the first out in the fields in the morning, the last home at night and the first to market with our crop. Who needed Las Vegas? Nothing could slow us down."

Bob loved being the area's star farmer. He farmed for others. A sick friend begged him to take on his 750 acres and he did, going $90,000 into debt. Bob never consulted Patty. "I couldn't have said no. He was lying on a divan and if he didn't take two or three years off, he'd be crippled," Bob said.

But then, almost as quickly as a hailstorm can destroy a spring's crop, the bottom dropped out. Former President Jimmy Carter's grain embargo cut the flow of exports in 1980. Interest rates climbed as high as 21.9 percent in the late 1970s. Land values plummeted. The rains never came four years in a row. Smith found himself "jumping over dollars to pick up nickels." Bob and others thought it was just a bad streak of luck. Things would get better next year.

They didn't.

To compound the problem, Bob decided to help his parents retire and bought their farm so that they could be financially solvent for the rest of their lives. "We sold to Bob as a way to maintain our health. Bob's grandfather had died in his 70s and my husband still believes that if he had quit earlier, he would have lived longer," says Mrs. Smith.

Bob eagerly took on the responsibility. "I figured it was better that Patty and I took the licks rather than them. We couldn't have lived with the guilt. We're fighters and we could make it."

Bob filed a Chapter 11 bankruptcy petition. He felt fortunate to get a 40-year payback period. He and Patty were down to 680 acres, 440 they owned and 240 they rented. "At least we were able to salvage Grandma's 240."

But having to admit defeat caused Bob to become depressed. Fear pervaded his life. Bob feared for his family and his parents. He became obsessed about the possibility of losing the farm. He fought with Patty more. He yelled at his children. He worried about his manliness. He stopped going to town and seeing people. All he did that winter of 1982 was sleep and watch television. He began taking a shotgun with him in the field. He considered driving off a bridge.

Pat brought Bob out of his depression. She told him to "get out of here and get something done. You've done it in the past, why can't you do it now," she kept hammering away. She offered support in spite of the verbal abuse he dumped on her. "I said things to her that other women would have left their husbands for. But I never took a hand to her. She learned to cope by turning away or blocking out the insults."

What pulled Bob through was a chance to be the consummate showman, like his own childhood idol, Uncle Wade, his father's eldest brother. "He was a high roller, a moneymaker, but one who couldn't hang on to it. Dad did all the work in the barns behind the scenes. And when they got into the show ring, Wade took the straps of the animals from Dad and got all the glory."

Like Uncle Wade, Bob sought public approval. He ran in the Democratic primary for the state senate in 1986 with a platform focused on farm issues. He loved the adulation. "I never wanted something as much as I wanted to win that race. It was one of the saddest moments when I lost," he said straining to stay composed. "It wasn't for the money, which would have been about $17,000. I knew I could help people." Bob plans to run again.

Bob came back fighting. In June of 1987, he helped organize a restless upheaval of farmers into a 145-day farm rally in Chillicothe. They embroidered the landscape with their trailers and combines. Bob recalled, "We were tired and dirty. But we didn't move, protesting during daylight and sitting around campfires of flashlights at night wrapped in blankets. We were fed up."

What began as a local grievance against an abusive Farmers Home Administration supervisor, who made it impossible for farmers to keep their holdings, turned into the biggest farm rally in history. It was a desperate attempt to change the lending practices of the Farm Credit System and the Farmers Home Administration.

For the first time, farmers in Missouri's poor rural areas were heard not just locally, where they were able to oust the FHA supervisor, but in Washington, D.C. "It was an empowering event," recalls Allison of the Missouri Rural Crisis Center, who campaigned to raise $40,000 for the rally.

Today, Bob keeps getting involved in other causes. "Maybe I can change things for the farm family." Almost every month, he gives a virtuoso performance at support meetings in farm territory. Take for example his oratory at the dusty red brick Andrew County courthouse in Savannah, a small town two hours west of Chula.

Bob speaks eloquently to the group of old and ill farmers whose faces and bodies reflect their poverty. Many have lost their farms which have been in their families for generations. The audience clings to every scrap of optimism Bob throws them. "We are so damned efficient we produced ourselves right out of a job," Bob shouts.

The fate of these people has been astounding. Alvin Bierman, a 70-year-old pinched-faced little man with a pronounced stooped, angular body reflecting his misery, tries several times to speak before he recounts his pathetic tale. He bursts into tears. After a moment he speaks. "We tried. Thought we were doing everything right. We listened to the bankers too much and when we got into trouble, the bank said sell out. We sold everything. If we had gone bankrupt in the first place, we could have saved a lot." Bierman, who lives in Mound City, says his family almost lost all back in 1929.

His wife, Esther, offers little support. She is emaciated, her face translucent and unadorned by makeup. She adds to the tale: "There isn't one night that I don't go to bed that I just want to go back. I'm not just thinking of myself but my sons and grandchildren." For people like the Biermans, who remember the Depression, there is little hope because of illnesses and age.

As Bob takes the floor, he asks, "What in the world are you going to do with people who are 60 years old and older, who have farmed all their lives, who have raised and educated a family? Are you now going to pay them $50 a week, give them food stamps and something to do when they should be enjoying their golden years and passing on their family farms?"

Bob suggests concrete ways to rechannel skills. "We all know how to fix a piece of machinery. Doctor a sick animal. Be a chemist, tax consultant, inventor and weatherman. And we're all good managers to boot."

Dave Ballwin, 39, of Chula, takes the floor. Ballwin felt compelled to come back to his family farm when his father took ill. He got into hog farming which is helping him keep his farm. "Hog prices are way up right now," he said.

But just three weeks later at another meeting in a private home, attended by a younger group of farmers barely eking by, Ballwin finds himself asking rather than offering advice. Hog prices have dropped $12 to $15 in the last 10 days. Ballwin's head tilts, his eyes droop as he speaks. He looks much older than 39. "We're losing money on grain every time we walk out the door. The hogs was what would help keep us afloat. And now we don't even have hogs. I'm real scared."

Bob tries to console Ballwin and the other 35 young farmers at the meeting. This is a different group, a more vocal and politically active group that still has energy to fight. What they most want is parity for their products, or a fair price equal to the wages that city workers get.

Despite reports that land, commodity prices and government farm subsidies are rising and debt is being reduced, Smith still contends the crisis hasn't peaked. "We haven't seen the last of the farm foreclosures. There have been two or three more foreclosures in our county this year. I know these are foreclosures when large farm equipment rather than small hand tools are advertised for sale in the newspapers," Smith explains. "What happens from here on in depends a lot on who's put in office in '88."

Doug Hughes, a Democrat, who lost to Tom Coleman in the 6th Congressional race in 1986, stands out in the room as an odd amalgam of farmer and politician. His appearance in a blue blazer and black wing-tip shoes is clean and well-groomed. Hughes believes the crisis is past. "I feel it easing up on me."

Bob Smith interrupts and asks, "What did you get for the crops this year?"

"Not much," Hughes replies. "But we've paid off a little debt and made some others eat some debt."

"What he really means," Bob Smith tells the group, "is that his family knows better how to operate under these dire conditions."

Some farmers haven't fared as well. Hughes is encouraged to recall the time that he led a group of 42 farmers to Washington to lobby. "Thirty-five percent of the people on that bus are no longer farming. Three or four of the couples are divorced and one committed suicide after a check was returned on him."

The others vigorously disagree with Doug and feel the worst is yet to come. The downside may be permanent. Hughes' wife, Marsha, says the rural crisis continues to undermine family unity. "There's not hardly a mother left at home. My kids are starved to death for attention. I'm torn between going with my husband to campaign and being with my kids."

Ellen Dolan quickly interjects, "The farm family has changed out of necessity for the farm wife to get out and do something for herself—at least to earn money for bread and milk."

Later, after the meeting, Bob and Patty concede they are glued to a family business they believe will not turn itself around for a long time. But they love their life and business and feel obligated to pass it down to the eighth generation. "I just love it out there," says Bob. "I wouldn't give it up for the world, even if I'm not making money. I was in the game for the long run, for my lifetime and my son's lifetime and his son's lifetime. That was my attitude from the start."

At the same time, farmers and other small family business owners like Bob are afraid that if they pull up stakes, they may not be able to carve out a better way of life. The Smiths have too many friends who have tried to plant old myths in new soil. Most are no better off. No matter why a business fails—poor planning, a downturn in the economy—owners must rationally weigh what has been against what will be for themselves and their scions. They must make a decision.

Bob's colleagues currently consider different options for farmers—growing new crops, changing grass and plants into fuel and developing land for condominiums. Bob tosses out slightly more novel ideas. For him, the emotional lure of farm life continues to win. With a giant sweep of his arms, he points to his remaining acreage and asks, "Can you imagine having some crops here and then setting up an entertainment center on this corner property? We could stage concerts, hold tractor pulls. Wouldn't it be great. Don't tell anyone about this, it's still pretty premature." Bob knows it would be difficult to convince farmers to part with money for fluff. More important, there may be nobody left in Chula to attend.

Epilogue

By May 1988, the farm crisis was deemed over. Farmers expected bumper crops, strong sales overseas and improved land values. Two months later, optimism throughout the Midwestern Farm Belt was squelched.

The spring and summer of 1988 brought a drought, reputed to be the worst in 50 years. Bob stayed up until midnight thrashing wheat in chalky, dusty, bone-dry soil. He rose by 6:00 A.M. to bail hay. "It ripped the farmers and our family apart. Things were pretty dim. The crop in the ground didn't grow. The cattle didn't sell and many died from the heat and lack of feed. The price of cattle dropped $150 a head from $700 in one week. You couldn't even throw a cigarette outside. It was so dry it could ignite. Here we go all over again," Bob said.

Dave Ballwin often stopped by during the summer to brainstorm as his family struggled to keep its herd.

Come fall, little had changed as Bob switched to selling some milo and other row crops and working in his shop where he butchered animals. The summer's terrible drought was still fresh in his memory. "All the wells in this area have quit working."

The results of the Presidential election proved disappointing. "I had enough of Bush for the last eight years and Dukakis wasn't much better. I had rooted for Jackson."

And FHA letters that went out on Tuesday, November 15, 1988, informing 83,000 farmers across the country that they had 45 days from the postmark to pay up their loans or to demonstrate that they are eligible for relief, proved another stress for most. Bob said he didn't know how he would pay the $13,000-plus amount, although Patty has taken another job to supplement her work at the Post Office. She drives a bus one or two days a week.

In addition, Bob's relationship with his parents had worsened, he said. "I haven't made any payments to them for a while."

But Smith, the eternal optimist, continued to find bright spots. The Smiths' son, Billy, won the local math competition and placed 11th in the state. Chula voted to keep its school open for another year. A bond issue passed by three votes. "It was the largest turnout in years," Bob said with pride. "Some services are more limited. Taxes will go up $1.12 per every $1,000 of assessed property. I hope we can pay. The University of Missouri at Columbia's Extension Service has proved more helpful, though they can't pay the bills."

And this past Christmas found the family warm, together and healthy with plenty to eat.

Bookstop
Austin, TX

I guess I got to light out for the Territory ahead of the rest, because Aunt Sally she's going to adopt me and sivilize me and I can't stand it. I been there before.

—The Adventures of Huckleberry Finn by MARK TWAIN

On a typical wintry day in March, 12-year-old Gary E. Hoover was shopping with his mother Judith in downtown Indianapolis.

While Mrs. Hoover combed the aisles of L.S. Ayres, the city's most prestigious department store, Gary wandered into the store's executive suite. "I'm here to see Mr. Peacock, the president, about some important matters," he told an amused secretary. She sat him down and told him to wait.

A short while later, a pesky and indomitable Gary was escorted into Peacock's office and seated across a massive desk from the president. In a voice that was bright and with a manner unflinching, he fired a round of questions—whether Mr. Peacock liked his job, what he did, what it was like to run a chain of department stores.

An hour later, when Gary told his mother about the meeting, she smiled and shrugged her shoulders. To her the incident was quite routine.

"Gary was always finding successful businessmen and striking up conversations. He'd wander into a bank and end up talking to the president. I don't know how he did it, but he always got in. And they always seemed to listen. When he was a young teenager, he asked us to start subscriptions to *Fortune, Forbes* and *Financial World* magazines," said Mrs. Hoover.

Gary's interest in business intensified. In high school, he collected every issue of *Fortune* back to 1936. He wrote to Proctor & Gamble Co., the giant consumer products manufacturer, for the company's history and its stellar roster of products because he considered a career in consumer marketing. Gary began collecting annual reports.

Twenty-five years later in 1988, Gary Hoover, age 36, remains a born talker, a born hustler, a born entrepreneur. Business experts and writers marvel at the retail savvy of the businessman who has turned the science of selling books upside down. Today, the success of his enterprise looms lofty over the idled drilling rigs of the Texas oil plains and the vacant offices in the skyscrapers of the state's largest cities.

Gary's brainchild, Bookstop, is a chain of 21 mammoth 6,000-to-11,000-square-foot bookstores, two to three times the industry average. Fourteen Bookstops are scattered throughout Texas. Six are in Florida cities. One is in the French Quarter of New Orleans. Gary plans to open a store in San Diego in the fall of 1989 in an old movie theater, and at least six other stores around California, Texas and Florida.

Each store stocks about 45,000 titles and 100,000 books, more than 1,000 magazines, hundreds of records and audio-cassette tapes, three to four times a typical bookstore's inventory. Prices are more surprising. Bookstop discounts all books daily at between 10 and 40 percent from list prices, almost unheard of in the industry except in large cities. Results are impressive. Sales per square foot are in excess of $250, twice the industry average.

Gary's success lies in putting tough, iconoclastic entrepreneurial skills to work. But Gary represents a different breed of entrepreneur from those of the past who risked all for their dreams to make a living, gain freedom and pass on their businesses to successive generations. He's also different from many of the present breed of entrepreneurs, who are the driving forces behind the majority of the 8,400 businesses that are started weekly in this country, according to *The Encyclopedia of Entrepreneurship*. Many of these entrepreneurships function fine when they are small, growing, on a limited budget and run by the founder and sometimes underpaid family members. An abysmal down-side may develop as the business becomes successful. The business may become too large for hands-on management.

Once entrepreneurs have achieved financial stability they often be-come complacent. This may cripple the company's growth and un-knowingly cause the business to stagnate as evidenced by rising inven-tories and receivables, flattening market share and lower earnings, according to Gerald Le Van, a trusts and estate attorney and family business consultant in Baton Rouge.

More problems surface when the founder wants to retire or dies. The business may not be able to survive without his personal attention. It's also unlikely the founder trained anyone to succeed him. Often he's been too busy or was afraid to face his own mortality.

Gary and many other "new" entrepreneurs—often young, female, minorities and immigrants—are better educated, better trained and more comfortable about bringing in experienced outside management than family to build a team rather than to operate solo. In addition, entrepreneurs like Gary vehemently oppose nepotism and passing on their businesses to spouses and children. They want them to make it on their own. To the "new" entrepreneur, nepotism connotes all the negatives of a family business—too many unqualified relatives vying for power and money.

Many of these new entrepreneurs are changing the complexion of the traditional American family firm by making it a more professional operation for the long haul. Their businesses have strategic goals, clear-cut organizational charts, job responsibilities based on mer-itocracy and succession plans. Non-family managers and staff become the extended family who are rewarded handsomely and take over when the entrepreneurs are gone.

Family business experts cite three prime reasons for the change in attitude: the increasing mobility of the American population which has left many family businesses without family successors; better trained and educated family scions who want to manage larger and more challenging businesses than their family firms, and the desire of foun-ders to avoid family rifts by eliminating the possibility of relatives working together.

Gary thinks this shift in attitude is more egalitarian and more beneficial for a business and its bottom line. "Business is complex enough without bringing in another element—the family and all that jazz," he says. "Sometimes kids are 50 percent brighter than their parents, but sometimes they're not. It's a 50-50 shot. You should encourage the people who work for you in a business by giving them equity and incentives rather than just handing something over to them because they're a relative. If I had children, there is no way I'd let them work with me. They need to go out and make their own mark in the world."

Entrepreneurs like Gary are still few in number, however, according to Robert H. Brockhaus, director of the Institute for Entrepreneurship at St. Louis University. He pinpoints their number at 10 percent of the total entrepreneurial population. "The vast majority, the remaining 90 percent, are very similar to entrepreneurs who started Mom-and-Pop businesses such as restaurants and grocery stores after World War II and passed them down, if they had an heir."

Gary, still a bachelor, talks animatedly about getting married and having children. He emphasizes that the way Bookstop is structured makes it highly unlikely family could ever take over. "I've never allowed myself a majority ownership position, even when the chain first opened. I originally had a 30 percent stake, which I've decreased to eight percent as a way to reward others, my extended 'family.' "

Gary's right-hand man and Bookstop's president, Steve Mathews, supports the same anti-nepotism stance. Mathews, the father of an eight-year-old daughter, developed his philosophy as a buyer at a small family-owned bookstore in Dallas-Fort Worth known as Taylor's. "At Taylor's nobody except the family shared in the company's success," Mathews said. "That's fine and the way it can be. But there are a lot of real bright people who have been in this business because they like books. They're no longer in this industry because they couldn't move forward. That's not been true of Bookstop."

Gary and Steve had developed a detailed plan of what they want to accomplish and are determined not to be the only ones to partake in Bookstop's success. It is a shared venture of their family of 300 employees, whom they refer to as "associates." Gary hopes to make all financially comfortable and has set the goal of making his senior managers millionaires. All are young and hardworking.

They have formed a board with eight outsiders to monitor management. It includes Gary, Steve, one of Gary's college advisers, Pat (an early investor), two representatives from a supermarket chain who put up money and three venture capitalists who invested several million dollars.

Gary's lifestyle reflects his business philosophy. He lives modestly in a 2,800-square-foot house in an integrated neighborhood. He drives a six-year-old big black Fleetwood Cadillac because it is one of the few cars roomy enough to accommodate his two mutts, "his girls," from the Humane Society, nine-year-old Bubba and 10-year-old Gretchen. They go on frequent driving excursions, one of Gary's few forms of relaxation.

Like many entrepreneurs of today and yesteryear, Gary has a philosophy about life, business and retailing that can be traced to his grandfathers, both preachers with the Church of the Brethren, to his parents and to the corporate mentality of his hometown, Anderson, Indiana.

Gary's plan developed after he wrote an eighth-grade term paper on another of his and his mother's favorite haunts, Marshall Field & Co. in Chicago. Gary thought Field's was the most impressive museum he'd ever been in. His parents would go to Chicago for his dad's meetings and he and his mom would spend most of their time combing the aisles of Field's. To Gary, it was the greatest American department store. "All these people and all these items in a public place and buyers trying to match the right people with the right things," he thought.

In addition to his mother's addiction to shopping, Gary gained a love of retailing from his father, who ran wholesale and retail grocery stores and later headed the sales and marketing division of a glassware company in Anderson, a town 40 miles northeast of Indianapolis with a population of 65,000. More than half of the city's residents worked at a General Motors assembly plant. Living in Anderson was a great way to learn about life, business and human nature. In the halcyon days of General Motors, Gary would have a person sitting next to him in class whose father was manager of the auto plant and lived in a big house with servants' quarters and the fellow on the other side of him whose father was head of the union. There would be two weeks every three years when the two kids weren't allowed to—and didn't—talk to each other.

Gary's insatiable curiosity about business and how companies were run was further piqued by conversations around his family's dinner table. Gary had a brother 11 years older and a sister six years older, and they talked, questioned and debated world issues and local town gossip. Such repartee taught Gary about people and about the world.

Gary's thinking crystallized when he studied economics under Milton Friedman at the University of Chicago. Friedman, a Monetarist, stressed that the economy is inherently stable and would stay on course if it weren't sidetracked by unwise monetary policies. Gary also believed that government shouldn't intervene in business.

"Chicago was a great university, where you were free to exchange ideas," Gary said. His parents had tried to talk him out of going there because he had a full scholarship to Butler University in Indianapolis. His parents promised to throw in a car if he'd go to Butler. Gary's guidance counselors tried to dissuade him from going to Chicago because they thought only Communists and Marxists went there.

While at Chicago, Gary became more enamored with Field's. It combined the finest retail ingredients—a good location, a reasonable price structure and honest, well-trained help. When Gary would wander throughout the store, he'd have holes in his clothes and the sales staff would be happy to see him, "unlike Saks Fifth Avenue in New York City where they were real snooty about things like that. You could enjoy yourself at Field's whether you bought or not."

It was at Chicago University that Gary tested his skills at making money. His venture was a charter bus company that offered great trips, great discount student fares and free drinks and wine while in transit. The business failed, however, after Gary and his partners overexpanded. "If we had just stuck to the New York route, we would have done well, but we got into trouble when we added Denver, Miami, Boston, etc." So he learned.

He tucked away lesson No. 1 for future endeavors: Don't expand too quickly.

Gary's second business, again a partnership, was buying old books cheaply at one of Chicago's large post offices and selling them to students for five times their original prices. In that case, his success taught him two more lessons for future endeavors: Sell in volume and set good profit margins.

Gary graduated in 1973 and considered going on for an MBA, but in hanging around the business school at Chicago he became disillusioned with the mind-set. He'd go up to the students and ask them why they were there and they'd answer, "Cuz I want to retire at age 36." Gary had wanted to hear them espouse intellectual business philosophies.

Gary decided he wanted to focus on retailing because it was the best way to have the most impact on society. It also was a simple business to get into and one of the least regulated.

Gary, a 6'4" beanstalk with a disheveled appearance, didn't go directly into the book business. He embarked on a series of brief, well thought-out detours. He knew that a void existed in retailing books after seeing the Toys "R" Us chain, the first stores to put games in a supermarket-size outlet and slash prices razor thin. The chain killed its competition through high volume and low prices. With Gary's strategy and affinity for numbers, the world of retailing books could be his.

Gary decided to go through financial boot camp as a retail analyst at Citicorp in New York in order to learn to crunch numbers, spot and study the best-run retail chains and make contacts with future investors. He loved his work. His bosses told him to study the industry.

After two years at Citicorp, Gary left in 1975 when he felt he had learned enough. He purchased a Greyhound bus pass for $100, which entitled him to three months of unlimited travel. He arranged interviews with 14 department stores around the country hoping to be hired as a buyer. After almost eight weeks, he got tired of riding the buses and took a job as book buyer at Sanger-Harris in Dallas. Gary was in charge of a small department, but he had control and was given a good salary—80 percent of what he had earned on Wall Street. But he decided buying books wasn't his forte. He had trouble being objective and was often unable to buy "the trash" that he didn't feel like reading.

The main lesson Gary learned in this chapter of his life was what made a bookstore work, which he mastered by studying the competition, Taylor's, which had huge stores, enormous inventory and a great reputation. He wandered in every day and browsed. Taylor's had books Gary had never seen at many of the big outlets in New York. Books on yachting, on bicycling, on ships. But Taylor's didn't discount. Gary devised his retail strategy.

Gary stayed at Sanger-Harris for two years and took a post in the corporate office of a competing retail chain, May Department Stores Co. in St. Louis. If he were going to be a retailer, he needed to learn how retail decisions were made from the top down. William E. Grafstrom hired Gary as a financial research analyst and charged him with identifying acquisition targets. May hadn't made any acquisitions since it bought the G. Fox chain in Hartford in the early 1960s and David Farrell, May's chief executive, wanted to make his mark. Farrell sent Gary to look at 400 to 500 companies—study the 10-Ks to grasp a company's financial strengths and weaknesses, analyze the balance sheets and find out if the companies were in good shape. Farrell settled on the Volume Shoe chain, out of Topeka, Kansas, and Gary did the leg work. May bought Volume for $160 million in 1979 from the Pozez family when Volume had less than 1,000 stores. May later expanded it into a chain of 2,210 Payless ShoeSource Stores.

Gary's two years at May were demanding, but invaluable. The work taught him how to produce quality under intense pressure, demand the best of himself and inspire others around him. "Farrell had the highest standards of any individual I've ever worked for. He was the kind of guy who thought that one mistake in 1,000 was completely unacceptable. He was determined to make May the greatest retail company in America and in that respect Farrell and I are of the same soul and spirit."

Gary learned quickly and again switched jobs after two years. He went to work for Henry A. Lay, who was in charge of May's real estate subsidiary, May Centers. There Gary picked up the knack for attracting good tenants and understanding the intricacies of real estate leases. Most important, he had the chance to help put together St. Louis Center, the city's enormous downtown enclosed mall that May built in partnership with Melvin Simon & Associates, a development firm based in Indianapolis. Lay wouldn't let Gary manage the center, believing he was too young and inexperienced. Because Gary also was convinced that May wouldn't make another acquisition in the immediate future, he decided to move closer to his goal. "It was time for me to start my company," he says.

Gary knew it was time to roll the dice. He asked a college friend to map out Bookstop's strategy. They shared a hotel room for a month, while writing a 200-page thesis. In September of 1981, Gary quit May Department Stores Co. cold. He was penniless. His parents pleaded, "Gary, you've got a great future with May. How can you quit?"

Grafstrom of May, who now heads May Center, said, "Gary had a unique combination of talents. He had financial, business and retail knowledge. He was exceptionally bright. You put a quarter in Gary, sit back and listen for endless periods of time to get his exceptional intellect and anecdotes. He was a character, too. He'd come in anytime between 10:00 A.M. and noon and work until 2:00 A.M. His office generally looked like a Boy Scout paper drive with stacks of invoices. I took a lot of questions and pressures about his uncanny ways, but I knew he was worth it." Gary went hunting for financial backers to raise $6 to $7 million to open his store.

But this time he wasn't as lucky. Potential investors were put off by the length and detail of Gary's plan. Most considered him too green at age 28. Gary kept getting the door slammed in his face. He was told he'd never be able to produce the volume or profit margins he projected. One investor offered Gary $1 million to open his store in Dallas on a smaller scale. Gary wasn't interested and the deal fell through.

Gary learned to handle rejections and cut his plan's number of pages in half.

Several months later, with no potential backers, he reduced his plan to its least expensive format. He would zero in on a city with a high literacy rate and a low cost of living. He would seek a total investment of $300,000. Gary compiled a list of potential cities and started analyzing. Cambridge was scratched because of the high cost of real estate. Berkeley was nixed because costs were even higher because of its proximity to pricey San Francisco. On and on. At last he decided on Austin because no city was better educated for its size.

In Austin, Gary found a secret weapon—Steve Mathews. He was the guy he knew he had to have to make Bookstop work because it was a project too involved for one person. Mathews was the consummate buyer. Gary had met him through a mutual friend. Gary promised him a lot of control, though a meager salary and hard work. Steve couldn't resist.

Together the men convinced the Pozez family to invest $150,000. They encouraged another family, which owns an envelope manufacturing company in Kansas City, into investing $70,000. They persuaded college friends and business colleagues, including Grafstrom, to put up another $80,000.

With money in hand and the project on go, Gary called Farrell of May and cancelled an interview for a new job that he thought he should consider if money didn't materialize for his business. The job at May would have paid $68,000. Gary didn't see that kind of money again for five years.

Gary, Steve and a third partner, who subsequently left because of a personality conflict, incorporated in March 1982. They made cold calls from the yellow pages to line up their first retail location. They found a site in a strip shopping center with flexible hours in an affluent neighborhood in Northwest Austin. They set up a warehouse in the back of the store.

The night before the first Bookstop store opened, September 18, 1982, Gary and Steve sweated out the wait in their offices. "It turned out great. It's a bit hazy, but I know we did about $10,000. A year later we opened a second store in the least educated city we could find in Texas—San Antonio. And we did well there, too." Their favorite locations are one-of-a-kind buildings such as a 1939 abandoned movie theater in Houston, which has become the company's hit attraction.

While good new concepts are usually quickly copied in the retail industry, Bookstop still stands as an island. Most competitors are convinced that Bookstop either isn't doing as well as Gary says or that he's keeping some strategies secret. "We're a private company." All he's willing to share is that by January 31, 1988, Bookstop produced its first profit on sales exceeding $30 million. Gary expects a double-digit gain in 1989.

Gary and Steve are an odd mix in demeanor, dress and management style. Gary's complexion is pale with blue eyes that pop out for their brightness and intensity. His horn-rimmed glasses make him appear even more intellectual than he is. So do his strands of gray hair which fall loosely across his forehead. Gary dons the suits and white shirts he first learned to wear at Citicorp, but, he says he can't be bothered with details—combing his hair, wearing a belt, tie or cuff links or pressing his clothes.

Gary is the idea man, dreaming up schemes and putting together numbers. For all of his unconventional ideas, he's an easy person to get to know. With Gary, what you see is what you get. He is a man gloriously gifted with rah-rah salesmanship, able to figure out and take advantage of consumer trends before competitors, able to thrive on hard work and irregular sleep patterns. He goes to bed about 8:00 P.M., gets up around 11:00 P.M., works until 2:00 A.M., takes a long nap and rises about 9:00 A.M. to get to his office between 10:00 and 11:00 A.M.

Stroll into a Bookstop with Gary and it's a crash course in learning about books and book retailing. His anecdotes are breathless. They keep a listener on the run. "Hi, sir. Can we help you?" he asks leading a customer in his Lincoln Village store in Austin to a section on bicycling. On the way, Gary stops. He scans every row to make sure no book is out of place. For a man who's totally disinterested in his appearance, he's fastidious about the look of his stores. Gary bends down to pick up a book that's been thrown on the floor and careens the aisles to find the exact spot where it belongs. A few minutes later as he passes through the mathematics section, he stoops again and rearranges titles out of alphabetical order.

In contrast, Gary's partner Steve carefully chooses words and attire. He dresses impeccably but surprisingly casual in starched shirts, ironed Levi jeans and black high-top Reeboks. Not a strand of hair is out of place.

Steve puts Gary's ideas into action and manages the "associates," who report directly either to Steve or his subordinates. "Steve's better with people," says Gary. Associates concur. Gary and Steve have veto power over each another, though they rarely use it. "We've spent so much time together—sometimes 10 hours a day and then another four hours on the phone—that we know how the other will respond," explains Gary.

The interiors of the Bookstop stores are well mapped out to categorize inventory and maximize sales. Parquet aisles weave through a sea of gray industrial carpeting. Walls are painted deep red. Simple plywood book racks are arranged ingeniously in long rows in a baseball-diamond configuration to help customers find their way around the field. This layout also allows browsers to scan the front of each book quickly, which is important when 6,500 new books arrive at the 21 stores three times a week. Best-sellers and magazines are placed in the second-base position so traffic passes through the entire store and doesn't block the front. Children's books, one of the fastest growing segments of the book market, are positioned near the best-sellers. Consumers thread their way through the aisles with the aid of a store marquee and printed directories.

Store hours encourage browsing. Most are open seven days a week, 362 days, and 12 hours a day, from 10:00 A.M. to 10:00 P.M. or from noon to midnight. Employees don't rush customers in and out.

Displays are minimal to keep the focus on books. Few extraneous gift items are sold such as cards, children's toys and games, mugs, stationery and pens. Associates don't wrap books. Purchases are never mailed.

Every book sold is tracked on a computer and beamed back to corporate headquarters which is in a building eight miles from downtown Austin amid uncultivated farm land that is being developed as the city expands outward. In the company's early days, offices were in one of the extra bedrooms in Gary's first house. The new corporate nerve center is much bigger but still is far from a showplace. The 22,000-square-foot building, which also houses a distribution center, is a Spartan, one-level concrete box with interior space partitioned into more than 60 offices with crisp painted white walls. Rent is $4.25 a square foot per year, or $99,000 a year. Many of the offices and conference rooms are located in the interior, without windows. Furniture is modest wood and chrome desks and chairs. The most obvious luxury is the plethora of computers and a separate computer room, which keep operations humming smoothly.

Stickers with a book's original list price, its Bookstop discounted price and an even greater discount if the consumer buys an annual $9 "Reader's Choice" card, are affixed to the jackets in either the Austin distribution center or a newer one in Orlando, FL, after books arrive directly from publishers and from book wholesalers.

The books arrive at the centers by truck in cartons or pouches and are stacked on pallets reaching five feet high. About 80,000 books pass through the Texas distribution center weekly. The Orlando center is expected to process a comparable number once all the new Florida Bookstops are operating.

A quality control team of employees unpack and check books for defects such as ripped covers and pages and wrong jackets. Damaged goods are returned to publishers. Acceptable books are sent to a data entry room where the computerized labels with the three price categories are slapped on.

Steve and the company's four book buyers purchase for 36 departments at the two main trade shows in spring and fall. In June, they stock up on Christmas books and in February buy spring releases. They also meet with publishers' representatives. Christmas is the busiest selling time when 17 percent of total company sales are made. The May-June period is the second busiest because of Father's and Mother's Day, weddings and graduations.

Bookstop's buyers have divided books into categories. They look at every title, unlike some bookstores, which consider only the best-known. Buyers base their decisions on which titles publishers think will sell well, on the size of a book's initial printing, on what other books the same author has written and how well they've sold. Bookstop specializes in backlist titles, those that have been available for at least six months and which other book stores have returned to their publishers. Bookstop's return rate is below the industry average.

Gary also considers it essential to stock enough special interest books for customers who want a book to help them strike out for new terrain, such as assembling a doll house, learning about bikes or writing a computer program. Not many copies may be carried.

The inventory of each store may vary slightly. Although the buyers pride themselves on their good batting average, occasionally they hit a foul or strike out, mostly by misreading consumer demand. Sometimes they can score quickly and reorder. For example, in the winter of 1988, the buyers ordered 40 copies of *The Rise and Fall of the Great Powers* by Paul Kennedy because the publisher, Random House, initially printed just 9,000 copies. Once the book hit the stores, it sold out.

"Readers quickly told us they wanted more," said Bookstop buyer, Dan Winn. Gary bought a copy with his Reader Choice Card, paying $16.95 instead of the $24.95 list price.

To move books off the shelves but keep advertising to a minimum, Bookstop ties into national publicity such as Phil Donahue who frequently interviews authors.

Books that don't do well within their first 130 days are kept on Bookstop's shelves if they are the definitive book on a subject. The chain measures the rate of return. The bigger Walden and B. Dalton Booksellers chain return about 20 to 25 percent of what they buy, while Bookstop returns about 10 percent because it carries more backlist titles and buys more carefully.

The youth and aggressiveness of the Bookstop team inspires Gary and Steve to fine-tune the chain's format. They test ideas and merchandise. Sometimes an idea works. For example, Gary and Steve added special order books and software. The software has been discontinued. When an idea flops, it is quickly dropped. They've also upped the price of their Reader's Choice card twice since the company's founding as a way to pump in more cash to operate smoothly after the company lost $200,000 on sales of $26 million in fiscal 1986. The first increase on the card was minimal, but the second one jumped from $1 to $8. A card now costs $9.

Gary and Steve were prepared to take flak about the raise, but decided to play it straight with customers. They told them in advertisements cash was needed. They raised $1 million from the readers' cards and from a major book clearance. In early 1987, they rounded up another $3.5 million from venture capitalists.

Bookstop executives are considering ways to edge out bigger discount book chains, which view Bookstop as a threat. Walden started discounting all its books to meet Bookstop's prices, but then backed off when it didn't make money, Gary says. Crown Books Corp. also tried to mimic Bookstop's discounting in its Houston stores, but ended up closing some because it couldn't compete with Bookstop in the same market, he continues.

Smaller booksellers have also gotten down in the bunkers to compete by cutting staff and inventory when they heard Bookstop was moving into their cities.

No matter how the Bookstop strategy changes, employees and management are adamant about not cutting back on the number of books the stores stock. "I could extend store hours and cut salaries, and they probably wouldn't squawk, but if I cut back titles, my associates would be up in arms," Gary says.

Despite the general consensus that the video revolution will make books obsolete, Gary and Steve seem unfazed. It's been more than a decade since VCRs appeared and more than 50 percent of all American households now own them. Video hasn't hurt book sales. Society has absorbed the technology, the way it absorbs everything else, Gary says. Industry experts back up Gary's perception. The proportion of Americans who read more than one book a month is increasing, according to the Book Industry Study Group, a nonprofit corporation in New York. Overall book sales are expected to grow through 1992 about 3.3 percent annually.

Bookstop's success has allowed Gary to start paying himself a salary of $85,000. When he wants an increase, he goes to his board and asks. Gary doesn't hold an employment contract or golden parachute, which could help him land with a fat nest egg if Bookstop goes public or is taken over. "This is a company that we all own," he says. About 100 shareholders hold the company's stock, but nobody owns more then 20 percent. Gary owns about eight percent, having cut his shares through gifts to co-workers, his family and the University of Chicago, which holds about 3,000 shares, currently valued at about $36,000, according to Gary. "I may be the parent, but I'm certainly not controlling all aspects of this business. I want the child to be independent and to be able to grow up." In spite of all Gary's talk of building a business for the future, he hasn't had time to draft a formal succession plan.

Can Gary be content staying with the company he founded as entrepreneurs traditionally have done, or will he, like many other "new" entrepreneurs, become restless and seek a new challenge? Some who know Gary expect him to move on or to expand so quickly that Bookstop becomes another look-alike chain. Either of those routes could be Bookstop's undoing, says John Plummer, a retail analyst and a partner at Ward Howell International in New York.

Fred E. Wintzer, vice president and specialty retail analyst at Alex. Brown & Sons in Baltimore, thinks Bookstop's discounts and huge selections will keep the chain a tough-to-beat competitor as long as it sticks to locations in smaller markets and suburbs where it has fewer competitors. "Selection is the key," Wintzer adds. "Generally when a reader goes in to buy a book, he's looking for a specific title and

Bookstop's usually got it. The downside to what Hoover is doing is that most people don't want to make an extra trip to a store that's not in a mall, which is one place the Bookstops are never located."

Gary responds that he still has much to do, including taking the company public. "We've got people who've got over 100 percent of their net worth in this business. You have to remember that I was a security analyst and I can't wait until I'm on the other side of the table. I could stay with this business for another 30 to 40 years as long as we keep moving across the country."

He explains that Bookstop's expansion will be carried out in an organized, controlled fashion. Gary learned the hard way. In 1985, the chain went from six to 12 stores in 105 days and couldn't handle the growth financially. Between March 11 and April 12 of 1988, the chain opened only four stores. Yet, at the same time, Gary says, Bookstop's bigger and better trained organization can handle faster growth without going haywire.

He adds that he's content pursuing a career he enjoys and believes will survive Steve Mathews and him.

Without the excess baggage of family and its built-in problems, Gary, Steve and their board have been able to focus on the business and run a lean and well-managed operation. Like any business, Bookstop rewards employees for hard work with good salaries, raises, stock options and a chance to climb. But unlike most family businesses, employees here have the chance to capture the boss's job.

Family business owners would be well advised to follow some of Bookstop's management strategy. "My father made it clear that if you were born with brains, you should help people, that you owe it to society to give your kids ethics and morals and a belief in themselves but never hand them money or a company." To do so may spell disaster for the individual, the family and the business and may squelch new entrepreneurial ventures.

On June 26, 1989, the board of directors of Bookstop forced out Gary Hoover and voted to bring in a more experienced leader, Thomas Christopher, former chairman and chief executive of Pier I Imports. Christopher was named chairman of Bookstop. Steve Mathews remains as president. Hoover will continue as a board member and substantial shareholder.

Ironically in this case, Hoover's parceling of his company to a wide circle of non-family, proved to be his undoing.

Fox Photo Inc.
San Antonio, TX

I'm very proud of my dad's name,
Although his kind of music and mine aren't exactly the same,
Stop and think it over
Put yourself in my position,
If I get stoned and sing all night long, it's a family tradition.
                    —"Family Tradition," by HANK WILLIAMS, JR.

Carl Newton III is tough, pragmatic, intuitive. He shakes things up and works hard to get his way. He's energy incarnate, moving with the speed of a sleek red fox running after its prey, the symbol of his company, Fox Photo Inc.

A long-haired, bleary-eyed, thin-nosed dandy, Carl is combed, shaved, starched, well-dressed and behind his desk by 7:00 A.M. His house is just five minutes from his office. It reflects his hobbies and interests. Snake skins. Moose heads nailed on boards. Stuffed trophies of his favorite animals from his hunting and fishing expeditions cover walls. A lion's rug, stiff like old parchment, lies underneath the coffee table.

Carl downs several cups of coffee and tall glasses of fresh grapefruit juice, scans his mail and studies his company's computerized sales sheets. He peers out a half-opened door, calls Diane, his administrative assistant.

By 10:00 A.M. he's out of his office to zip over to San Antonio's International Airport just around the corner. He's on his way today to Southern California to check on Fox's new one-hour photoprocessing retail sites, known as mini labs, and check on acquisitions for his 83-year-old, third-generation family company. Seventy-five percent of Carl's life is spent on the road cheerleading the troops, checking the quality of finished prints, meeting the managers of his labs and working on ways to increase sales at each location. "I go around and mix and mingle. I check things out—how nice the managers are to customers. I want my managers to stop what they're doing and look me in the eye and say they'll be with me in a moment. A lot of them don't recognize me. I start firing questions: 'What's good? What's bad? What can we do differently?' "

Carl's a horizon cat. He tries to focus on the larger business picture. A lot of facts are important and need to be considered to run a business, but not just by him, he scoffs. He has surrounded himself with an experienced staff to fill in the gaps, just like his father, Carl Newton II, did. But Carl's operation is much leaner because of Fox Photo's highly leveraged status.

Six months ago, Carl decided to buy back Fox Photo. He and his dad had sold it in late 1986 to Eastman Kodak Co. of Rochester, NY, for $95.5 million, or 30 times Fox's earnings, an offer they couldn't refuse. But Carl found out that money isn't the main criteria to being satisfied. Being your own boss and continuing a family tradition are.

"I consider myself an entrepreneur which is quite unusual for someone running a third-generation family business," he says winking and smiling devilishly. This isn't any family business. It's one of the country's three biggest photofinishers.

Fox Photo was founded in 1905 by Carl's grandfather, Carl Newton I. With a portrait camera and an idea, he left home in Canada at age 16. While passing through St. Louis, he saw a portrait studio and was intrigued by the operation. He figured he could duplicate the concept and went down to sparsely populated San Antonio to try his luck. He heard about General John J. Pershing and his American soldiers chasing Pancho Villa, a Mexican bandit who held up trains and shot those on board. Newton captured that action on film. He came back to San Antonio and opened a studio with a partner, Arthur Fox, for whom the company was named. He reasoned that Fox was an easier name to remember than Newton.

Six months later, Newton wanted total control of the studio and bought out Fox for $800. Newton opened the first studio in downtown San Antonio. It was across the street from the Alamo, the two-story convent building and thick-walled Spanish-style stone mission church where Colonel William Travis and an army of 189 men, including Davy Crockett and Jim Bowie, tried to fight off General Antonio Lopez de Santa Anna, president and dictator of Mexico, and his 4,000 soldiers beginning February 23, 1836. They lost their fight for Texas' independence from the Mexican autocrats in 13 days.

Newton went around town taking portraits of children on ponies. He enlarged the prints, which no one at that time did. He simultaneously thought up another gimmick—photofinishing prints and shipping them by mail. He aligned his company closely with Eastman Kodak, and by the 1920s made Fox the largest mail order photofinisher in the world. Newton died young at 47 in 1932, in Kodak founder George Eastman's office.

Carl Newton II, his only son and the eldest of his five children, was 13 when his father died. His stepmother, Carrie, took over the business by default. She had never worked. It was the Depression and few people had money to spend on picture taking. A year after Mrs. Newton took over, the company made just $1 per employee or a total of $200.

After a stint in the Navy and graduation from the University of Pennsylvania's Wharton School of Business in 1945, Newton II came home to the family and the business. Fox Photo, which had one store and one plant, was in a precarious financial state. It had sales of $600,000, along with 200 employees and profits of a paltry $5,000. But Newton was ambitious and determined. He worked 72 hours a week. Wherever he went, he carried a card listing his goals. The first was to make $1 million in sales. That took two years. The second was to make $1 million in profits. That took six years. The last was to do 100 times what the company had been doing in sales and profits. He did that, too, a few years later, "all without ever borrowing a nickel," he would brag to his friends.

"When I came back from the Navy and took over this business, they said I was the worst S.O.B. in the world and I was. I had an attitude: you put more input into something and you get more pay, and if you don't, you won't be here any more. When I was president, nobody got here ahead of me and no one left after me. I kept going through the plant and out into the offices."

To improve sales and profits, Newton had to expand. He moved into Houston, then into Dallas, outside the state to New Orleans and Memphis. Newton merged with other photoprocessors. The business grew. Sellers got cash, not stock, and all but two of the 34 companies with which he merged would later make more money with Fox Photo than they could have on their own.

After 20 years, Fox Photo's sales climbed to $60 million and profits to $3.5 million. Newton's four sisters and their husbands got restless waiting for proceeds from the business. They wanted hard cash. They wanted furs and cars instead of their 20 percent shares. Newton tried to reason with them. "Sell 20 to 25 percent of what you own, but hang on to the biggest chunk. You'll never get anything as good as what you have with me," he urged. The sisters were getting $12,000 to $15,000 a year in dividends. For every dollar they left in the business, Newton made them $3. But that didn't mollify them. They insisted on selling.

To raise the cash, Fox Photo merged in 1961 with Stanley Wurtz of Stanley Photo in St. Louis. Newton had known Wurtz for 30 years. Wurtz wanted to retire. Wurtz had one plant and four stores.

The new larger company with $9 million in sales went public a few months later in 1961, much to the satisfaction of Newton's sisters. With fattened company coffers of $5 million, he went wild opening stores throughout the country. The stores continued to carry cameras, but the bulk of the profits were generated from photofinishing.

Carl Newton III, the eldest of three sons, knew from the time he was knee high that he wanted to follow his father into the family business. His father wanted that, too. The two had spent a lot of time together both in and out of the office. "When you're from Texas you need to learn how to hunt," Newton II told his five-year-old son.

They'd go out into the woods, and after they shot a deer they'd build a big campfire and gaze at the stars. Newton II would gather his buddies around and ask his son, "What do you want to be in life?"

Carl would reply, "I want to be president of Fox Photo and I don't want to go hunting with women." His father's buddies were suitably impressed. This father had trained his son well.

Many years later, when the elder Newton was in the hospital, Carl told the family, "Don't worry. I know how to get daddy well and fast." Carl tiptoed into his father's room. Newton's eyes were closed. Carl crept over to the bed, knelt down and whispered, "Dad, this is Carl. I'm here to tell you something. Can you hear me?" Newton squeezed his son's hand. Carl said, "Daddy, I just want to tell you one very important thing. Be sure you understand. I do not want to be president of Fox Photo and I do want to go hunting with women." The reverse psychology worked.

Newton got well and Carl came into the family business after graduating as a marketing major in 1967 from the University of Texas in Austin. He had a new bride and a new job. The late '60s were a time when the photofinishing industry was in its heyday. Carl knew what had to be done to reap results. "Creativity through marketing and aggressiveness" was his credo.

But Carl's father was smart enough not to start his son at the top. He made him a traveling salesman. Carl drove 1,000 miles a week to visit the Fox Photo stores scattered around Texas. After two to three years, his dad promoted him to the mail order department. His two younger brothers also worked at Fox for brief periods but were never considered for managerial roles.

Carl next moved into the operations side of the company and was named executive vice president. When father and son worked together, the father had final say. But his father didn't hover. Other people trained Carl. Newton knew it would be easier because both were aggressive and outgoing and because employees would resent his son's presence less. Yet, at the same time, Carl didn't hide the fact that he was the boss' son. He always referred to his father in the office as "Dad."

Together they worked well. In the early 1970s, they began building small 9-by-4 foot inexpensive—$7,000 to $10,000—drive-up prefabricated kiosks made of steel and glass. Kiosks were the darlings of the photofinishing industry, but their popularity would wane by the end of the decade because film had to be sent to a central lab to be processed which meant that consumers waited to get pictures returned.

As Carl moved up the corporate ladder, he found it increasingly uncomfortable to fight the old regime. Many resented Carl's quick rise to the top. Carl was determined not to let this get in his way. He made sure that whatever he did, he did better than the next guy. "Only the person at the top can cut out that bullshit," he told his father. His father didn't want to interfere.

Newton II tried to make it easier for his son. In 1979, after mulling over the decision for two years, Newton moved himself down to vice chairman, moved his president, Don Becker, 54, who had started with Stanley Photo in 1946 and became Stanley Wurtz's right-hand man, up to chairman, and named Carl president. But the promotions caused friction between Becker and Carl. "There was bad chemistry; it was impossible for those two to work together," Newton II recalled. He tried to stay neutral. "Carl, you have to fight your own battles," he told his son. "It's always fifty-fifty because no one is ever totally right."

It became a knockdown between the two executives. Don stayed seven years and left. Carl had been determined to outlast everyone. "When you get down to it, blood is thicker than water," he said.

Carl and Becker haven't seen each other since the rift. Becker became an independent investor and consultant for the retail field in San Antonio. Becker refuses to discuss Carl or to judge his performance, but says that he had a great business relationship with Carl's father.

John L. Brack Jr., 50, Fox's chief financial officer and company controller, said that Becker was a good but conservative businessman. "He wasn't a risk taker. He was too detail-oriented. My assessment is this: He was the opposite of Carl. Carl is a big picture guy. Don would have analyzed whether to open mini labs for five years and then perhaps opened one. And Don could tell everything down to the nuts and bolts about a mini lab. But with Don at the helm, we would not be into mini labs as big as we are today."

After Becker left Fox Photo, Newton II named himself chairman, but let his son control operations. It wasn't easy making the change, but the father knew it was good business. "It's never easy to give up power," he said. "There's nothing like being boss; running your own show. But I thought it was the thing I should do. My stepmother bowed out when I came back home. You can't have two bosses." Newton II continued to hold non-voting preferred stock in the company.

When Carl took over, the amateur photofinishing business was changing again. A new phenomenon was on the scene: one-hour labs sprouted across the country and offered shutterbugs quick, cheap, quality prints. There were only about 600 one-hour labs in 1980 and Carl knew what direction the company had to take to remain competitive. He also knew how to capitalize on Fox's solid relationship with Eastman Kodak by using its products to process film.

Carl didn't select locations willy-nilly. His gut reactions told him that he needed to put one-hour Fox labs in high density shopping centers in affluent areas all across the country. Carl looked to buy independent photoprocessors' sites and build his own. He was an ace at picking profitable sites and drawing in customers by offering top-quality photoprocessing and Kodak film and products. Company sales and profits shot up. Yearly increases attracted the attention of Kodak, which wanted a bigger slice of the wholesale and retail photoprocessing markets.

In December 1986, Kodak made Fox the attractive offer: $95.5 million in cash, or $30 per share. For Kodak, it was a clever way to secure Fox Photo's photography business. "It was a case of buying Fox or possibly losing that market," said Eugene G. Glaser, a security analyst with Dean Witter Reynolds Inc. in New York. A Kodak spokesman describes the offer slightly differently. "We wanted to buy Fox Photo because the company was for sale and it seemed to be a good business fit."

Carl and his father were tempted. Both knew it would make the family rich. "It's really good for Kodak and really good for us," the father told his son. "You cannot be a publicly-held company and not do what's best for your stockholders unless you want to be sued."

Carl replied, "I know. The stock is trading at $12 and here's an opportunity right under our noses to sell for $30 a share."

"But," his father said, "I have to tell you, it's still going to be terribly difficult for me to give up the company. I think if you or one of your brothers had a son instead of all those daughters I wouldn't do it."

Nevertheless, the senior Newton was comforted knowing that Kodak would let his son have major control because of the long relationship between Fox and Kodak. Whenever Kodak executives had come to San Antonio, Newton II never let Kodak take him or his son out. Newton entertained and put them up in his guest house. "My dad had that kind of relationship with George Eastman," Newton II said.

He also knew that his son had maintained close relationships with Kodak's current leadership—J. Phillip Samper, vice chairman, and William J. Prezzano, group vice president and general manager, photographic products. The deal made Kodak a photofinishing colossus.

Their decision reflected a nationwide trend, though one that's difficult to peg because it's hard to separate family businesses from all businesses sold, says Raphael Amit, associate professor of management at the J.L. Kellogg Graduate School of Management at Northwestern University in Evanston, IL.

Not all family businesses make the decision under the ideal conditions that Fox Photo did. Sometimes a business must be sold because an owner dies or heirs don't want to go into the business. Other times the business may be failing.

Fox's business changed little after the takeover. "Kodak left me alone," Carl recalled. The big difference was that it took longer to make decisions. Fox represented an infinitesimal percent of Kodak.

But competitors started crying antitrust and charging Kodak and Fox with conspiring to monopolize the photofinishing and photographic paper and chemicals markets. Newton II says the scenario probably played like this: "Hey, we don't like what you've done and we'll consider switching off Kodak products if you don't get rid of Fox."

Brack, who was head of Fox's wholesale division at the time, said, "Kodak had to buy us originally to protect its investment in wholesale, which is a much more competitive segment of the industry and which has had a history of problems with markdowns and discounts. Competition would come in and underbid. So, we'd lose business or take a price cut." The wholesale operation is important for processing film for large accounts such as department and drug store chains.

Instead of slugging it out in court in an antitrust law suit, the leaders at Kodak decided about seven months after buying Fox to unload the retail end of the subsidiary. "We sold the retail portion because it was not our intention to compete in the retail sector," said a Kodak spokesman. "We retained the wholesale photofinishing operation to augment our own Kodak processing labs."

Forty buyers came forward. Almost down to the wire, Carl decided to bid and paid a premium or a little less than $50 million for a company that had a book value of $20 million. The decision pleased Newton II. "I knew if Carl didn't buy it back, I would have. But I wanted Carl to make up his mind that he really wanted the company."

"It was the right decision for me." says Carl who owns 51 percent of the company. "I'm a guy who can't work for a large corporation. I don't follow all their little rules. But I made money for them. So they couldn't bitch. I was also the high bidder. Anyway, Kodak knew my track record."

"Family owners have a lot of attachment to their businesses and legacies that goes beyond monetary value. It has to do with a real sense of tradition almost like a family heirloom," says Mary D. Korman, a consultant with Hubler-Swartz in Minneapolis.

Carl's now trying to bat a thousand with his new company. "I made a home run once, so why not again." He's not dismissing the idea of taking the company public once more to reduce the bank debt.

"I could see doing it in five to 10 years depending on the market, although I'd still want to stay in control until I get bored. This is not work to me. I go all over the world. I meet fun people. I learn new things. I'm having a first-class, fabulous life. I have a lot of friends who sit home doing nothing but clipping coupons. That's not for me."

Carl has no patience for ideas and people who don't work and for office politics that get in the way of good business. He wants results and wants them now.

Every detail of Fox's photofinishing business is calibrated to quickly become a new niche for the industry. "I think up a hundred million ideas. Some work. Some are dogs such as our Fox Photo point system," Carl explains. He tried to copy the airlines and give credit toward developing and enlargements. Bob Crandall, president of American Airlines, was a buddy of his, and Carl figured why not do what another company does well. It didn't work and he didn't know why. "Ten ideas look like they should work and one does. We do more things right than we do wrong. It's the same with employees. You can tell in an hour or a day. It's a gut feeling that you're either born with or you aren't."

Putting his nuggets of information into action required a vastly different management style from his father's. "Dad was low-key. I'm abrupt. Dad tried to be nice to everyone. I tell a person right off what's wrong. Dad was hands-on. I'm a delegator. Dad didn't have a plan. He tried to do everything himself. I'm more of a team player. I hired Brack and Ted de Buhr for my top aides. We get together hourly. Sometimes I tell them, 'I love you, but I don't give a shit to do this.' I always listen. I also believe in paying high salaries and incentives. I give all the cookies up front and then go in there and check and check on performance."

Carl also formed a new professional board with outside directors who meet for one hour six times a year. "Board meetings here used to be all day. Each member of the board gets 15,000 shares or one percent. I can't pay since we're so highly leveraged so I gave board members stock. It's important to me to have people 10 times smarter than I am to tell me our faults though I can tell them to stick it. I have made sure with our board also that there is a great deal of capital around me so when an opportunity comes up and I need money, I don't have to screw around with the banks down here. I've got lots of power-houses on the board."

Most family business owners who put outsiders on their boards find they help bring credibility to their firms, expertise family members often don't have, and power to help negotiate family differences. The number of private family business owners who have done so is still estimated to be small, only about 10 percent, according to John M. Nash, president of the National Association of Corporate Directors in Washington, DC.

One vocal dissenting voice about outside boards is Roger H. Ford, director of James Madison University's Center for Entrepreneurship in Harrisburg, VA, who found in a survey he conducted that many owners believe outsiders slow their entrepreneurial drive, especially when the business is in the first generation. "Outsiders aren't an automatic panacea," Ford says.

At Fox, the outside board sets the annual budget, declares dividends, raises salaries, and approves capital expenditures and acquisitions of more than $1 million. Carl III maintains day-to-day control of the operations. For example, Carl had the power to quickly chop the retail staff by 20 percent to 1,600 from 2,000 employees. He slashed the advertising budget. He tightened quality control. "I needed to make every penny seem like $1,000," Carl says. "My bank debt and interest payments are $6 million a year above the $50 million I spent on buying the company back from Kodak. "When you borrow $50 million to buy back a company, you cut the living hell out of expenses. Fortunately, it's worked well. In the first three months that we've owned it, our profits were $1.5 million more than those in last year's first three months. But still the biggest challenge we face in this business is to get people in that front door of our labs," he emphasizes.

There are 230 labs in 18 states in 150 cities, plus 100 of the smaller kiosks. Nationwide there are 14,000 to 16,000.

A typical Fox lab resembles a radiologist's office with the black mini photoprocessor in the center. Fox strives for a clean, pristine look in its labs and demands the same from its employees. Drop off film and the manager, usually a woman in her mid-20s, clad in a white lab technician's coat, writes the order and guarantees it will be ready in an hour. The manager drops the film into an extractor to remove the exposed roll, puts the negatives on a leader card, then into the paper processor and finally into the mini-lab processor, which takes about 45 minutes. The manager removes the prints and checks quality.

Most of his outlets develop between 150 to 500 rolls a week. A manager carefully tucks the 4-by-6-inch glossy borderless prints into a gold-colored plastic photo wallet. The cost of building and equipping a steel and cement lab varies from about $120,000 for one in a strip shopping center to $210,000 for a modular prefabricated drive-up unit. Sites are leased rather than purchased.

Carl thinks the key to turning a profit is increasing cash-flow and sales and controlling labor costs. "Hugeness is not best. We are trying to scale down the size of our labs from 1,200 square feet to 700 to 800 square feet."

Fox's financial man Brack reveals that "just to break even, Fox needs to do $1 worth of sales for $1 worth of investment in a mini lab. Our most lucrative lab is in Maui, Hawaii, which has sales of $1.2 million a year. Most labs bring in annual sales of $150,000 to $300,000 a year."

Most photofinishers such as Moto Photo Inc. in Dayton, OH and CPI Corp. in St. Louis—Fox's biggest competitors—offer comparable inventory and prices. Only 20 to 25 percent of the total number of customers, however, will retrieve their pictures within 60 minutes, says David Yun, former president of KinderFoto, a baby portrait studio and photoprocessor based in Reno. Yun, who now owns his own industrial lighting firm in Reno, claims the one-hour service is a marketing gimmick.

Disagreeing, Carl says that in our high tech, high energy society, speed is mandatory and as important as quality and service. His father concurs. "Our customers want good resolution of pictures and they want them fast. We eat $1.5 million a year in returned customer pictures. A lot of people don't take good pictures, so we have to get good prints from bad negatives."

Carl hasn't stopped hunting for sites. He pulls out a report from the Photo Marketing Association International which states that the one-hour photofinishing business has seen compound annual growth of more than nine percent during this decade and is the fastest-growing segment in the $4.1 billion amateur photofinishing segment. He explains that the jump has occurred for two reasons: the advent of less expensive and smaller processors that allowed pictures to be developed in small quantities on site and the popularity with amateur shutterbugs of fully-automatic and less costly 35mm cameras.

Carl isn't interested in certain areas of Florida or Phoenix where there are older adults without disposable income to spend on pictures. Yet he doesn't hesitate to open labs near a favorite beach, ski slope or winery. He shoves a bottle of Santa Barbara Cabernet Sauvignon into the hands of a visitor. "Here try this. It's a steal; a $15 taste for just

$5." He grins broadly. He put two stores down the street from the winery so he'd always have a good supply of wine. He put a store in Aspen so he could go skiing every year with 15 men on a stag trip. He opened a minilab in Santa Fe because Stanley Marcus of Neiman-Marcus likes it there. Carl started vacationing there. "It's amazing how we've gotten good stores."

He loves to drop names. He's put not only Marcus on Fox's board but also Randy Fields, husband of cookie mogul Debra Fields of Mrs. Fields Chocolate Chippery in Park City, Utah. At one time John B. Connally sat on Fox's board. Sam M. Walton, founder of Wal-Mart Stores, is another of Newton's pack. He comes to San Antonio and frequently hunts with Carl. Carl refers to him as a retailing genius.

When Carl bought Fox back from Kodak, he phoned Walton and said, "Tell me in 30 seconds, how you structured your business?" Carl says that Walton doesn't allow an officer to sit at his desk more than 50 percent of the time, but insists they manage by walking around. The most important space in business, Walton told Carl, are the last three feet across the counter between the sales person and customer.

Carl rewards his lean staff for their long hours, dedication and courteous service. Fox's 230 lab managers, one per store, average $20,000 a year. They are given quarterly bonuses. The top 20 receive an additional bonus of 20 percent of their salary. "We use the same doubling factor until we get to the top one or two people," Carl says. Officers, of which there are 13, receive bonuses of 30 percent above base. Carl depends mostly on two young professionals to handle company finances, marketing, promotions and advertising.

Brack, a seasoned veteran, oversees finance, administration and personnel. He is as much a taskmaster as his boss. When he came into the company in 1981, he was appalled at the inefficient accounting and computer systems. "This company was behind the times. The people were too conservative. Carl and I agreed that they had to go. I replaced all but one," he said. "Most went with Kodak. We're now rebuilding our half of the company."

Ted de Buhr, 40, senior vice president of retail operations, had worked for one of Fox's big competitors. He has the operating, marketing and real estate people at Fox report to him and he can spew forth which locations crank out how many rolls of film and how much advertising should be spent to bring customers into the mini labs. "In Los Angeles, our largest market where we have 40 stores, it's too expensive and too dispersed an area to spend a lot of our advertising dollars," de Buhr says. His style is smooth, slow, deliberate—a good contrast to his boss and his counterpart Brack.

Carl pays his two sidekicks "above-scale salaries," though he refuses to be more specific. He's also given Brack and de Buhr five percent of the company in stock. He's signed over another 10 percent to other high levels of his management team. A little less than 30 percent is split among Fox investors.

He takes a salary and gives himself a bonus tied to how well the company performs. Carl doesn't tolerate fat expense accounts, however. "We never fly first class. We do automobiles but nothing fancy. We don't do country clubs. Do you want to do social stuff or become a millionaire? We used to do that in the old days, but it's a different world today," he says with typical hot-blooded sureness.

Carl's father, who still comes to work daily at age 68, picks up the gist of the conversation as he saunters in and eases into a chair. "The world sure has changed," he says in a Texas twang. He speaks and looks like the late President Lyndon B. Johnson with his casual attire of plaid sport shirt, jeans and boots. This father and son clearly respect and enjoy each other as they verbally joust about work and family.

A proud father assesses his son's performance. "Carl is doing so well and is so enthused, it's wonderful for me. He's a natural salesman."

As much as Newton II misses being the boss, he tries to abide by the nameplate on his office door that says "First Assistant." "I've asked Carl to let me attend some meetings, but I know if I am in there all the time a lot of people will say, 'What does he think?' But, oh God, do I want to be in there."

On most days, Newton II studies reports and figures. He spends half his time wandering the corridors and popping into other people's offices and continuing to espouse the principles he's always had. "If I see a guy sloppy with his gun, he probably doesn't make his bed up nice. It tells me what he's like. I don't care where he went to school or who he is or anything else. I know then he'll also be sloppy here."

If it's an ugly or cold day or if there's a Fox board meeting, Newton II may stay all afternoon. If it's a nice day, he usually leaves after lunch to go to son Larry's cattle ranch in Persall, 60 miles south on the way to Laredo, or visit his other son, Billy, who's looking to buy another business, or laze around on his own property of 50 acres north of town where he raises Arabian horses with his wife of 44 years, Mary Jane.

He also oversees the Newton Family Foundation for Christian Work. As a much younger man, he and his sons frequently joined Billy Graham's crusades.

Carl III keeps walloping into new cities on a self-imposed whirl-wind. He plans to open 25 labs this year at an outlay of $4 to $5 million. Some may be start-ups, others acquisitions. "I like acquisitions more because they offer built-in sales and profits. Otherwise it takes a year for a business to become established. Our goal is to earn a 25 percent return after taxes over a five-year period on each $1 invested in any project whether it is a store or a new business," Carl notes.

The company is contemplating putting mini labs in retail stores and is negotiating with Kroger Co. and Safeway.

Throughout the country, corporate-owned mini labs, franchised operations and independent Mom-and-Pop photofinishers are everywhere. Yet pundits predict the decline of the photofinishing industry and herald the burgeoning field of electronic photo equipment. Kodak's Prezzano has set up a separate division to work on electronic cameras, which will require no film. But Kodak says that it's far off.

"We won't let video or electronics bother us," Carl retorts. "What makes our business is that there's always another Christmas and birthday. The work after Christmas and New Year's is our biggest. A lot of people get a camera and the first thing they do is shoot a roll of pictures."

In the meantime, Carl considers new niches. On the horizon are half-frame cameras that double the number of pictures on a single roll. Some photofinishers may balk because the half-frames complicate the automatic developing process and they doubt whether consumers will want so many shots on a roll and will put up with grainier pictures. But Carl sees it as more business for his labs. Carl also debates whether to jump on the bandwagon and install do-it-yourself enlargers.

This competitiveness not only runs through Carl's thinking and work, but dominates his personal life as well. "I love my family, but I'm a loner. I don't like people knowing what I do which is one of the luxuries of owning a private company. I'm always itching to get things done."

This may be one reason he's no longer active in civic affairs. "I used to be on boards and then decided it was a bunch of hogwash, especially after buying this business back." But he is proud of San Antonio and pleased with how the city has become the country's 10th largest with a population of 914,000 and moved out of the depths of poverty and illiteracy.

Father and son debate the company's future. Says the father, "I see this company going public again sometime, paying off its debts and making a killing. Carl would then have Ted and John run the business and he'll take off and do other things. He's unlike me. I never wanted to do anything but sit right here, but that's not my son's style."

Carl is not one to let others talk for him. "I'll never not work. Ted and John could run this company if I ever left. That's why I've surrounded myself with the right people who are aggressive. This may never be their company, but they can make a lot of money here. Some day, maybe in the next three to five years, we could go public again, though I also hope the company will go some day to my daughters."

Carl is determined not to let his quarry get away a second time. He's learned from experience. He and his dad sold the family business for megabucks, but they found that money is no substitute for a family heirloom.

Koss Corp.
Milwaukee, WI

John C. Koss, 58, was a fast-talking hotshot who had it all. He owned a fabulous 10,000-square-foot home along the bank of the Milwaukee River in the posh suburb of River Hills, modeled after friend Billy Graham's North Carolina retreat. Two Mercedes-Benzes. Membership in the Milwaukee Country Club. A condominium in Florida.

He had gained his riches by developing and manufacturing the first audio listening headsets for the home market in 1958. He was a pioneer who was quickly dubbed the "Father of the Stereo Headphones." Like so many entrepreneurs of that era, John was in the right place at the right time. He had it made.

But in a highly publicized Chapter 11 Federal bankruptcy on December 20, 1984, John was almost wiped out. It happened when John didn't trust his gut instincts, hired a professional manager to run the family business, Koss Corp., after hearing such advice at his Young Presidents' Organization meetings, and gave the manager carte blanche to expand sales at a time when his company was thriving. This proved Koss Corp.'s undoing. The manager overspent and diversified the product line too far.

John looks like six feet of conservative Midwestern reserve in a

175

sensible coat and tie. On the surface, he's as bland and colorless as a Lawrence Welk medley, but underneath lies the mind and heart of a hustler, the daring of a deal maker who thrives on a challenge whether he wins or loses. After he knew the company was in serious trouble, John took back control, played his hand one more time, and came up with the cards to save his family business and turn his life around.

Koss Corp.'s office and plant today, located on North Port Washington Avenue in suburban Glendale, WI, is a $27.5 million public company, which has grabbed an impressive 35 percent share of the $100 million retail headphone market. In its last fiscal year, net income rose 49 percent to $2.7 million. It also is a supreme example of a family business run by a father with help from two sons and two sons-in-law. It no longer employs a professional manager.

John's rise trumpets a typical entrepreneurial saga. He grew up on Milwaukee's East Side, the son of two teachers. He played stickball in the alleys of his working class neighborhood. He never liked school. "My father was always telling me, 'You're not going to amount to anything if you don't finish.' " John knew otherwise.

Koss wanted money in his pockets. He dreamed up new ventures to get it. He took old bicycles, fixed them up and sold them. He ran a lemonade stand. He organized a newspaper route. He loved music and took up the trumpet. He formed his own band and traveled with it after he graduated from high school in 1948. He met some of the industry's greats: Dizzy Gillespie, Oscar Peterson, Bobby Hackett. Koss knew a good sound.

John worked a variety of jobs—on an assembly line at American Motors, as a carpenter's apprentice, as a Fuller Brush salesman. He was drafted into the Air Force during the Korean War and played in the band. In 1952, he got out, married and started his first family business with his father, his brother and a $200 wedding check. Under the name Koss Hospital TV Rental Inc., they rented televisions to patients in Milwaukee hospitals. His wife, Nancy, helped until she got pregnant.

Competition from bigger rental companies caused John to lose business. He sold out, took the cash and some savings, and borrowed a bit to start a new venture with a friend, Martin Lange, Jr. Martin would prove to be the most important person in John's career.

John and Martin met in a Milwaukee night club in 1947 where John's band played. The two talked. Martin casually mentioned that he repaired television sets. John couldn't believe it. He said that he needed a crackerjack repairman for his TV rental business and hired Martin on the spot.

Martin always tinkered on the job. One day, he put together a gadget to test television tubes. John liked it and thought he could market it to local drug stores. It worked.

They conducted business from the tiny unfinished basement of Koss' modest three-bedroom brick ranch in suburban Glendale. John and Martin were a good team. Martin was the behind-the-scenes guy who crafted the tube checker. Cerebral. The quiet engineer, who cared about how things worked, not about money or fame. Not John. He cared about appearances. He was the perfectionist. He wanted the fast buck. He knew there was little money to be made in checking tubes.

Martin loved to tell this story about their different styles. Shortly after they first met, John had a car he was working on. It was polished perfectly. It gleamed. It was gorgeous. But the trunk handle was missing. Martin asked John, "Where is it?"

"I didn't like the way it looked so I took it off."

"How are you going to get into the car?" Martin asked.

"I'll just climb in," John said.

Martin had a car, too. It was painted with cheap black paint. It wasn't pretty. But it got him around.

The two partners toyed with the TV tube checker for three years, but found "it had no sex appeal," John recalled. They also almost got caught and fined for manufacturing in a residential neighborhood.

Undeterred, they tinkered and invented. With old phonographs and pieces and parts from World War II B-29 headphones, John and Martin built a prototype of a portable phonograph at a time when hi-fi's and stereo records were the rage. To help promote the phonograph, they added a gimmick, a stereo headphone jack and headset to provide private listening.

The men completed two combination phonograph and headphone sets in time to show them at the regional consumer electronics show in Milwaukee in 1958. Consumers were timid at first about trying on the headsets. Once on, they were wowed. "Hey, come hear this, Aunt Mary," listeners screamed. "You've got to hear this." They lined up to test and buy them. The public was intrigued. The headphones rather than the phonographs were a hit. Only airline pilots and telephone operators had used headsets at the time. Developing a product for home use was revolutionary.

Back home, John and Martin went to work to produce the best sound possible from their stereo phones. This meant perfecting their speakers to get a big sound. They mixed and matched parts. They crossed wires, took odds and ends, bits and pieces from different components and put them in various configurations. One day, John donned the speaker phones and started yelling, "That's it. That's the sound." It was like hearing Glenn Miller in the room. From then on John and Martin worked with Scott and Fisher and other speaker companies to upgrade sound. They used musician friends to test their theories and glean advice about how to beef up the bass or soften tenor sounds.

The partners also played both ends of the business to increase sales. In order to sell stereo phones, they needed major hi-fi manufacturers to add jacks to their phonographs. They told Herman Scott of H.H. Scott that Avery Fisher was installing jacks on Fisher phonographs. They told Fisher that Scott was adding jacks. Before they knew it, both had added headphone jacks. Orders poured in for the Koss headphones. The company manufactured more headsets of different weights and prices. John added loudspeakers, portable stereophones, cordless stereophones and cordless loudspeakers. John wanted the company to be the first and best in the consumer electronics audio market.

Bigger stakes, bigger costs, bigger risks. John moved too fast for Martin. John bought his partner out but kept him on to oversee manufacturing of the newly formed Koss Corp. Martin started his own small firm, but remained a consultant to Koss Corp.

Audio experts began to laud Koss Corp.'s products. *Consumer Reports* gave the company's first Pro/4A headphones its best rating in 1962. Issues of *Stereo Review* and *High Fidelity* magazines gave company models high marks. The perception was that Koss Corp. offered the No. 1 quality in stereophones and that it created the industry, John said.

John continued to make the right moves. He was at the center of the action. He loved the excitement. The wheeling and dealing of business. Orders poured in for his products. He shared the spoils with employees. He started doling out stock in the early 1960s.

The company grew. Production was at capacity. John could do no wrong. In 1966, he took a bold step and went public when he merged with another company, Rek-O-Kut. It made John a rich man.

Along the way, John and Nancy produced the perfect American family: five attractive kids. John was a strict disciplinarian. He believed in maintaining the same control at home as at the office.

The children were expected to have summer jobs. John told his eldest, Mike, then 13, that Mike was going to go to work at Koss the next day. "You're not going to lay around all summer." Mike went to work in the shipping department, then in maintenance and then on the line. By age 15, Mike started traveling to Europe during summer vacations to learn about the business. At 18, he and his father traveled together.

Mike and his siblings received minimal wages, ate with employees in the company cafeteria and had no special privileges. "But we got great experience," said Debbie Koss Sosey, the second oldest child and oldest daughter. She started repairing stereophones and worked her way up.

But John also bared a soft side to his children. When Mike was young, he was dying to stay up and watch the Beatles on the Ed Sullivan show. He had misbehaved and lost the privilege. Yet his father broke down and recorded the audio part of the show.

Later, when Mike wanted to go to private school, his father agreed. But nine months after Mike started, he wasn't getting good grades. He had a 75 or C+ average. His father said, "You can high tail it over to the public schools if you don't raise your grades." Three months later, Mike's grades showed improvement. His father let him continue.

When it came to choosing a college major in order to prepare for working in the family business, John stressed liberal arts. He told Mike, "Major in history or art. You'll learn about business in business. It's learning about people that's the harder part."

As graduation neared, John exerted subtle pressure on Mike to join the company. John felt Mike could learn on the job and that the togetherness of family superseded skills Mike could master elsewhere.

Mike joined Koss Corp. in early 1977 after getting his B.A. in anthropology and art from Beloit College in Beloit, WI. He worked in London for 1½ years overseeing the European advertising campaigns. He moved to Ireland and managed marketing services for all European outlets for a year. He returned to the States in 1979 to become product advertising manager and promote a digital delay system, an electronic piece of equipment that hooks to a stereo system to add the resonance of a theater hall. John promoted Mike to vice president of marketing in 1983, to executive vice president in 1986, to president and chief operating officer in 1987.

John Jr., known as Johnny, didn't feel the same pressure to join the company. "Dad and I always had a good relationship, but primarily as golf buddies." Johnny joined in 1982, becoming a sales representative in spite of his initial disdain for what the image connoted. "I wasn't going to be one of those guys making cold calls and wearing white shoes and a patent leather belt. But I quickly realized that it was crazy not to grab an opportunity that others would have killed for."

He was assigned the Wisconsin territory for eight months and then transferred to San Francisco because it was decided that a salesman with the Koss name would have the edge. He doubled his territory's sales and was promoted to national accounts manager. He moved back to the home office in 1983. In 1985, he was named national sales manager. One year later, he was promoted to vice president of sales.

John C. Koss exuded self-confidence like a daredevil race car driver. In spite of this, his expanded family team, an enhanced position in the community and greater success and visibility in the consumer electronics industry, he began to doubt his entrepreneurial instincts.

It happened slowly, almost imperceptibly, as he socialized more with successful CEOs in toney board rooms around town, at fancy dinner parties and on the golf links of the Milwaukee Country Club, which he joined in 1978.

A good listener, Koss kept hearing peers talk about fancy organization charts and detailed long-range plans. He mused that maybe his success, which had been founded on the basis of shoot-from-the-hip instincts and without benefit of a college degree, had come too quickly or been a matter of luck. Just maybe, he concluded, his good fortune wouldn't last. Koss' business cronies egged him on to professionalize. Koss couldn't resist. He was impatient. He had not come this far by waiting on other men—he was a man to lead, especially in his industry. Others could catch up.

He brought in a professional manager, James D. Dodson, whom he met at a Young President's Organization meeting. Koss was wowed with Dodson's Big Eight accounting credentials and his years of heading a variety of family firms such as Hankscraft, a division of Gerber Products Co. "He was 43 and a young superstar in his field," Koss said in his low gravelly monotone that at times sounds like a car shifting gears.

Koss made Dodson president and chief operating officer in 1979, signed him to a five-year term and gave him autonomy over operations. John, as chief executive, would maintain control over strategic decisions, according to Dodson. Dodson knew he was a hired gun to expand the company. He was audacious and shrewd. He knew Koss

Corp. was in a small niche market. Within that market, Koss had a major brand share. But that market was drying up. It had peaked in 1978. Consumers shifted their buying to new forms of entertainment—home computers, TV, games, VCRs.

Dodson moved swiftly. He told his boss that he needed to expand into other markets such as portable radios and cassette players. Dodson switched from independent sales representatives to an in-house sales staff whom he thought he could better control. He replaced part-time factory workers with full-time ones, a costly move, but one that would also give more stability. In 1981, Dodson convinced Koss to buy a small Florida audio and video care products manufacturer in Lake Mary.

Dodson took Mike on as a protege. John's YPO buddies concurred that someone else should train the boss's heir, and who better than the president and a non-family member.

When Dodson joined the firm, sales were $25.02 million. Two years later, in 1981, sales moved up a slight $200,000 to $25.2 million. Net income almost doubled to $2.3 million from $1.02 million because of a productivity program that John introduced the year before. Everything seemed perfect.

At the 1981 Consumer Electronics Show in Chicago, the Koss Music Box, Dodson's novel pet project of a $90 portable AM-FM stereo radio with Koss headphones produced in Taiwan, was a hit with $5 million in orders, or 100,000 music boxes. Nobody else had anything like it. It would give the company a financial boost just in time for crucial Christmas sales. More good news.

But only 20,000 boxes came in. "We missed $4 million in orders on the item. The rest of the deliveries came in between February and June. They dragged in," Mike said. In just two months, every electronics company in Asia had copied the Koss music boxes—and for much less. Unsold boxes filled the Koss warehouse. The sales staff became anxious. The management couldn't believe how quickly their luck had turned.

Johnny, working in the company's sales office in San Francisco, begged his father to cut losses by slashing prices. Koss wouldn't go up against Dodson, the pro.

Slowly, the company realized that the foreign competition was stiff. Mike thought that Koss Corp. never should have competed with the Japanese. "The problems arose when we tried to compete against Sony, Sanyo, Panasonic in their own backyard. They were better known. Also, we shouldn't have imported at that time because it diverted our efforts and meant we weren't introducing any new stereo phones," Mike said. "We should have stuck with just our radio music boxes. But Dodson kept adding additional products to get retailers to take our line. It still didn't work. We were left behind panting."

Dodson was determined to gun ahead. He told family and board members, "The stereo headphone market is mature. It's dead. We need to go on to new items. Electronics is the direction in which we must go to grow." Reluctantly, John agreed to expand as sales slipped to $23.9 million and net income declined to $1.7 million in 1982.

The company gave away 50 unsold radios to their city's baseball players. "I remember standing in the aisle of an airplane that was taking our Milwaukee Brewers baseball team to St. Louis during the 1982 World Series and giving each team member one of our radios with a headphone," recalls John. Johnny went with the team to St. Louis.

Mike chuckled recalling the incident. "I told my brother, 'You can be the one kid to go. But only if you come back with an autographed ball for me.' " Johnny did.

Mike and his father still thought Dodson knew what he was doing, though it was hard for them to ignore the more frequent rumblings from the staff about Dodson's autocratic management style. Employees did not like his contentiousness. They complained that he humiliated them and usually with an audience present. Morale sank. The Kosses paid closer attention and witnessed the behavior themselves.

"At various meetings, there would be a lot of pressure and Dodson wouldn't like what he was hearing from one of his subordinates," John said. "He'd get carried away and cut him down in front of the group. It became his standard modus operandi. A lot of employees learned a lot from him, but they had to have pretty thick skin to come back for more. Communications closed up. People became less open as a result."

Dodson viewed his style differently. "I'm perceived as tough. I expect a lot, a quality performance, but I'm fair. If a guy doesn't perform, I can destroy him pretty easily. I have the experience and intelligence level to do that."

By June 1983, Mike had nagging doubts about Dodson's ability when Mike went into the hospital with back trouble.

Dodson wanted to import 150,000 digital radios that could automatically switch to another station. Again, Dodson pushed his theory that doing so would broaden the line. Mike tried to convince him to take just 25,000. "He wound up buying 75,000. And he hadn't consulted with the sales guys at all to see if they could move the merchandise. I was in the hospital so he was out there on his own and did what he wanted," Mike said.

The digital radio was manufactured, but the Asian source dropped the line after delivering 1,000 units Koss had ordered. "We were out of the money we invested in this, about $2 million," Mike said. "We still haven't collected and never will."

Through autumn 1983, the company's lenders asked Dodson questions and scrutinized profit and loss statements as pretax income plummeted and turned to a loss, a gigantic sea of red. "Dodson kept telling us, 'Don't worry. It's not a problem. I'll take care of it,' " John said Dodson kept assuring him. John shouldered most of the responsibility while his son, Mike, was readmitted to the hospital in October for five weeks. Mike's hospital stay was followed with intensive therapy at home for three months. He did business by mail.

By the beginning of 1984, the company faced problems across the board, including difficulties with headphones which hadn't been updated. Cheap imports flooded the domestic market and overshadowed sales of Koss products. Koss Corp.'s share of the domestic market dropped. As the dollar rose in value, the company's European share was slashed by one-third.

Dodson says he went before the board and pleaded with it to diversify outside the electronics field. "If you're a public company, you've got to justify your performance to your stockholders. You've got to grow."

Months elapsed, but John couldn't warm to the idea of diversifying. "He represented a small company in a small niche but with a high profile and he liked it that way," Dodson explained.

In spite of all the debates, no major changes in strategy were made. To make matters worse, the company had neglected its core business in stereo headphones and missed the boat on getting into the under $20 headset market, which its Far Eastern competitors had cornered, Johnny explained. Dodson had his reasons. "He said the stereophone market was dying and wasn't worth more attention or money."

But without a complete line, some retailers decided they weren't going to buy anything from Koss Corp. How could the company sell Chevettes if it was only producing Cadillacs? Competition got tougher. A lot of unknown Asian manufacturers got their feet in the door.

Liabilities reached a staggering peak. They climbed to $13.7 million from $5 million in just nine months. A plan was in place which management thought would rectify losses, but the company kept slipping away.

On April 26, 1984, John, Johnny and Mike went to a Milwaukee Brewers' afternoon baseball game to celebrate Mike's 30th birthday. Their attention was barely focused on the game. As they sat behind home plate in the seats of Ben Barken, one of the Brewers' owners, lunching on Jake's hot dogs and drinking Miller beer, the Kosses made several major decisions.

They decided to get back to basics, which meant dumping more inventory. They concurred that John needed to take control and make sweeping changes. Family and non-family executives would beef up their only trump card, the company's basic headset and speaker lines. They would aggressively go after the under-$20 market. A couple of days later, John stomped into Dodson's office and threw the headsets on his desk and exclaimed, "This is what we're selling now." Mike recalled, "My dad caught Jim off guard. It was the crack in the dam that finished their relationship."

After five years and one month working for Koss Corp., Dodson walked out. John took over. "I should have trusted my gut instincts, but I figured I didn't have a college degree so who was I to question MBAs," Koss says in retrospect.

In the fall of the year, John was desperate for funds. He went to borrow $1.2 million from two banks and an insurance company to pay suppliers, who had been waiting for their money. The lenders gave him one year to pay the money back. John got the funds in September and the borrowed sum was added to the company's existing debt of $13.7 million. All was secured by company assets.

John consulted a bankruptcy attorney he had called in a few months before, Leon S. Forman, with Blank, Rome, Comisky & McCauley in Philadelphia. Forman advised John to file for bankruptcy under Chapter 11 rather than lose everything if he couldn't pay back the loans. Dodson also had suggested filing for reorganization before he left the company.

Some of the family agreed that filing was the best way out. "Family meetings became shouting matches," Mike said. "We begged Dad to file. I was in there pleading even 10 or 15 minutes before Dad signed the $1.2 million loan agreement. I felt we could cut a good deal with banks."

John disagreed. He told Mike and the rest of the family that by signing they would learn a good lesson—"to live within limits and stick to their knitting." John won.

They repackaged and promoted their $20-plus stereophones with the tag line, "Born in the U.S.A.," a play on the hit Bruce Springsteen song.

Cuts came quickly. John cut 45 staff members. He cut expenses. He cut inventory, mostly in the electronics division, and dumped unsold inventory at 25 percent of cost, including the music boxes, a tape player with headphones and a tape player with a radio built into it. The company switched to independent sales reps and let go their in-house team. Savings over the next 12 months totaled $2 million.

In November, as losses mounted in the company's Irish facility, the family decided to close it. "We were under water," said Mike, who had once headed the branch. "I had hired a lot of those people and now I had to go back and fire them." He also closed operations in France, Germany and England.

A boost to the company's coffers was the sale of the company's Florida subsidiary in a leveraged buy-out to management for $2 million. The family will never forget the date.

The family pleaded with the banks to give them more time to raise funds to pay down the loans. Friction heated up between John and one of the lead lenders, Rich Peterson of First Chicago. Peterson turned down the family's request.

On December 20, 1984, in Federal Bankruptcy Court in Milwaukee, Koss Corp. filed for protection from its creditors under Chapter 11. At that time, Koss Corp. scheduled total liabilities of $17.2 million and book assets of $16.4 million. The company stock had fallen to 75 cents after the filing from $3.50 a share.

But the company was able to show that it had filed 89 days after it had signed the $1.2 million loan agreement. It asserted that Koss Corp. was insolvent the day it signed and the agreement could be challenged in court as a preference under the bankruptcy laws. If a company restructures its debt within 90 days of filing a bankruptcy and gives collateral, the borrowings may be treated as unsecured claims because they are preferential, attorney Forman explains. As a result, Koss Corp. was able to negotiate with the banks for a favorable settlement of its debt. The banks lost their ability to force Koss Corp. to pay them in full and enabled Koss to treat the other shareholders and creditors on a comparable basis. Banks, the secured creditors, got approximately 75 cents on the dollar in cash. The general unsecured creditors received 100 percent over three years with 10 percent interest.

"I should have filed back in the fall," Koss reflected.

The family and bankruptcy attorney Forman went to work around the clock to orchestrate a plan to take into court that would demonstrate that Koss Corp. needed more freedom to operate its business to improve cash flow. "We wanted to stretch the debt out over a period of time and give some stock rather than all cash. We tried to persuade the judge that the projections the Kosses made were reasonable because Koss was able to keep selling to its suppliers, who weren't out any money as a result of the bankruptcy. Some lenders were unusually harsh in restricting how Koss could use its cash," Forman said. Forman finally told John, "There's only one way to solve this case and that's to get rid of these lenders and go to someone else. These guys just don't like you. I think some are annoyed with your lifestyle."

Forman wanted Koss Corp. to be one of the 30 percent of those companies with less than $25 million in sales that emerge from Chapter 11.

John gathered his family in the basement of their riverfront Colonial to map out a strategy. Recouping losses was like crawling out of a ditch. Chapter 11 wasn't the panacea they thought it would be. It was more akin to a stay of execution. Pressure became intense. Bankers audited the books regularly, questioned expenses and family salaries and perks. Decisions had to be made on spending to bring out new stereo products to keep the company's name visible.

Each Koss working in the business took an assignment. John worked with his lead bank, First Chicago, and unsecured creditors and suppliers. "Without a believable plan done in blood, there was no way the judge would rule in our favor," John believed. His two lawyer sons-in-law helped interpret the legal mumbo jumbo and draft reorganization plan after reorganization plan. Altogether, they formulated 18 plans.

Mike, more conservative than his father, compiled five-year financial statements for the banks.

Johnny, the sales superstar, hit the streets. He hustled retailers such as J. C. Penney, Montgomery Ward and Sears Roebuck & Co. and his wholesalers to hang in, which they did. Radio Shack even increased orders. Sears switched from selling "Sears Audio by Koss" to a private Koss brand, another coup for the family.

Mike praised his brother. "Johnny was our accounts manager and he had the unenviable job of saying, 'We're still here to stay and we'd like to service you.' We had developed close relationships with our accounts and gave them good service and quality products." Johnny convinced suppliers to wait to be paid.

Debbie used advertising and promotional skills as a liaison between the company's internal operations staff and the community.

Michael F. Moore, Linda Koss Moore's attorney husband, was busy franchising a do-it-yourself paint business when his father-in-law asked him to help out on an hourly basis. As hours mounted, Moore shelved his paint store to sign on permanently with Koss Corp.

The Kosses took more action. They cut the data processing department from eight persons to one. No factory workers were cut, however. Remaining non-union factory employees took 30-percent pay cuts. Managers and clerks took five percent cuts and officers took 10 percent cuts, except for John who shaved 50 percent off his salary. Nobody balked or quit.

Even worse than the stigma of going bankrupt was the guilt. John blamed himself for letting someone else take control of day-to-day operations—writing reports, compiling monthly statements—many things John said he should have checked. But John rationalized that Dodson needed to have control and that he had the experience and credentials. John trusted someone when he let him take charge.

Dodson refused to take the blame. "There are enormous cycles in this industry. It moves in extremes. When stereo is hot, people buy accessories. When it's not, people don't. I wanted to buffet the down periods. John wouldn't let me. I wasn't making the final strategies."

A major lesson Dodson said he learned was that family does not belong in public companies. He would also never let any of his six children work with him. "It doesn't do anything to build their self-esteem. It doesn't let them develop."

John decided it would help to talk to others who had gone through a similar bankruptcy. He gathered three friends for lunch, all of whom he had met through his Young Presidents' Organization 49s group. Only one had not faced bankruptcy and that was because he had sold his business. Koss convinced that friend, James L. Dorman, a former accountant at Arthur Andersen, to serve as a consultant. He paid him $10,000 a month and later named him a director.

A natural reaction for the family would have been to panic and to close itself off from everybody. Said a worried Mike, "My God, if we don't make it, who will hire me? I had my own personal debt problems. I had leveraged myself to the hilt." On the advice of a family friend who had survived a Chapter 11 filing, the Koss family kept a high profile. They showed up at the country club. They shopped at the same neighborhood market. They attended dinner parties. Few friends shunned them.

Only Nancy Koss stayed home. She needlepointed, played tennis and prayed. She had raised a family and helped build a business. She planned to protect both. But there were days when things seemed out of her control. For Nancy the worst moment came when a reporter with the *Milwaukee Journal* phoned her at home and asked if her dream house had foreclosed. It was an ugly misunderstanding. The banks had sent a foreclosure notice when John was out-of-town on business. He had seven days to come up with the money to keep the house. On the sixth day, he returned and thought it wasn't serious. A reporter got wind of the foreclosure action filed in court and called the house, which John had refinanced. Because he didn't refinance immediately, the papers printed the story. The family later got a postage-stamp-size retraction in the paper which was buried toward the back of the business section.

The Kosses subsequently decided to sell their home, but not until February 1986. It was an all-cash contract for $1 million, what the family sought. They moved into an apartment.

Peterson of First Chicago continued to be John's nemesis. He refused to accept John's offer to repay the debt in cash and stock with a return of seven percent, John said. He insisted on 12 percent. Finally, on December 17, 1985, the court approved a plan for a $9 million cash settlement to be paid on the 31st. The company had raised the money from a variety of sources: $3.5 million from sales of obsolete inventory and new products, $2 million from the sale of the Florida plant, $1.5 million from the seven-year sale/leaseback of the company's Milwaukee headquarters, $1.3 million from a stock sale to five friends and a working capital line of $2.7 million from First Bank of Milwaukee. John felt elated. "I could have floated around the ceiling."

John breathed easier. To celebrate, he threw a party in the lunchroom of his factory. The champagne flowed. Music blasted.

The Chapter 11 bankruptcy proceedings took their toll on the family and employees. The aftermath of the reorganization was analogous to a postpartum depression. The company was reborn and had to figure how to channel its adrenalin. It found temporary highs. For instance,

John offered to fly down to St. Louis and counsel CMC Electronics, which filed a Chapter 11 bankruptcy in fall 1987. The company declined his offer.

When the highs wore off, the routine returned to normal. Workers rolled more products off assembly lines. In June 1986, Koss Corp. introduced a cordless stereophone as JCK/200. It was modeled on the infrared technology used in television remote control. It consisted of a miniature transmitter that hooked into the main audio receiver to give off an infrared signal to a lightweight headset. This enabled sound to travel up to 200 feet from the main source without the annoyance of long cords.

Some of the stereophones were known as circumaurals because they blocked out all background noise. Others are referred to as supra-aurals because they allowed listeners to hear some background noise such as telephones and doorbells.

A year later in June 1987, Koss Corp. again made history. It introduced the first and only cordless loudspeaker, the Koss JCK/5000 Kordlesspeaker. The system consisted of two speakers and a transmitter that converted audio signals from a receiver amplifier into a beam of infrared light. Light was picked up by sensors in speakers.

Koss Corp. also began manufacturing a complete line of mini portable speakers and four different audio/video speakers that augment the sound and picture from televisions and VCRs. Some of the new stereo technology such as the compact disc players' popularity is expected to fuel sales of headphones more.

On December 30, 1986, Koss felt secure enough to repurchase his company's 130,000-square-foot Milwaukee plant from the owners to whom he had sold it. Today, about 300 full-time workers man the assembly lines in the spartan cavernous factory. They produce a total of 23 stereophones and six speaker models. The headphones represented a whopping 91 percent of company revenue in 1987. Workers earn $8 an hour. They pride themselves on making products precisely.

Koss Corp. has so finely tuned its manufacturing process that it can boast about an adjacent tool room where other workers build all equipment needed to produce headset and speaker components and test them.

New advertising campaigns continue to hit the street and keep the Koss name well known. Among the latest is Koss' version of E.T.'s message, "Phone home," which shows Whistler's mother wearing stereophones and reminding passersby to "phone your mother." The company received much attention for its innovative billboard and ad campaign featuring Mona Lisa in headsets.

In the fiscal year ended June 30, 1988, company sales hit record levels. Domestic market share rose to 35 percent. Individual domestic accounts number 1,600. Products show up in more than 15,000 retail outlets that include audio specialty stores, catalogue showrooms, chain department stores, military exchanges and national retailers, including a company-owned store adjacent to corporate headquarters.

The company has defied industry trends. It exports almost 25 percent of its products. In some foreign countries such as Canada, it captures about 50 percent of all sales.

The Koss family, which thrived on its hard work, even during the bad times, rewarded itself. The family has bought 40 percent of the 3.9 million outstanding shares of voting stock. John increased his salary to $150,000, plus a $75,000 bonus. He still holds forth from a large fancy office with windowed sitting alcove. The walls of John's corporate office are covered with reminders of the golden age of Big Bands.

After work and on weekends, John oversees the building of his second dream house—slightly more modest than his first but still an impressive 4,000 square feet of wood and stone at the end of a winding road on another of River Hill's finest. John leaves day-to-day operations to Mike, 34, who is a head taller than his father and has well-chiseled features. He considers himself heir apparent. Mike exhibits a different management style than his father, more patient, more cautious, more hands-on, according to both. He looks the part of a young, prosperous and somewhat stuffy fair-haired star in his starched white button-down shirt, tiny red bow tie and blue blazer. He earns $100,000, plus a $60,000 bonus.

Johnny, 31, vice president of sales, is the family member with the best people skills. He has the look of one of the boys. He's thin and athletic with short brown wiry hair and a bushy moustache. He earns $55,000 a year, plus a 100-plus bonus because of impressive sales commissions. "I hope Johnny makes more than me each year. Then I have it made in the shade," Mike jokes.

Moore, who was Johnny's college roommate, is vice president, legal counsel, credit manager and director of personnel. He considers his brothers-in-law his equals, but earns a lower salary of $50,000.

Debbie, 32, used to earn $22,000 in a part-time position, but recently elected to stay at home. Pammy, the youngest Koss daughter who was in high school when the company filed for Chapter 11, also worked for Koss Corp. part-time compiling the company's history, but is now home with her first child.

The nine-member board of directors consists of just two family members, John and Mike, and executives from Allen-Edmonds Shoe Corp., Brooks Stevens Associates, Oster Co., Shadbolt & Boyd Co., Cade Industries, Hunter Business Direct, and Eyecare One Inc. The board meets quarterly in a handsome room lined with Koss headsets and speakers.

The company continues to share its newly-expanded riches with employees. It contributes cash for hours worked. Most recently, workers gained the equivalent of five weeks of salary for nine months of work and eight to nine percent of their salaries are contributed into the company's Employee Stock Ownership Plan. "You do these things to motivate employees rather than as a way to keep out a union," John said.

John C. Koss can be seen today zigzagging around Milwaukee in a large silver 1978 6.9-model four-door Mercedes-Benz. Mike is in the front seat wearing Koss Corp.'s JCK/200 headphones and listening to the pure sound of Barbra Streisand's "Funny Girl" that emanates from Koss M60 speakers. It's a typical routine, a perfect way to relax and think up new schemes for the future.

The Kosses know they must be on their toes if they are to grow. Consumer electronics sales have been slower because of saturated markets. Overall factory sales rose less than one percent last year, according to the Electronic Industries Association. This reflects greater competition from more chains, a lack of exciting new products and consumer wariness because of stock market fluctuations. The company plans to introduce 10 new products this year all in the stereophone segment.

John wants to move into new but related niches with industrial products for telephone operators, National Football League players and coaches. Mike wants to go after manufacturing sets for the hearing-impaired, theaters, libraries and schools.

Both also are interested in new high-end product lines that can be kept from the deep discount retailers. Koss Corp.'s Pro/450 $175 stereophone with dual elements—two in each earcup, a special new magnet, two cords with oxygen-free cable and all leather headbands—

is an example. It's for the studio musician and recording engineer who make records.

But above all, what John and his children must do to maintain the company's niche and to keep peace in a family business that employs several members of two generations is for each to capitalize on certain strengths and carry on with assigned roles:

John must remain the dealmaker, the antithesis of most entrepreneurs at this stage of their lives, and also the caretaker who doesn't let a professional manager take control.

Mike must remain the heir apparent, the role he's been groomed for since childhood. He also must keep the company on track to manufacture and sell quality sound equipment.

Johnny must follow in his dad's footsteps and maintain good sales relationships with clients to close deals.

Mike Moore, the lawyer, must fill in where needed without stealing thunder from his brothers-in-law.

Debbie, if she returns to the business, must promote the company's reputation and be content not to threaten her brothers' control.

Ironically, it was the bankruptcy that convinced the Koss family that clear-cut roles are crucial and that family has to maintain day-to-day control. Says John, "Don't you know that I engineered the Chapter 11 to teach my kids that valuable lesson. In a way, the bankruptcy was the best thing that ever happened."

Elyachar Real Estate
New York, NY and Sarasota, FL

They offer many words of wisdom—
Do their children hear what they say?
How do they work with one another, day by day?
They look so natural together
Just as two land-barons should be—
Are there some dividends in store for mc?
> —Dana and Peter Elyachar-Stahl
> quoted from song dedicated to their 60-year-
> old father and uncle, who are twins.
> Sung to the tune, "Sunrise, Sunset."

The plot has all the ingredients of a pulp best-seller—a conflict waged amid the towering skyscrapers of New York City by 60-year-old identical twin sons, Daniel and Ralph Elyachar (pronounced LHR), cast out of the family business, deprived of what they consider to be their companies. The twins were at war privately and publicly with their father, Jehiel R. Elyachar.

On May 2, 1984, in a New York City courtroom, they squared off in a costly eight-day lawsuit against their father, then 85. At stake was whether the brothers own an approximate 40 percent interest of the

193

stock of four corporations that hold four prime Manhattan buildings, plus the degree of management and financial control that the ownership gives them.

Are the twins justified to sue because of their holdings? Or is their father, who still manages the properties, and gave them the stock, entitled to call the shots until he retires or dies?

This has been a tale of antipathy since the sons joined their father in business in 1950. The feud became a collision after the senior Elyachar reneged on a real estate deal in 1980 that his sons had initiated in Sarasota. The father withdrew $550,000 from the project. "We were forced to go to the bank and borrow the money at a high rate in the middle of construction," said one of the twins. Two years later, the father stopped payment of each of his sons' $18,200 dividend checks. Rich and powerful Jehiel Elyachar did not try to resolve the dispute amicably with his sons.

After much soul searching, the twins sued their father, one of the most painful decisions of their lives. Suing is against everything they believe in because of the family's long Spanish lineage and the Talmud, an interpretation of the Torah that teaches respect for parents.

"Great is the honor one owes one's parents—for God raises it even above the honor one owes Him. . . . How do you honor God? With wealth in your possession . . . But with 'Honor your father and your mother' (Exodus 20:12), it is not so: whether you have the means or you do not, honor your father and your mother; even if you must become a beggar at the door."—*Jerusalem Talmud*, Kiddushin, chapter 1, paragraph 7.

"It didn't occur to us to go up against our father until we discovered he was going to rewrite history," said Daniel, the more outspoken of the twins.

They concluded that enough was enough.

Suing was the only way Daniel and Ralph thought they could obtain what they say was rightfully theirs, based on the words and actions of the senior Elyachar during happier family times. Not surprisingly, the court's initial verdict confirmed that the stock in the corporations was owned by Ralph, Daniel, their sister, Ruth Dvorkin, and their respective children, but would be held in trust for their benefit during the Colonel's lifetime. This verdict satisfied neither side and produced further legal entanglements. Whatever the outcome, it will be a hollow victory. It has eliminated the family ingredient from a family business and has caused irreparable damage to the happiness of 25 family members.

The saga of the Elyachar twins is similar to dozens of other families in business together who allow personal conflicts to spill over into the business and public arenas.

Laurence Price, 41, son of Sol Price, 71, founder of Fed-Mart and The Price Club in San Diego, both discount chains, hired ace attorney Marvin M. Michelson to sue his father in the Supreme Court of San Diego for $100 million in damages and lost business after Sol broke Laurence's employment contract.

Laurence operated a tire mounting subsidiary of The Price Club. Total corporate sales exceeded $4 billion in 1988. "The bigger it got, the worse my relationship with my father got," he said. The son's division was bringing in between $50 and $100 million when it was taken away from him in a classic struggle between a controlling father, who refused to treat his son like an adult, and a son, who needed to be independent.

All hell broke loose between father and son over Laurence's divorce and custody fight. Sol ordered Laurence to give up custody of his two sons. Laurence refused and the boys moved in with him. Enraged, Sol ordered Laurence to send the children back to their mother. Once again Laurence refused. In retaliation, Sol grabbed the tire business from Laurence. An ugly court suit ensued where father and son tried to resolve differences in arbitration. "Our father-son relationship was never good," says Laurence. "Going to court was the only way I could get my father to reason with me. My older brother Robert E., 46, who is chief executive, was always considered the good son because he went along with what my father wanted."

Laurence received $3.7 million, which he considered paltry because of staggering lawyers' fees and taxes.

Michelson pointed out that there's no law stipulating that a parent has to give a child anything. "You always hope that bitter disputes can be healed and that people can change if they always do what the other person wants. But by the time someone walks into a lawyer's office he's already usually been to his rabbi or priest. There's almost no longer a viable relationship that can be salvaged."

Family struggles like the Prices and Elyachars turn on three key questions:

Is there a point at which the head of a family business should be forced to step down and hand over the reins of a family firm to younger members, especially if he's too old and perhaps senile and if his children are qualified?

At what point should children break from a family business and pursue their interests if they realize a parent will never let go?

In the Elyachar case in particular, were the family members in business doomed to suffer because of the makeup of the players?

—A father, born in 1898 and reared in Jerusalem where the patriarch ruled the household. His sons describe him critically. Authoritarian. Ruthless. Unwilling to allow anyone to make even minor business decisions.

—Two sons, once financially and emotionally dependent on a father who never treated them as adults and peers.

—An older daughter, inactive in the business, torn by loyalties, but siding with her father more out of duty than for money, a modern version of the caring, dutiful Cordelia in Shakespeare's *King Lear*.

—Grandchildren, confused by the rifts and longing to bury the hatchet, but unable to devise a way to do so.

Once family members reach the point of airing their problems in public by suing, the family unit is destroyed and the ties usually are severed, says Dr. Florence Kaslow, clinical psychologist and family business consultant in West Palm Beach, Florida. Kaslow sees the possibility of more family business lawsuits because of a more litigious society. "Young people grow up feeling entitled to what they think is theirs. Most parents want to provide their offspring with as much as they can and would rather have a child than a stranger take over a business. But there is nothing in the law that says this must be done. What the law does stipulate is that a parent's obligations end when the child turns 18."

Kaslow is concerned how these lawsuits will affect family relationships down the line.

The weekend of November 13, 1987, held promise. It was the Elyachar twins' 60th birthday. Second-, third- and fourth-generation members gathered to celebrate in Florida and rehash family issues. The Elyachars, a seemingly close, caring group, relaxed and reminisced. Their more private conversations were bittersweet, revealing the nagging feud between the first and second generations. The Elyachars' older sister, Ruth Dvorkin, who also owned shares in the building corporations, her husband, Spencer, who at one point had worked for his father-in law, and their four daughters had not come from suburban New York to celebrate. They had not been invited.

More significantly, the elderly patriarch of the clan wasn't there. Extremely frail at age 89, and according to his sons, suffering from Alzheimer's disease, the father, Jehiel Elyachar, had not even sent a gift, telegram or birthday card. His office manager of eight years and one of just three employees, Harriet Leeds, had responded, but at the prodding of one of the 12 third-generation members. "I sent a birthday card to the twins for their 60th like a gullible jerk," Leeds said. "David called me up and said it would be the classy thing to do."

All eight children of Daniel and Ralph Elyachar flew in from across the country for the celebration. Many of the grandchildren were present, from four-month-old Isaac Elyachar-Shuster from Evanston, IL, to four-year-old Rachael Elyachar, in from Wilkes-Barre, PA, with her father, Jonathan, and her younger brother, Justin.

Family members flocked around the pool of the Hilton Hotel in Longboat Key, the part of Sarasota that extends into the Gulf of Mexico on the West Coast like a long, pointed finger. The temperature had climbed into the 70s after being chilly for several days. The sky was a brilliant blue with few clouds to cast shadows. The crowds of people that can choke a winter haven had not yet descended. All was peaceful.

Memories were saved for a birthday dinner at the hotel's restaurant that Saturday night. The brothers held court at the head of a U-shaped table. They resembled each other closely in physique, voice and mannerisms. Ann Elyachar-Shuster, Daniel's only daughter, reminded them that at times even they couldn't distinguish one from the other in 40-year-old family photographs.

They still resembled one another with deep-set brown-eyes, prominent features, 6-foot-tall statures, slight paunches. A few strands of gray hair covered the tops of their heads. In conversation, Daniel's voice was slightly gruffer and lower. Ralph stood straighter and cut a more dapper figure, outfitted by his dark, stylish wife of 35 years, the former Alice Feuer. She was the family member known for paying attention to details—clothes, shoes, jewelry.

This was a competitive lot, the 16 adults present. Each vied for laughs and tears as they recalled funny and sad tales about the men, each other and their grandfather.

The third-generation Elyachars talked of the difficulties of either finding a place to hide or a way to be noticed in a big family. No matter how different the stories, one message came through. The twins had always been there when their children needed them—whether it was coaching a basketball team when other fathers didn't want to give up precious Saturday mornings or picking up children and dates late at night. "Children are the best assets a man can have," said Daniel.

Daniel and Ralph were overwhelmed by the extent of their family closeness, something they never experienced with their father.

They had gathered some Sundays and for most of the major Jewish holidays at their father's 50-acre suburban estate in Harrison, NY, Ruradan Farm, an acronym for his children's names (Ruth, Ralph, Daniel). But attendance at the dinners was mandatory rather than spontaneous. Listening to their father's soliloquies and berating of their mother, the Colonel's late first wife, Jean, was uncomfortable. When the twins were 14 years old, their father went to serve in the Army. The boys had little contact with their dad until they worked in the business together after they completed their own Army stints and graduated from college in 1950.

The three Elyachar men had grandiose plans. They would build a real estate dynasty, as great as any in Manhattan.

If you were to capture Jehiel Elyachar in a photograph, the image would be blurred. Even a finely calibrated shutter could not fix on this man caught in the whirlwind of his enterprise. He is a paradox—a highly domineering private man; a sometimes charming, philanthropic public servant who established the Elyachar Welfare Fund, a private foundation funded by 10 percent of the profits of the four building corporations. His face is broad and fleshy with dark-ringed eyes, his body stocky and powerful. The combination gives him the look of a proud immigrant.

Elyachar's family had been merchant bankers in Palestine. But he wanted to go to America, about which he had heard great things, and carve his own niche. He emigrated to the U.S. in 1928 and a year later started his real estate business. The Depression had sent real estate prices plummeting. Banks were foreclosing on properties. They willingly sold and gave away buildings for little or no cash. Elyachar bought two prime locations at 8 East 48th Street and at 222 East 56th Street.

As a prominent landowner, Elyachar assumed his place in Jewish

Sephardic society, an elite group that had arrived in New Amsterdam years before the German Jews. Sephardim believed that their ancient Jewish heritage put them on a higher social plateau than the nouveau riche, pushy German Jews.

After the outbreak of World War II in Europe, the senior Elyachar enlisted in the Army as a private in 1941. He rose quickly through the ranks to become Lieutenant Colonel. Later, because of his engineering skill, he joined General George C. Patton's fight in Germany. He became a decorated hero and dined at the White House with President Eisenhower several times after he returned to his real estate business.

But Jehiel ruled autocratically at home, at his office or on the few fishing trips to Canada that he took with his sons. Father and sons shared few happy memories. The twins respected yet feared their father. He screamed. He ranted. He raged. He hit. The twins thought that their father was disappointed in them, didn't consider them to be as bright as he had hoped and found it difficult to accept them. Their happiest childhood remembrances were of their mother when their father went into the Army. She ran the business for her husband and gave her boys freedom to mature.

The twins' fear of their father made them apprehensive about joining the business. Nevertheless, the idea of working as a family pulled them in. They believed that family feeling was the root of what's important in life.

After spending summers working part time, the twins went to work full time for their father when they earned their undergraduate degrees. Daniel, who had planned to become an attorney, graduated from the University of Michigan. Ralph graduated from Purdue University. The senior Elyachar gave his boys the impression that he needed them in his business. The threesome built motels in Indiana and Pennsylvania, a nursing home in Brooklyn and two apartment houses in midtown Manhattan at 1100 Madison Avenue, a full block between 82nd and 83rd Streets, and at 250 East 39th Street.

The work involved choosing a location. In one case, a supervisor in their company found the 39th Street property crowded with tenements. The Elyachars tore the tenements down and put up a new apartment house. Their work involved acting as general contractor. They arrived at a site as early as 6:00 A.M., sometimes seven days a week. They assigned the contracting work and supervised construction. They checked that walls went up correctly, the electrical wires were properly installed, that plasterers did their job. Daniel and Ralph corrected problems. It usually took a year to oversee construction of one building. They also acted as office managers, negotiated loans and okayed alterations on other buildings, including ones the senior Elyachar had bought from the banks years before. They drew up leases, collected rent checks, supervised superintendents.

The twins considered themselves equals with their father. They were touted as a successful team by others in the industry at a time when real estate was less competitive. They upped their salaries. They had what was most needed to succeed: family unity.

Slowly, arguments began between the Colonel and his sons. He began to treat them less as equals and family and more as underlings. He ordered them about as office boys. He listened in on their telephone calls. He began firing and rehiring them.

The twins remained with their father in business because he gave signs that succession would take place. Starting when his sons were 18, the senior Elyachar sold and gave them shares totaling 40 percent of the stock of the buildings. The Colonel continued to dole out to his children and his grandchildren shares in his buildings piecemeal like chocolate bars awarded for good grades. He repeatedly told them from the time they were young that they eventually would own everything.

Nevertheless, disputes became commonplace. Daniel severed family ties when he couldn't handle the disagreements between him and his dad. His father shouted, "Get the hell out." Daniel moved to Chicago in 1956 with his wife and three children.

A year after moving to Chicago, however, Daniel returned to New York and started his own construction company. "My roots weren't in Chicago," he said. But his father got involved in Daniel's projects as a ploy to keep Daniel on a tight leash. Daniel tried to minimize contact. He didn't fully succeed.

In the late 1950s, the senior Elyachar lost interest in his business. He put a stop to new construction. He was content to collect rent checks. He had no desire to improve buildings or to convert them to the more lucrative cooperative status as his sons wanted to do. They wanted to take the bricks and mortar and turn them into the beginnings of a real estate empire, "as great as what the Tishmans, Roses and Horowitzes were doing," dreamed Daniel. Those were three highly successful and also Jewish New York real estate dynasties. Instead, the senior Elyachar retreated to other worlds. His circle of Army pals. His charitable organizations. The State of Israel, including the American

Society for Technion, a support group for the Technion-Israel Institute of Technology, that country's main technical-education institution.

He also established a chair at Yeshiva University and the Sephardic Home for the Aged in Brooklyn, NY.

Ralph stuck by his father. He rationalized that his family problems were no different from countless other family businesses headed by entrepreneurs, who founded a company, succeeded because of their tenacity and began to focus on non-business interests and hobbies. Perhaps his father would change and give him more autonomy and control, Ralph hoped. But his father didn't budge. With little to do, Ralph joined forces with Daniel in 1958. They built a large one-family housing development in White Plains, NY, called Twin Properties. They acquired walk-up apartment houses that they remodeled and managed. In 1965, they put together a $6 million 221 (d) 3 project in Newark, NJ, consisting of two seven-story apartment buildings of 260 units. They built the first 236 Federal housing project in Bridgeport, CT.

In 1970, the twins started building a sleek 25-story tower as a cooperative at the southeast corner of Madison Avenue and 80th Street in Manhattan. The brothers needed additional capital after a slump hit the residential housing market. They tried to convince their father to put in some of their family's money because they believed the market eventually would come back. The senior Elyachar refused. His sons had to sell the building, just when they were about to complete it.

Daniel moved to Florida in 1972. He started his own development firm, LHR Construction, to build and manage apartments and condominiums.

Ralph, who had been better able to deal with the Colonel, stayed in New York longer. But a turning point came for him as well and for several reasons.

By 1978, the Colonel had transferred and sold the bulk of the shares of his buildings to his sons, daughter and grandchildren. But he kept the stock certificates themselves hidden in a closet, as if this gave him power to revoke the gifts. Like King Midas hoarding his gold, he refused to share the accumulated earnings of the building corporations until he was forced to do so by his accountants. They told him that to resist further would result in tax penalties. The first dividends to Daniel and Ralph in 1978 were meager checks, each for $2,195 for their interests in the building at East 56th Street.

The sons came to believe that their father's reasons had to do with his wanting to see them fail so that they would have to grovel to him. Why would a father turn against his children? They rationalized that their father was afraid that they might be more successful with the business than he was.

The Colonel also began to act irrationally with other family members and outsiders. At his grandfather's urging, David Elyachar, Daniel's oldest son, moved to New York from Chicago where he had been a carpet mill representative. He dropped everything and showed up for work the first day at 8:45 A.M. His grandfather fired him, handed him *The New York Times* and said, "Prove yourself in New York and find another job." The Colonel didn't help at all. David left the business and moved away.

Ralph couldn't stomach such family bickering any longer. He joined his brother in Florida for a six-month trial in 1978. He concluded that his financial position as well as his physical and emotional makeup would not permit him to continue as his father's lackey. Ralph decided to make his stay permanent and he and Daniel worked together at LHR Construction. Ralph also continued to commute frequently between his apartment in Sarasota and a house he kept in Scarsdale, NY, one of Westchester County's loveliest suburbs.

The brothers continued to hope, once again, that their father would change and that they could all work together again. The Colonel came down to Florida in 1980 and said, "We have so much wealth, so many buildings, so much income. Let's get together."

The twins agreed. But just a few months later, the Colonel reneged again on an executed construction loan for 176 condos the sons were building in Sarasota. When the father withdrew all $550,000 of the corporate funds in the Sarasota deal, the bank informed the twins, "No more money." They called their father and demanded an explanation. He matter of factly replied, "I don't like the deal. I don't think it's a good investment. Not only am I not going to give you any more money, but I want my money back."

Construction hadn't been completed. The twins were forced to go to the bank and borrow the money at a higher interest rate. It was either that, get out of the deal or lose their shirts. They told their father it was their money and they didn't have to pay it back. Jehiel didn't give in.

The Colonel kept acting oddly with other family members and outsiders. He wrote his son-in-law, Spencer Dvorkin:

I (will go) to the lawyer, go to jail if necessary and spend $1 million to cancel everything (I have) ever done for (you and your) children.

The Colonel asked one of Ralph's friends to come into the business, but then berated the friend so much once he joined that he soon left. Ralph was so embarrassed that he never spoke to that friend again. Ralph wrote his father in May 1981:

This week you told me that I was wasting my time in the office. I could not nor do not disagree with that statement of fact. Basically, because without authority and responsibility to an organization, an individual cannot function efficiently.

Nine months later, the Colonel again asked Ralph to come back to the business. Ralph responded in a letter he sent his father:

Dan and I have tried over the past several years to build a bridge which would connect New York to Sarasota. The bridge has collapsed every time. On several occasions, Dan and I almost drowned. If you, in your wisdom, want to do what in our opinion is good for you and what would be good for the family as a whole; namely, to retire and to allow Dan and myself to take complete control, we would reconsider. . . ."

Two months later, the brothers again told their father that they would not come to New York as he requested unless "we had complete authority." The sons tried to reason with their father and their father's new attorneys at the blue-chip New York firm of Paul, Weiss, Rifkind, Wharton and Garrison, to turn over their stock certificates which the father continued to hoard.

Their father wrote his sons in a more businesslike than paternal fashion:

Dear Ralph and Dan:
    I am enclosing a dividend check from Gerel [one of his corporations] for each of you. The least you can do is to send a receipt, and a thank you note, and also a check for the Elyachar Welfare Fund. This is very important to me. Ruth has sent her check. I would like an answer by return mail.

Sincerely,
JRE

When the twins deposited their dividend checks, they bounced. The father had stopped payment. No resolution came.

The twins consulted experts. What could they do? Do sons sue their father? They were afraid of setting a family precedent. But they felt they had no recourse.

In April 1982, they sued their father in Federal court in Manhattan to confirm that the stock was indeed theirs and also to gain possession of the certificates. The father claimed he never made such gifts and that his refusal to deliver the certificates proved this. Even Dvorkin, his son-in-law, believed the Colonel engaged in secretive behavior because he wanted to disavow everything, according to the opinion of the judge, Abraham D. Sofaer. That opinion sheds more light.

> He placed 'X' marks through some stock certificates he wished to cancel, and destroyed or hid others. He also appears to have thrown away letters and other documents that might have shown even more conclusively than has been demonstrated by the remaining records that the transfers were intended as gifts and were effectively delivered and accepted . . . in letters, in tax filings and in corporate reports. . . . Colonel Elyachar's delivery could not have been more complete.

Furthermore, in the court's opinion, Judge Sofaer said that the father had suppressed evidence by refusing to turn over corporate records that would have proved his children's ownership claim. Sofaer concluded the father had transferred ownership, but that he wanted to retain control of the certificates and the business until his death. The judge let the senior Elyachar stay in charge. He ruled that the father could hold the stock certificates as trustee for the beneficial interest of his children and grandchildren until he resigns or dies.

In effect, Sofaer's decision meant that, except for limited dividends, the brothers' combined ownership included between 40 and 43.8 percent of the shares of each of the four buildings. But control would remain in the hands of the Colonel until his death. The brothers could not oust the Colonel from his post and could not force the buildings to be sold or refinanced. At best, the decision insured that the business would be preserved in its twilight state until the Colonel's demise.

The twins' sister felt torn. But because Ruth knew her father respected her for her intelligence, she tried in the summer of 1982 to resolve the conflict, her brothers explained. She wrote her father:

I agree with Ralph and Dan that by this time they should have their stocks. . . . You have given the stocks away—to all kinds of people. That was your absolute right. But once given, they cannot be taken back by you.

Sofaer's decision similarly affected the twins' sister, even though she hadn't participated in the suit. Worse yet, it meant that the brothers would be forced to return to court periodically to make sure that their assets would not be lavished on charities or depleted on other projects.

The twins lost patience. When the senior Elyachar refused to resume dividend payments, which he had stopped in 1982, or to pay out retained earnings, which at that time they calculated at about $8 million, they sued in New York State Supreme Court. Their goal this time was more final—to dissolve the various real estate companies and to distribute all assets to themselves, their sister and their respective children. At the time of the suit, the properties were said to be debt free and worth more than $100 million.

By this time, Sofaer had been appointed to the post of legal adviser to the State Department and a new judge, Vincent Broderick, replaced him. The brothers waited for Judge Broderick to end the feuding.

In the meantime, the sister continued to urge her father to repair the damage. In a letter to him, she said:

You have always taught us that no one is above the law. And you must know that no one can rewrite history. Is it so terrible that you have given shares in your corporations to your children and grandchildren? Why deny that you did so? . . . Their actions were taken to restore their legal rights, not claim more. It is time to stop this way you have fought against your sons . . . Only you can do it. You are not perfect and neither are your children . . . Let us try and be a family again. It's all up to you.

Relations were patched together temporarily. The Elyachar clan gathered at Ann's wedding in August 1984. It was the last time they were together. The family closeness pleased the bride, though her grandfather's gift surprised her. He had given her and her husband the same check that he had given to newlyweds 10 years before. It must have been a mistake, she thought. She remembered in great detail how her grandfather sat at the head of the table at family dinners and told her, her siblings and cousins that they never would have to worry about money. "You own land," he bellowed.

As late as Father's Day, 1987, Ralph wrote his father one last time to reconcile.

THERE IS VERY LITTLE TIME LEFT . . . THE TIME TO END THIS STRUGGLE IS NOW! . . . FATHERS AND SONS NEED ONE ANOTHER FOR MANY REASONS. FOR THE SAKE OF THE ELYACHAR FAMILY AND ITS DESTINY, IT IS NOT TOO LATE TO MEND OUR WOUNDS AND TO ADDRESS THE WRONGS AND TO REMEMBER THE GOOD PAST. LET US, TOGETHER, ON THIS FATHER'S DAY, TRY TO BURY THESE PAST FIVE YEARS AND ATTEMPT TO WALK HAND IN HAND INTO OUR SUNSET YEARS.

The Colonel never responded.

A question haunts the Elyachar twins. Did they do the right thing?

The twins think so and hope other wealthy family business owners will be able to forestall intra-family wars before differences permanently divide them. Their revelations provide a rare glimpse into a collection of dashed dreams.

Perhaps they might have been content to bide their time, work with their father and take his abuse if he had been a warmer and more supportive father.

Perhaps they might have waited if their father had proved a sharper businessman. The Colonel had never offset his tax liabilities with tax shelters to avoid paying high corporate and individual taxes. Instead, the senior Elyachar set up his real estate holdings in corporations rather than partnerships which meant that they paid double taxes.

The Colonel also had never developed his properties to bring in the current high prices of elegant cooperatives or expensive office spaces as other real estate moguls did. The buildings are still rental units, stuck in time. The brick facades look old, tired, down-and-dirty. Room air conditioners and black wrought-iron fire escapes protrude hideously from two of the buildings. Entrances and lobbies are seedy.

The most shocking building in the Colonel's portfolio is the East 48th Street building where his office is located on the second floor in a modest space. It stands smack in the center of glitzy mid-Manhattan's labyrinth of steel and glass, making its unkempt appearance of worn, grimy brown bricks, cemented windows, dirty front entrance door and ugly, faded green awnings more startling. Said his office manager

Leeds, "He likes things status quo. You should see this office. We don't go in for the plush. This and the other buildings were like his children. He didn't want to alter them and he didn't care about making money from them."

One New York real estate executive agrees with the brothers' assessment that the Colonel has not made the wisest use of his buildings. "Clearly by turning the units into cooperatives and selling them, they could have made a staggering sum. Without question. The building at 1100 Madison Avenue could be renovated with units going for almost $148,000 a room or a two-bedroom apartment probably selling for more than $425,000."

The Colonel could not be reached to comment and his attorney, Leslie G. Fagen of Paul, Weiss, said his client "refuses to be interviewed or cooperate at all. I will say the lawsuit has caused Jehiel Elyachar great pain. So has their (the brothers') going to *The New York Times*." A story appeared on the front page of the business section on February 23, 1987.

The twins' sister also refused to cooperate. "I am horrified that the family feud would be written about in a book." she said in a telephone call from her 1950s-era wood and frame split-level suburban house in the Edgemont section of Scarsdale.

Leeds chuckled when asked if she feels the twins are justified in suing their father. "I can't see why they're bragging about suing their father? I recall many times when the senior Elyachar bailed them out of tough situations. He paid to educate all the grandchildren and helped buy their homes. They've been on the brink for a while."

The twins refute Leeds' comments.

Others say that the brothers had no alternative but to sue. They had similar experiences with the Colonel. An established New York real estate developer and member of a well-known family firm explained, "We bought a building from him and he reneged on the deal. I have the sense he's not functioning, not acting rationally or the way a father does with his children." This developer asked to remain anonymous.

Still another New York real estate developer remarked that he had often seen the Colonel's hot temper. "I recently heard him yelling at his wife at a fund-raising dinner in front of hundreds of people. I understand he's not easy to get along with."

A recent visitor to the Colonel's office was subjected to his bad moods. She related: "I was in the office to rent an apartment in the 1100 Madison Avenue building, when a young man sitting across the room smiled at me. I smiled back. At that exact moment, Mr. Elyachar walked out of his office. And he started shouting at both of us, 'What are you here for? Why are you laughing at me? Why? Do you know who I am? Do you know who I am?' I left. There is no way I'm going to rent from a guy like that."

The brothers are convinced that their father will never be able to make business decisions because of ill health and age. "The last time someone asked him where he was, he said he was in Milwaukee and it was 1900," says Daniel. "His Alzheimer's has been confirmed by doctors, though the medical experts refuse to testify in court because of doctor-patient confidentiality," he adds. Dr. Ronald D. Adelman, former head of the Alzheimer's Clinic at Mt. Sinai Hospital in New York who is chief of Geriatrics at Winthrop United Hospital in Mineola, NY, evaluated Jehiel Elyachar in early 1987 at the request of Elyachar's second wife, Dr. Adelman said. "It's highly confidential stuff and it's too convoluted to go into," he said in a telephone call.

The brothers console themselves by rationalizing that the largest part of their predicament has been caused by factors beyond their control.

Yet one observer, Abraham Zaleznik, a Harvard Business School professor, disagrees and contends the twins have control. "They are in a teasing relationship, a game, in which the father is keeping them psychologically and financially on the hook. They are tar babies who are stuck in a situation on some level they enjoy. But it takes two to play the game. These men can't change their father, but they can change and let go of the situation."

Mary D. Korman, a consultant at Hubler-Swartz & Associates in Minneapolis-St. Paul, describes the relationship as an emotional dance. "Children spend their lives trying to get parental approval and also to do better than their parents or beat the old man down. It's the young and old buck syndrome. Only these kinds of families are fighting it out in the courts."

Other children in other family businesses have been able to close the book on a difficult relationship, though it's usually once they've become successful in their own right. The Elyachar twins have had their share of licks.

Daniel describes his own family as independently wealthy with most of the money tied up in land. Yet both brothers are vague about their Florida holdings. Ralph talks more straightforwardly of a lifestyle that "we might have been able to have . . . if." He and Alice rent a two-bedroom apartment in a nice but unpretentious building in Sarasota. "We're not paupers, but we don't have large sums of cash in our hands and hence the ability to parlay this pyramid into bigger and better land packages," Ralph said. "We have had to liquidate some of our holdings to get cash to live on. We don't believe in selling but in buying, building and holding. That's how big wealth is amassed."

The headquarters for the brothers' LHR Construction Company confirms that they have not established a real estate dynasty. They lease office space in a two-bedroom model apartment at Rolling Green South, a complex of brown and white two-story concrete block and stucco condominiums adjacent to an 18-hole golf course that they built and sold. It's difficult to tell whether the neighborhood is climbing into middle-class chic or slipping, though land values had soared in prior years before Florida real estate values began leveling off. The brothers say that they own the land bordering the golf course where they can build 314 additional units. They value the property at $3.5 million.

No Sarasota area real estate observers, building and trade associations or the local Chamber of Commerce and Better Business Bureau are able to shed light on their operations. None has heard of the brothers or their company, which may not be unusual for a company that hasn't built new projects in the last few years, explains one New York real estate developer.

Either way, the twins say they are eager to end their exile in Florida and return permanently to New York. Alice prefers the social life up North and the closer geographic proximity to her two daughters. One lives in the 39th Street building in Manhattan where she owns five percent of the stock. The other lives outside Boston. Daniel's wife, the former Michelle Henden, is concerned about Sarasota's schools. Their four-year-old son Joshua will start kindergarten next year.

None of the brothers' seven grown children has joined them in their business. Daniel describes their business as a rubber band. "It constricts to just the two of us when work is at a standstill or expands to include others as new projects come on line."

During the twins' 60th birthday weekend, after playing a hard game of poker, the grandchildren talked into the wee hours of the morning to map out a plan to end the feud. Daniel's children, in particular, reached some conclusions. They want to end the rift out of loyalty and love to their father. He had been both father and mother after his wife left them when Adam, the youngest, was five months old. But they have no solutions.

A major reason is that there is little logic to the Elyachar plot.

It would have been logical for Jehiel R. Elyachar to have stepped aside in the interest of family unity and good business. But he couldn't let go. While he won't reveal his reasons, others try to. According to Judge Sofaer's opinion, "The buildings are his 'children,' and he seems to feel that if he quits working he will die." Leeds added, "Mr. Elyachar is a workaholic. He comes in every day, he passes the time of day here. He signs checks. This is not a big time operation. If he makes money, he's content."

It would have been logical for the sons to have accepted the abuse or broken all ties. But they never did either, as often happens with scions in an unhealthy family business.

The Elyachar twins contend they care only about the shares already given to them or that they bought and not about the contents of the Colonel's will, about which they have no knowledge.

Even when the Colonel dies and the twins gain control of what is theirs, together they still will own just a minority share of the four corporations. They won't be able to exert control. Ralph and Daniel, for example, own 40 percent of one corporation, with their sister owning another 40 percent—with their father owning the remaining 20 percent. They believe, however, that they will have a majority because they hope their sister Ruth and the third generation will band together.

Perhaps, the only good to come out of this family feud is the direction in which the third generation has headed. Because of the bitterness between their parents and grandfather, all seven grown children pursue independent careers and have forged healthy relationships with their parents and each other.

In particular, Daniel's children, David, Matthew and Adam, live, socialize and work together in Kansas City for the four-store carpet company that David started and that employed 25 people in 1987. Big Bob's Carpet earned about $3 million in 1987 from used and cut commercial carpeting and from carpet cleaning. It hit sales of some $4.8 million in 1988.

Although the Colonel's demise may come too late for his twin sons to rejoin the business and to rekindle a healthy father-son relationship, it ironically may create a chance for future generations of Elyachars to work together and breathe life into an established but stagnating family firm.

Epilogue

On November 25, 1988, Judge Vincent Broderick ruled that Colonel Elyachar be removed as trustee and that the stock certificates for two of the buildings be delivered to Spencer Dvorkin and the Elyachar twins, who would then have the sole right to retain physical possession of them, vote the shares, and manage and control those companies.

The stock certificates for the other buildings were ordered to be delivered to Dvorkin, his daughter Elizabeth, and Ralph Elyachar.

Dividends were also ordered to be paid, totaling $5 million, according to a set schedule. Each twin received a total of $1.02 million. Their sister received $1.26 million.

On March 29, 1989, Jehiel R. Elyachar died of a heart attack at 90 years of age in Manhattan. He is survived by his second wife, Anna Tulin, three children, 12 grandchildren and 10 great-grandchildren, according to a lengthy obituary in *The New York Times*. Many charitable organizations expressed sadness at his passing.

A memorial service was scheduled for April 17 at the Spanish and Portuguese Synagogue at 8 West 70th Street in New York. One grandchild, Ann Elyachar Shuster, said she had no plans to attend the service. "I received the invitation too late," she explained by telephone from her home in Evanston, IL.

The brothers would not respond to queries about the funeral and whether they attended the service. They also would not respond to whether they have reached an accord with their sister over the future course of how the four buildings will be handled.

Blake-Lamb Funeral Homes
Oak Park, IL

In Him who rose from the dead our hope of resurrection downed. The sadness of death gives way to the bright promise of immortality. Lord, for your faithful people, life is changed, not ended. . . . When the body of our earthly dwelling lies in death, we gain an everlasting dwelling place in heaven.

—Preface for *Christian Death I*

Hundreds of mourners begin to gather around noon for the 1:00 P.M. service in Oak Lawn, IL. It is a typical workday for Blake-Lamb Funeral Homes, a South Side Chicago institution. This is one of five funerals scheduled that day in this location.

Silk-tied, black-suited officials stand guard outside the homey brick building on tree-lined Main Street in one of Chicago's most populated suburbs, 35 miles from the city. The funeral officials direct traffic to the parking lot.

Solemn and dignified, the mourners file into the chapel, where another contingent of officials directs them to the appropriate service.

In more than 60 years, this picture has barely changed. Several generations of Catholics have relied on Blake-Lamb to oversee every detail of their family funerals. The routine is as precise as the inner workings of a Swiss watch. Choosing the right casket. Selecting flowers. Planning a wake. Having pallbearers in attendance exactly on time. Each service is impeccable, tailor-made for the family who requires support in a time of sorrow and vulnerability.

The assignment is especially challenging because this is no tiny one-man shop. Blake-Lamb is a seven-figure business with 17 branches, 150 employees, six limousines, 10 hearses and 50 other vehicles. It brings in $8 million a year in revenue from 3,200 funerals, about 250 of which are cremations and 65 percent of which are Catholic services. Of Chicago's 5.7 million residents, 2.4 million are Catholics. Chicago is the second largest Catholic archdiocese in the country, after Los Angeles.

A recent company venture into pre-arranging funerals, the industry's fastest-growing trend, rings up another $2.5 million in sales for Blake-Lamb.

Inspiring such entrepreneurial flair are brothers and partners, Matt III, 56, and Dick Lamb, 47, who grew up in the business, living above the original funeral home. They bought it from their father 20 years ago. The business has provided the Lambs with flexible work schedules, generous incomes and affluent lifestyles.

Every morning, Matt Lamb is chauffeured five blocks from his elegant apartment at 1550 North State Street, which is two blocks from Lake Michigan, to his office in the long, low dun-colored motel-type Blake-Lamb Funeral Home at 1035 North Dearborn. Lamb's driver parks one of his two Rolls-Royces or his Lincoln town car in the building's underground garage. Matt gets out and follows a maze of passageways up to his office on the first floor. Blake-Lamb's Dearborn branch spans a valuable parcel of land. Matt walks through the funeral home like a proud father checking arrangements and making sure all runs smoothly. Lamb runs his hands over a crack in a wall, covered by his large abstract paintings titled with such names as "Peace Star," "Dachau" and "Nativity." The decor presents a somber vision, the elusive colors of the walls tied to the grays and browns of the upholstery. Visual valium.

Matt is the Bohemian of the family. Artistic. Soulful. Flamboyant with gaudy gold and diamond rings on both hands. A craggy-faced Irishman with a great appetite for the best surroundings.

He leaves in the early afternoon to go home. A white-gloved uniformed doorman guards the entrance to the building which reeks of old money. The Lambs' 11,000-square-foot, 18-room penthouse on the 10th floor overlooks the lake, Lincoln Park and the mansion of his friend, Cardinal Joseph Bernardin.

The apartment is furnished opulently with paneling imported from Scotland, English Victorian mantles and antiques. The 54-by-25-foot living room is lined with red silk damask wall coverings and wall-to-wall Matt Lamb original oils. Each room has a different style and many are named.

When Lamb wants to become the artist, he steps into the elevator and travels down 10 floors to a two-story apartment, connected by a spiral staircase. Rooms are cluttered and sloppily stocked with art supplies, paints, canvases and watercolors. Paintings are mostly abstract oils in garish primary colors done in frenzied thick brushstrokes dabbed on with a palette knife.

Matt's painting is a "second full-time career," he explains. He took it up five years ago after he was told he would die from chronic hepatitis. "It gave me time to sit back and look at my life. The one thing I regretted was that I had never made a statement through art," he was quoted as saying in *Inside Chicago*, a bi-monthly city publication in which an exhibition of his art at Galleria Renata was touted. "All my life I wanted to express deep feelings on social and economic subjects and religion," Lamb is quoted in the Chicago tabloid.

In the evening, Matt mingles with well-known Chicago politicians, religious leaders and artists. He craves the limelight and drops names of individuals and organizations with whom he's involved with the frequency of a tree shedding leaves in autumn. "We move through the social, economic and political structure of this city. I was at a party with Rich Daley the other night," he says in one breath and then quickly adds, "In 1985 I was appointed Papal Knight of the Holy Sepulchre by Pope John Paul II and a Knight of Malta in 1986."

Matt's brother, Dick, lives and works in the suburb of Lisle, 25 miles west of Chicago. Although they bear a striking resemblance, Dick is taller and more conservative looking. He's also the family pragmatist. He's a paper-and-pencil man who maintains an insouciant presence and spends most of his work time on a new venture he started three years ago, Silver Quality Life Plan. The plan allows consumers to select and pay for funerals in advance of their deaths, a service termed pre-need. "It's peace of mind," says Dick. "They have control over the kind of funeral they'll get and their heirs won't have to worry about all the details or taking money out of the estate to pay for it."

Dick is home on a Friday afternoon relaxing with his wife, Sue, and their five children. Their Tudor-style six-bedroom home reflects a successful life. In the garage is Dick's Mercedes. His wife Sue drives a

BMW. Their home is in a tidy subdivision of large houses on half-acre plots. All houses back up to two lakes and lie within a few yards of an arboretum. This bucolic setting is the perfect place to raise a large family.

The Dick Lamb home is as well-run as his business. It's right out of an interior design magazine with splashes of colors in pleasing, muted tones reflecting conventional good taste. In their two-story redwood paneled sunroom with a vaulted ceiling is a deck with a tarp over it. The Lambs point out that this is the hot tub they installed but they rarely use. Dick grabs a soda and props his feet on a fluffy ottoman nearby.

Because of their different personalities, interests and nine-year age difference, the brothers work independently and often have no idea what the other is up to. Matt likes to talk over the phone. Dick prefers to meet in person. They rarely see each other during the day. They also rarely socialize. Matt's 56th birthday celebration underscores the emotional distance between them. Matt's daughter Colleen is throwing her father a party. Dick and his family weren't invited. "It's his birthday today?" Dick asks. "Sue, did you know that?"

"You have to remember Matt was a lot older and I went off to college in Massachusetts at a time when he already was in the business," says Dick. He quickly switches topics, explaining he'd rather talk about the nine members of the third generation and how some are coming into the business.

So far, five work for Blake-Lamb. Rosemarie, Matt's daughter, who's usually referred to as Rose, oversees the Oak Lawn headquarters. Matt Jr., actually Matt IV, is a funeral director, who lives with his wife Janet above the funeral home in Lombard. Colleen, their younger sister, manages and lives above the Oak Lawn home and oversees the crematorium. She's known as the politician in the third generation for her public relations finesse. Sheila, the youngest on this side of the family, manages and lives above the Becvar Funeral Home at 52nd Street and Kedzie in Chicago. She had been a licensed hairdresser who decided to join the business almost two years ago.

Only one of Dick's children, his eldest child, Maureen, a recent college graduate, is old enough to work in the business. She mans the shift from 12:30 to 8:30 P.M., answering the switchboard and learning the ropes in the hope of becoming a funeral arranger.

"Having the Lamb name will probably get you the job, but it sure won't keep you. You earn what you earn," says Dick.

Walt Becker, one of the company's three regional managers who has been with Blake-Lamb for 10 years, agrees. "Matt Lamb Jr. is an example. He came into the business but he's not going to rise to the top like his sister Rose has done. This is a demanding business . . ."

The fear of not finding enough jobs for their heirs and trying to expand their business as the funeral industry began to consolidate forced the Lambs to think about the future.

In spite of the highly-charged emotional nature of the funeral business, the Lambs have remained coolly detached and clear-cut about goals and how to attain them. They know it's important to be compassionate to customers, whom they refer to as "their families," but they've never let compassion interfere with the company's bottom line.

Blake-Lamb represents the essence of professionalism. Its goals are simple. To capture a bigger market share of an increasingly older population. To expand into new geographic areas by taking over competitors' operations and building new chapels. To make a profit.

The Lambs' vision and focus for what they want to do enabled them not just to plan for the next year or two, but to adjust the lens and aim farther down the road at where the $6.5-to-$7-billion funeral industry is headed over the next 20 years. Most of the country's two million annual funerals are performed by Mom-and-Pop operators, who arrange just 100 funerals a year. "There's probably no other industry which is so dominated by families," says Michael Fritz, director of communications for the National Funeral Directors Association, the industry's main trade group in Milwaukee.

The Lambs saw little way that small funeral operators could survive in a highly regulated industry that has high fixed costs averaging between $500,000 and $1 million, according to Fritz. A chapel, land, supplies and payroll eat into profits. Margins are as slim as three percent. The Lambs also saw another discouraging trend developing. Service Corporation International, the country's one national funeral chain, and a host of large regional conglomerates such as Arlington Corp. in Arlington, VA, were dangling before the small independents attractive cash and stock packages, greater financial backing, larger trained staffs and a full complement of funeral services from caskets to flowers.

"If you're not moving forward, you're moving backward," philosophizes Matt. He sits in a conference room in the company's Dearborn office tugging on his beard and offering his well-thought out diatribe. "What happened to all the businesses that were never going to change?

What would happen if my brother and I died before we could sell? We didn't want to be caught in a desperate situation and sell for less than we were worth because we had to. If we didn't keep current with industry trends and expand, what is the worst that could happen to us?" Matt analyzes. "I'd have to move out of my apartment and sell the Rolls. The kids would be out of jobs. I'd be the one with holes in my pants wondering what went wrong. Obviously, the risk of not selling was worse. And we couldn't afford to expand on our own. Why would someone in their 50s want to take on a lot of debt. If you're 32 and you sign up all you have, you don't give a damn. But it you're 55 and you have all you want, then you really start worrying."

The brothers were also concerned that too many third-generation Lambs coming into the business would not be able to work together as well as they had and concerned that there would be too little family money to pay large estate taxes upon their deaths.

Four years ago, the brothers began weighing their options, much more methodically and analytically than most family business owners do. They sought the advice of a family business consultant, John L. Ward, professor of free enterprise at Loyola University in Chicago. At Ward's urging, the Lambs brought together a board of outside advisers and paid them a modest stipend in exchange for their expertise— Ronald L. Taylor, president of the Graduate School of Management at Loyola University; Mark A. Levy, a restaurateur and real estate developer, who works with a brother, Larry; Edward R. Schwinn, Jr., president of Schwinn Bicycle Co., another old Chicago family company.

The Lambs also met with venture capitalists to see if they could raise money to expand on their own. They talked to interested buyers to get a handle on what their funeral business was worth. Matt came to the conclusion, before Dick and Rose, that they had to sell. With so many cousins possibly going into the business, Rose agreed. "I knew it would never just be my company," she said.

The Lambs were bombarded by offers from venture capitalists and conglomerates. It was November 1986. The Lambs felt under the gun. They had two months to decide to sell before the tax laws were to change on January 1, 1987, under the Tax Reform Act. They wanted to gain the lower capital gain which pushed the rate up to 28 from 20 percent.

They also tried to assess the intangible advantages and disadvantages of a family business, though it's hard to put a price tag on a family name, a tradition, a culture and a potential place of employment for future generations.

Matt, Dick and Rose held marathon meetings. They felt pressured to decide. The offers weren't tempting enough. January 1 rolled around. They still hadn't sold. Work returned to normal, but each of the Lambs had a nagging feeling that it was sell now or never.

Enter Service Corporation International (SCI) with the sweetest and most lucrative plan to make Blake-Lamb part of its giant funeral chain and to keep the family on to maintain customer loyalty. SCI's highly-structured funeral network represents a small but rapidly growing six percent of industry sales. SCI performs 120,000 funerals a year at its 453 funeral homes and 120 cemeteries in 36 states. It sells more than 100,000 contracts for pre-need funerals, and sales here are booming— $222 million during its last fiscal year, up 43 percent from the previous year. Revenue for the fiscal year which ended April 30, 1988, hit $540 million and net income for the same period was $63.5 million.

The Lambs found the decision process agonizing. From the moment Matt rolled out of bed on Wednesday, November 25, 1987, the day before Thanksgiving, until he and his brother signed the dotted line and handed over Blake-Lamb to SCI that afternoon, he found himself soul searching over how well the two cultures would meld. Corporate marriages aren't always blissful as H. Ross Perot's Electronic Data Systems and General Motors' dismal union proved. Over breakfast and as he was being driven to his office, it was the power of positive thinking that kept him afloat. He had spent four years fine-tuning his vision. He knew it was the right thing to do.

Rose was relieved. She says that 1987 was the worst and the best year of her life. Once the Lambs made the decision that SCI was the best way for Blake-Lamb to survive as a family business and that the decision would prove financially sound for each family member, they breathed a sigh of relief.

"It was very, very scary, representing a sense of loss. It doesn't matter that our children won't be able to pass on the business. It would have been much harder for them to all work together. In the beginning it was just my father and mother, then my brother and me. Now there are nine cousins. It's better to pass on an opportunity," Rose reflects. "I've seen too many family businesses destroyed, often brought on by successive generations that have earned so much money and gotten so far away from the family that they didn't care."

Both SCI and the Lambs benefitted from the deal. SCI attained a bigger foothold in the large and profitable Chicago funeral market, where it already had bought 11 different companies. Blake-Lamb sold its 12 funeral homes, excluding property, and gave SCI the option to buy its real estate within two years, excluding the parcel at the corner of North Dearborn and Maple streets. The price was a tax-free exchange of SCI stock.

The brothers say their sales contracts don't allow them to reveal the number of SCI shares. "I have no problem personally telling the amount," Dick says, "but SCI asked us to keep it quiet." An industry source has pegged the value at $22 million. The brothers promised SCI they would hold the stock for at least one quarter before selling it.

The Lamb brothers also were asked to stay on at their jobs and continue the illusion of a family business, important in a personal service industry. The brothers signed five-year employment contracts. Matt retained the title of chief executive and chairman of Blake-Lamb. Dick became president of Blake-Lamb and chief executive of Silver Quality Life Plan. In addition, Rose, 32, became chief operating officer and executive vice president of Blake-Lamb. The contracts stipulated that the Lambs had autonomy to run their funeral and pre-need divisions, including deciding where to build or buy new chapels. Control would be theirs as long as they doubled business.

Robert L. Waltrip, 57, SCI chairman and chief executive, talks animatedly about a bigger empire. He plans to keep buying at least 50 to 60 funeral homes and cemeteries a year. Waltrip, a fourth-generation funeral owner, started SCI on a shoestring 26 years ago. He began with three funeral homes. Waltrip's son, W. Blair, 33, has joined SCI and is a senior vice president and board member.

Since the sale, the Lamb family has added five funeral homes to its network with more in the offing. The lifestyle of the Lambs has also improved. "We figured what all our perks cost—cars, country clubs, eating out—and put them into the purchase price," said Dick, who has already cashed in two-thirds of his SCI stock. "I don't want to have to look in the paper every day to see how the stock is doing. Matt has held on to most. It is a difference in attitude toward diversification and has nothing to do with our faith in the company."

Do Matt and Dick have any regrets about letting go of the business that their father, Matthew J. Lamb, Jr., bought from the Blake family heirs in 1928? They hedge. They say they could have kept cashing in on their goodwill for decades, but needed to sell in order to gain more capital to expand, grab a bigger market share and cement their family's destiny.

The gamble has paid off. One year after the sale, little appears to be different at Blake-Lamb. Blake-Lamb carries the family name. It maintains the same high level of service and quality. There is room for every Lamb heir who wants to come into the business if he or she is willing to work, learn and start at the bottom. Family members continue to live above some of their funeral chapels in order to be available day or night. Many long-time employees remain with the company.

The daily routine also hasn't changed since the takeover. Business never shuts down. It operates seven days a week, 24 hours a day. When a family calls in to report a death, one of six embalmers, who work mostly at the Lombard branch, is contacted. The grieving family arrives. The family wants someone to take care of every detail, but, Rose cautions, "we don't want our families to feel we are taking advantage of them." As an additional service, families are invited to join one of the company-sponsored support groups operated by a widow on staff.

Funeral arrangements are completed in about 90 minutes. By the time the family leaves, the type of service and length of visitation has been determined, the casket and flowers selected, the cemetery plot picked out. About 65 percent of the company's families now opt for a shorter visitation, one night rather than three as was the custom. The least expensive funeral costs $2,000. The average costs are about $4,000 and can be the third most expensive cost a person incurs, right behind a home and a car, says Rose. "We never turn people away if they can't pay."

Hiring and firing employees remains Matt, Dick and Rose's domain. The Lambs have been told by SCI that their jobs are secure as long as sales remain strong. In turn, if they have to fire another family member who isn't doing his or her job, they know it may be necessary. "A business decision supersedes a family decision," Dick explains. "The two have to be separated. But obviously there is a fine line. Now that we're dealing with a new corporate parent, we must think differently than in past. The family must be secondary here."

For the most part, the public isn't aware that SCI owns Blake-Lamb or other acquisitions. The SCI corporate name doesn't appear on the buildings, in contracts or on promotional materials.

Yet subtle internal changes have taken place since the sale. Major financial decisions are no longer made on the spot. They must be approved long distance by SCI and there's more of a hierarchy to run decisions past. Before the Lambs acquire a new funeral chapel, they must get SCI's approval. But because the Lambs have done their homework, SCI has approved five acquisitions in new neighborhoods. The Lambs are currently negotiating with 14 other independent funeral homes. SCI scrutinizes expenses more closely than the Lambs did. Gone are the automatic perks, some as simple as going across the street to the drug store, buying a bottle of aspirin and charging it to petty cash, Rose says.

But Becker, the Blake-Lamb regional manager, says, "You have to remember the Blake-Lamb business was in great shape to begin with. SCI would have made a lot more changes if it hadn't been. What they've done is offer more to the Lambs—more accounting help, more personal service, the advantage of being part of a purchasing consortium to get better prices."

Quarterly meetings are held with SCI and Blake-Lamb executives discussing industry trends and selling techniques. The atmosphere at Blake-Lamb's funeral homes has become more disciplined.

Sue Ann Fraher, a Blake-Lamb funeral arranger for the last nine years, says the one negative of the SCI affiliation is the "atrocious amount of paperwork that we now process."

Perhaps, the biggest difference since the brothers decided to sell is that a third-generation family member, Rose, heads Blake-Lamb with SCI's consent. They knew Rose had the experience of working in the business and training under her father and uncle. They knew she had the right image the family and its parent company wanted to project. She's as sweet as a sugar cookie on the surface with a determination underneath that's as tough as an old-time Irish cop.

From the time she was 14, Rose worked in the business after school and during summer vacations. She answered phones, helped arrange funerals, tagged along with the embalmers and learned to get around Chicago.

Rose hated school and was eager to drop out of college to go to work full time. When her father told her he needed help with a new funeral chapel on Western Avenue in Chicago, Rose jumped at the opportunity even though she was one semester shy of graduating.

Once in the business, Rose found the hardest part dealing with some old-time non-family employees. "People try to divide and conquer.

They like to see the boss put down or they pumped me up to get to dad. It was the 'I used to change your diaper syndrome.' " She acquiesced where she could. "I wanted everyone to stay. A lot of the employees were valuable. Some of those people are still here and some aren't. I had no doubt that I was going to win."

Becker of Blake-Lamb substantiates that employees gave Rose a hard time. "Employees fought and resented her. She won most of the battles and now commands respect. They've learned she's fair."

No sooner had Rose adjusted to one situation than she was forced to deal with SCI's brass. "I thought, those Texas good old boys, they don't know from having a woman in authority." Rose was also concerned that her lack of a degree would be a strike against her. She thought about finishing her bachelor's degree, but dreaded going back to school. She could hone up on her skills on the job.

SCI signed Rose to a five-year contract and put her in charge of three regional Blake-Lamb managers and a chief financial officer. SCI also offered Rose "very broad shoulders" in the form of John Morrow, the head of one of SCI's divisions. He was there to help her market Blake-Lamb's showrooms to generate more sales—turning the showrooms into a stage with the right lighting, the right props and the right music. Placing caskets was crucial. They are the most profitable part of a funeral sale.

Rose isn't an anomaly as a female funeral head. About 42 percent of the 1987 enrollees at the country's 40 mortuary schools are now women and minorities.

Rose has earmarks of success. She drives a Cadillac, lives in a townhouse in the southwest section of the city, owns a downtown condominium with her sister Colleen that they rent out, owns another house with her sister at Lake Geneva, WI, and takes a vacation every other year.

But Rose, a product of a down-to-earth home and family, is happiest when she's at work and overseeing several projects.

Rose describes her style as a combination of her father and uncle. "Dad is not a dictator but a strong, strong personality and has a definite way of doing things. He lives or dies with a decision," she says. "He's reactionary; shoots from the hip. That style is effective for certain situations and people in smaller organizations. My grandfather was much the same way, though he delegated even less than dad does. My uncle is conservative in his manner and appearance and also his planning. He plans and implements slowly. He rarely gets angry."

Rose's management is more appropriate to a large public conglomerate. "I take into account what others say. I don't come in and chop off heads and then ask questions. I plan faster than my uncle, but put into action a little slower than my father."

Fraher agrees. "She's definitely a lot softer than her dad who could be very explosive. Rose can explode occasionally but she doesn't yell as much. Dick is the quiet one in the family but you always see the wheels turning."

Rose enjoys her new position, but in putting in long hours she has sacrificed a personal life. Rose would like to marry, but doesn't want children. "A divorced guy would be fine," she jokes. "Stepchildren would be great. I'm too driven to start a family and I enjoy the corporate environment."

Rose wants to make Blake-Lamb SCI's most successful division. She plans to triple the number of funeral homes within five years, which she thinks is feasible now that Blake-Lamb is in a six-county region that includes Milwaukee. "I would like to go from $8 to $14 million and I'm sure we can."

Rose is also excited by SCI's innovations. Its "Partners Program," started in 1987, allows companies that sell out to buy back 20 percent of their business in five years at the original selling price if they achieve a 100-percent sales increase over that five-year period. Sales increases, her uncle Dick adds, would have to come primarily from acquisitions because most of the neighborhoods the company is in are fairly mature and death rates aren't increasing.

Rose sees Dick's pre-need division as a major coup for the company. Although pre-need has been in existence for more than 60 years and become much more popular in the last 10 years, it still has its skeptics. Some worry whether there will be enough money in the plans purchased at the time of death to pay for all the services desired. Others think the average cost, about $4,500 which is comparable to the cost of a regular "at-need" funeral, can be better invested in tax-free instruments. Still others think such plans appeal mostly to ethnic groups who equate a lavish funeral with paying proper respect. But such groups often are least able to afford all the hoopla.

"This type of protection is not respected among most professional insurance people," says Allan Silverberg, a chartered life underwriter for First Financial Group of St. Louis. "It is extremely expensive compared to what pure life insurance would cost which covers not only funeral costs but the total needs of the surviving family members. Unfortunately, among lower income people a funeral is overly important and they end up paying more than they should."

Rose and Dick disagree and think Blake-Lamb's Silver Quality Life pre-need plan is almost fool-proof. It is insurance based and allows buyers to make a single deposit up front or to pay premiums over a period of time. It also includes an inflation rider so that death benefits increase as inflation does. "People are guaranteed to get the funeral they selected and survivors aren't left dealing with more than they can handle," Dick says. Most of their pre-need contracts are based on a life expectancy of 73 years.

Silver Quality Plan's sales climbed steadily from $600,000 a year in 1987 to $650,000 in the month of April 1988 alone. Dick estimates that within a few years the company's total number of funerals will be split between pre-need and at-need because of customer demand and support from SCI which pioneered marketing the concept in 1977. SCI's pre-need earnings have grown from $200,000 in 1982 to $28 million in fiscal 1987, a 71 percent compound annual rate of increase.

Rose's brashness and self-confidence have not endeared her to some of her younger siblings and cousins. Rose knows what she's like. "My father and I cast big shadows." In front of her parents, Maureen, Dick's oldest child and daughter, is asked how she likes working for Rose. "That's an unfair question if I ever heard one," she says rolling her eyes and refusing to answer. Her parents chuckle self-consciously at her response.

Always the consummate professional, Rose had tried to encourage Maureen to enter the business after she graduated from Holy Cross College. "Tell me what job you want?" Rose asked her cousin. Maureen said. "I don't know. I've decided to go into advertising." She didn't find a job and the family business suddenly looked appealing. But when she called Rose and told her she was ready to come into the business, there wasn't a slot and the company wasn't owned by family any longer. Rose told her cousin, "I can't fire someone who's been here forever to make room at the top for you." She convinced Maureen to sign on as a switchboard operator with a chance to learn about arranging funerals.

Today, Maureen seems indifferent about her job and shrugs when asked whether she likes her work. When Rose is questioned about her cousin's ambivalence, she says, "Maureen hasn't been in the business long enough to gain a position of authority, which is what she wants. We all have to wait our turn and learn the ropes."

The thought of Blake-Lamb as part of an enormous public conglomerate would have been unthinkable 20 or 30 years ago.

The original business was founded by another family, Michael and Thomas Blake in 1880 at a time when funerals primarily took place in the privacy of the home of the deceased. In 1892, the Blakes purchased property at 712 West 31st Street, which had been the post office for the town of Lake before the area was incorporated into Chicago. The chapel was on the first floor. The Blake family lived on the second floor. The horses to drive the hearses were stabled in the basement.

As Chicago grew and the neighborhood expanded, the funeral home business burgeoned. After Michael's son, Thomas, died in 1928, Matthew J. Lamb, Jr., who had a thriving livery business, bought the Blake company from Tom Blake's heirs. It included a home at West 31st Street. Lamb combined the names.

Matt and Dick Lamb grew up above that funeral home with their older sister, Margaret Dillon. The Lamb children knew no other life. They hung around families in mourning who came for advice and to eat. "We had lots of our clients up for dinner all the time," Matt said. "My father had the philosophy that life and business are all pretty simple. You can make them complicated. But if you lay out things, the choices become obvious. Nothing comes by happenstance, but by design."

As the city's population migrated south, Lamb in 1941 opened a second chapel at 1413 West 79th Street. Matt III came into the business in 1945. "There was never any doubt that that's what I would do," Matt says. "I worked all my life in it. I liked it. I drove the hearse starting when I was 15. I joined the Teamsters' Union 40 years ago. You have to remember it was around the time of the Depression. There were no real debates about anything. You were told what to do."

In school, Matt seemed bound for failure. He attended three colleges, then embalming school and came back when his father took ill in the early 1950s. He and his dad operated two funeral homes and conducted about 250 funerals a year. The payroll was large and Matt wanted to trim it. He also didn't like what he saw in the business.

"There were a bunch of old-timers. They'd work when my father was there and slough off when he wasn't. I wanted to get rid of them. My attitude is always do something. My father was a great thinker, but not a great doer. It drove me crazy, but he told me, 'Do what you want. I don't give a damn, because I'm dying anyway.'"

His father recovered. "I understood the tribal laws that I'd have to wait to take over the business even though I had been running it."

While working with his father, Matt did his own planning for the future. His brother Dick came into the business after graduating from Holy Cross College in 1958 and became a valuable ally. Together the brothers talked of building a big business that could effectively cater to the needs of individuals. With their father, they formed the 103rd Street Building Corp., a real estate adjunct of the company, named for a new funeral home they built at 4727 West 103rd St. in Oak Lawn in 1960.

Their father insisted that they buy in, which they wanted to do but couldn't afford. "We had no money," Matt said. "I was earning a weekly embalming salary. I didn't have a heck of a lot of perks. My wife Rose and I sold our house for $8,000 and cashed in our $25,000 insurance policy which gave us $2,000 more. We took an apartment for which we had to pay $132 a month. We had no furniture in the living room for a year. We had three small kids. If I would have died, my wife would have had zero. For all that we only received six to seven percent of the corporation."

As Dick and Matt amassed funds, they scouted for properties to increase their network and income. They formed the Matt-Rich Investment Co.

They grabbed choice locations at 3737 West 79th in Chicago in 1964, at 63rd Street in Chicago in 1968, and at 229 So. Main Street in Lombard in 1968. In 1977, the family purchased the former Lain F...eral Home at 1035 North Dearborn and bought another home on 51st Street in Chicago in 1984.

The ethnic mix of a neighborhood always was crucial. "You can't put a Mexican funeral home in a Polish area or a Roman Catholic one in a Jewish area. You don't run them the same way," said Matt, who is currently negotiating to buy 14 different independents. "It's a long, long process. Besides the neighborhood, you care about the people who own the company. If they leave, will the customers stay?"

The love for the business was bound to filter down to Rose, Matt's wife, and to the third generation. Nothing about it was sacred or a secret, especially for Matt's family who lived upstairs and were privy to the daily goings-on.

Says Matt's wife, Rose, a tall and stylish chestnut blonde, "I had to get involved in the business. It was the only way I was going to get to see Matt. I figured I would be good at promoting Blake-Lamb, but instead of doing internal public relations, I went to work for several organizations, mostly through hospital boards, as a way of meeting people and making contacts indirectly."

Like her in-laws, Rose routinely invited clients, colleagues and business leaders to dinner. "I'd often start cooking at 4:30 P.M. and have as many as 200. They'd roll in and roll out and my three girls would help."

In contrast, Dick and his wife deliberately lived away from the funeral homes once they had children. Sue says, "It was interesting living above a funeral home when we were first married, but it was also an intrusion."

Traditionalists may mourn the loss of family-owned funeral, or similar, businesses. But such companies can survive in a different and stronger mode and still retain the flavor and service of a family business.

The Lamb family still works together and for now appears to be better off under the financial thumb and watchful eye of SCI. It has ready access to SCI's professional expertise and more sophisticated communication systems.

As a neutral mediator, SCI may be better at diffusing the inevitable intrafamily power struggles that surface so often among family members vying for greater control and salaries when so many work together. SCI will also prevent the third generation of Lambs from taking too much financially out of the business.

Some disagree and have termed SCI a "corporate wolf" for gobbling up family businesses, eliminating owners and paring service. Says one SCI critic, an independent funeral home operator, "A funeral business is not a retail store where you go in and just buy a product. The funeral business deals with a family and its grief."

But Dan Johnson, SCI's director of investor relations, says that SCI has never gone into a market and forced the family out of the business or eliminated service. "Mom and Pop funeral homes will always be the backbone of the industry."

Rose agrees. "We've heard all kinds of things on the street about SCI. Some good. Some bad. But when we got ready to sell, SCI was totally ethical, and as far as a partner, we couldn't go to a bigger force in the industry."

On the other hand if Rose doesn't meet SCI's objectives, she and her relatives know they won't have a protective family safety net to catch them and they could lose their jobs.

Rose thrives on change and the challenge of melding her family business culture into a more synergistic corporate structure. Her family's Irish Catholic roots come through: Rose has rolled the dice, but she hasn't cast her fate to chance. She's in control and confident about the outcome. Her business is destined to outlast the present generations.

Unified Services Inc.
Washington, DC

The problem of holding the Negro down, therefore, is easily solved. When you control a man's thinking you do not have to worry about his actions. You do not have to tell him to stand here or go yonder. He will find his "proper place" and will stay in it. You do not need to send him to the back door. He will go without being told. In fact, if there is no back door, he will cut one for his special benefit. His education makes it necessary.
  —Carter G. Woodson, *The Miseducation of the Negro*, 1933

Jerry G. Davis, Jr., was determined to make it beyond Oak Grove, LA, a small farming community in the northeast part of the state. As his high school graduation neared, Jerry, as he was nicknamed, and his father sat in the family kitchen late one night, nursing beers and brainstorming about Jerry's options.

Jerry had big plans. He wanted college and had won a scholarship to Southern University in Baton Rouge. Jerry wanted a better life than he had growing up amid the fields where his father sharecropped 20 acres and where Jerry helped out as a youngster.

The Davis family worked hard. For entertainment they listened to the radio. On Sundays they attended the local Baptist church. Segregation was an accepted way of life. Blacks couldn't eat in the same

229

restaurants as whites, couldn't use the same drinking fountains or bathrooms, and had to ride in the back of a bus.

Jerry Davis, Sr., listened to his son, but as the family autocrat, "Big Daddy" would have the final say. "We don't have the money for college even if you have a scholarship," he explained. "And if you leave the family farm, you're likely to be drafted into the Army. You're better off enlisting. Don't let the Army tell you what to do. Make your own choice."

Jerry headed south to New Orleans to work in a defense plant and was drafted not long afterward for World War II, joining the 40th infantry division.

Troops were segregated in the Army and blacks got the dirty jobs, but that didn't hold Jerry back. He stood out. At 6'4", Jerry was tall, handsome and winsome. He was full of fight. Within eight months, Jerry at age 20, became a sergeant.

In 1946, he went off to Paris, where he gained his ultimate symbol of success: a big desk. Jerry had never seen a black person sit behind a desk. But when Sgt. Davis was assigned his desk, people showed him respect. He sent his mother a picture. He would never be without a desk again.

It was also in Paris that he lost his complex about being black. Having grown up in Louisiana he always had the misguided view that whites were better than blacks. "But by working side by side with whites, I learned that we're all people with the same hopes, fears and dreams."

Jerry next entered Officer Candidate School. He was one of only five blacks accepted and the only one to graduate. He was commissioned a Second Lieutenant in 1952. Jerry stayed in the Army. The Vietnam War was being waged and he wanted to be in on the action. Also, it was the beginning of the 1960s, an era of major change for blacks: civil rights and equal opportunity.

After fighting long and hard in Vietnam, where he had been promoted to Lieutenant Colonel in 1967, Jerry returned home a hero the following year. Jerry was ready to retire. Financially, he was in good shape with a nice nest egg from his Army pension. He didn't need a job, but at 42, was too antsy to sit around. Yet realistically he wondered what was out there for a black man who had risen through the ranks in the Army and seen the world, but who didn't have a college education?

Jerry never bought into the belief that blacks are victims of society, born into an environment that loads the dice against them. He thought why not take his military skills and apply them to business. He knew he could sell. He knew he could captivate a group. Most important, he was willing to take the risk.

Getting a break took scratching and climbing. He used his Army contacts. Friends set up interviews. Jerry and a friend, Theodore A. Adams, Jr., decided to start an engineering consulting firm for minority businesses in Washington, DC. One of their accounts was a black-owned company in Portland, OR, that manufactured ammunition containers for the Army.

Being in business felt good. Jerry liked the income, the prestige, the respect, the perks. He supported President Nixon's philosophy that black economic development was the key to the so-called black problem of black poverty.

There was one hitch. Working with a partner wasn't enough. He wanted to be in charge. That opportunity came after he met G. Jean Cotton, whom he would later marry. She would give Jerry the idea for a new business and help him run the company.

Divorced from his second wife, Jerry relished his role as bon vivant. He had been dating a string of women, but no one seriously. One day Ted told Jerry, "I've got a great woman for you named Jean. She is dating some stupid lawyer up here but don't worry." Jean worked for the ammunition company. She was smart. Ted knew that Jerry put a lot of stake in that.

Ted told Jean, "Don't do anything till you meet my buddy Jerry."

Jean, who was 29 at the time, was behind a desk when Jerry first saw her. It didn't take long for Jerry to agree with Ted's assessment. It didn't take long for Jean to be attracted to Jerry.

Jean was smitten with Jerry's joie de vivre. "He spent a lot of money. He was fun. But most important, he projected the image that I wanted for my six-year-old son, Robby."

Jerry admired Jean for different reasons. She didn't push for marriage as Jerry's other female friends were doing. "She caught me," he said. "We both had the same kind of drive and people smarts, I think, because of a similar upbringing."

Jean, the daughter of migrant farmers, grew up near Shreveport in rural Minden and 130 miles from Oak Grove. Her mother was determined that her three children receive college educations. The Cottons lived on the corner of an all-black block which backed up to an all-white street. Their yard abutted an Italian family's property. The families became friendly. The Italians had no daughters and treated Jean like their own.

A major influence on Jean's upbringing was her mother's addiction to soap operas. Mrs. Cotton watched, memorized and copied every move Nancy Hughes, the matriarch on *As the World Turns*, made in rearing her daughter. "Whatever Mrs. Hughes did, Mamma did," Jean recalled.

Jean and her brothers were drilled daily—how to speak without a Southern accent and in complete sentences. They had to enunciate. "Mamma was a bear and a stickler for what was proper. Her thinking was that I should have a choice in life. If I wanted to get married and have babies, that was fine, but at least I should be able to do something. I'm not sure why she was so different than others. But I know that she hates the drudgery women did."

Jerry and Jean's union proved fortuitous. It got Jerry to act quickly. Once they became serious, Jean moved to Washington and went to work for Jerry and Ted's consulting firm. After Jerry and Jean married, the partners thought it best that Jean work elsewhere. She took a job as an executive secretary at the Department of Transportation's National Highway Traffic Safety Division, when John A. Volpe was Secretary of Transportation. After working there three years, she switched to the Department of Commerce and then returned to work for her former boss, who had become president of the Recreational Vehicle Industry Association.

Although both Jean and Jerry worked, money was tight. Jerry loved to spend.

After talking to friends and management consultants about business possibilities, Jerry hit upon an idea at age 46 in 1971. He realized that the big government buildings like the one Jean worked in needed cleaning daily. Jerry knew the trend was to use outside cleaning crews rather than in-house help and that there was no substantial black-owned competition.

What better business for a black person to go into, Jerry reasoned. "After all, blacks are supposed to be great cleaners, but they can't do anything else. Right? I hadn't gone to college, but I'd spent all this time in the United States Army so I certainly knew what clean was and I knew how to manage people."

The managers of different buildings were thrilled to see Jerry. Government agencies had to contract a certain amount of business with minorities. "When I walked in and said, 'I'd just like to clean your

building,' they were relieved and said, 'Come with me soooooooon,'
They were real receptive that I didn't want anything else from them."

Jerry tested his theory. He went to the manager of the 150,000-
square-foot National Labor Relations Board building at 1717 Pennsylvania Avenue across from the White House. He threw the manager a
bluff to get his business. "I told him I wanted to clean. He responded,
'You want me to take a chance on you and lose all my tenants?' I said,
'Aren't most of the people who work in your building black?' "

The manager responded, "Yes."

Jerry shot back, "Why, you'll feel awfully strange at 5:00 P.M. when
nobody shows up to work, wouldn't you? You ought to think about it."
Jerry left.

At 3:00 P.M. that day, the manager called and gave Jerry the job.
Jerry hired the crew of 21 that was already working in the building. He
bought their equipment. It was his first big contract for his new
company, which he named Unified Services Inc.

Jerry opened an office at 17th and Elm in downtown Washington.
With the help of $5,000 in savings from his Army retirement pay, a
loan of $15,000 from the Small Business Administration, membership
in the SBA's 8 (a) "Set-Aside" program—a way for small minority-
owned ventures to win government contracts—plus chutzpah, Jerry
hawked his service.

At the time, the janitorial and office cleaning business in metropolitan DC was a highly fragmented $500 million industry of small
companies. Business took off by dealing with more government agencies, the General Services Administration and individual businesses
that contracted their own cleaning. Most of his business came from
blacks.

Next Jerry lined up the Federal Aviation Administration Flight Control Center in Leesburg, VA, and the Army post at nearby Fort Myers.
Contracts were for one year and then up for renegotiation.

Jerry used his cunning to sign up more accounts. He adjusted sales
pitches. "If I'm talking to an extrovert I talk real nice. If it's an
introvert, I go real low key. You kind of sense how to do it. I learned in
the Army how to deal with all kinds of people."

Office cleaning was easy to get into and master. It didn't require
much technical know-how. It wasn't capital intensive. All that was
needed was a telephone and a few supplies. Most cleaning took place
at night. One person could clean 3,000 square feet an hour using high
speed floor machines and vacuum cleaners. Each worker was assigned

a zone. Jerry preferred one person cleaning a space. That way he could fix responsibility and count on better production.

Insurance costs were high, as great as eight percent of labor costs. But the most difficult part of office cleaning was finding and keeping good help which consumed at least half of the total revenue of a small job and as much as 66 percent of a large job. "Who wants to clean? If you kept a janitor 90 days, you were doing well," Jerry said.

As USI grew, it needed professionalizing. Jerry's younger daughter, Amelia, thought one way to do so would be to hire a sharp black female she met who had graduated from the Harvard Business School in 1969. Davis took Amelia's advice and in 1973 hired Lillian H. Lincoln, daughter of a Virginia subsistence farmer, to be a consultant. Lillian was a good fit and Jerry offered her a full-time slot as executive vice president.

Three years later, Lillian walked into Jerry's office and announced that she was leaving to start her own office cleaning firm, Centennial One Inc. of Crofton, MD, but she would stay at USI for six months until Jerry hired a replacement. He appreciated the gesture that meant she'd be in charge while he attended Harvard's Summer Executive program.

Jean seethed. She told Jerry why Lillian couldn't stay. "I know you like her a lot and trust her, but I don't," Jean stated. "She needs to go immediately."

"She can't go. I'm leaving. There's no one to run the company," Jerry said.

"There's no way you're going to leave her here for three solid weeks while you're gone," Jean told him. She gave Jerry an ultimatum. "If you don't get rid of her, I will. I'll run the company. If you're in a key position in a company, you go immediately, especially if you're leaving to go into the same business. There is no way she is going to devote 100 percent of her attention to us knowing she has a competitive venture in mind."

But Jerry couldn't fire a woman. He let Jean do it and then Jean took over Lillian's job. Lillian formed her own company.

Jean took a hands-on approach while Jerry was gone. She demanded to know why things were done the way they were done. "If employees couldn't give me a convincing argument, I wouldn't give them the go-ahead."

Jerry returned and was impressed at how well Jean had managed in his absence. "Man, she did great. She gave us the best profit we ever had in one month. She had a way of getting people to teach her because she let them know she needed help. Some were resistant but knew they had to be tolerant because she was the boss's wife."

Even Luther Pounds, the company's crusty old operations man, was won over. Jean made everyone feel they had an important part to play. She exhibited sensitivity. She frequently told those under her to be patient with the cleaning staff. "Most of our cleaners aren't educated. If they were, they wouldn't be cleaning. Some aren't always going to dress right. Some don't always talk right. But they're doing our work. That's what we get paid for."

After filling in for Jerry and Lillian, Jean returned to her former job. Jerry had a slot to fill. He hired an Army buddy.

Two years later, Jean's boss left. She hesitated about working for someone new. At the same time, Jerry's business had grown to 12 accounts and sales of $2.8 million annually. He needed a full-time personnel manager to hire and fire employees and to deal with unions. Jean said, "Why not hire me, Davis?"

Jerry balked.

"Oh, come on, Davis. Don't be such a chauvinist. You know I can do the job. I've worked in private industry and in the government. I know so much about the business from stories and strategies you've shared with me. Most important, I already know most of the employees."

Jerry still resisted, but he arranged a dinner with close friends to help him decide. By the end of the evening, the arguments convinced Jerry. Jean started the next week at $19,000 a year.

With two such strong personalities, the Davises knew from the day Jean walked into USI that they had to establish ground rules. They divided responsibilities and kept business and home life separate. "If working together ever threatened our marriage, I agreed to step out of the picture," Jean said.

At home, Jerry rose first and served his wife coffee in bed. They headed to work in separate cars so that Jean could get home first and switch into her role as wife. Jerry wanted his dinner waiting whether she had cooked it or brought it in. He told Jean years ago, "Your job is to see that the family eats in the evening." Jean knew that Jerry wasn't big on change.

The Davises also decided to avoid talking about business at home, though that was hard at times when they had a rotten day—no sales, nothing in the hopper, difficult clients and unruly employees. Jean found it tougher than Jerry to avoid rehashing problems. "If I had a really lousy day, I'd want to discuss problems with Jerry, but he'd sit in his Archie Bunker chair and didn't want to get involved. Sometimes life is like a checklist and you have so many things to get done and no energy or time to do them. Then you especially don't feel very romantic. There are times when I've needed an old-fashioned wife."

Through the years the Davises polished their routines. After a year, Jean moved up to vice president of administration. After another year, she was promoted to executive vice president and became Jerry's right hand.

The Davises expanded their company. They bought a wholesale janitorial supply company, Consolidated Maintenance & Supply Inc., and put Jerry's son-in-law Richard S. Frazier as warehouse supervisor. They purchased one master franchise of The Maids, a residential cleaning company, which had three outlets. They brought in Jerry's daughter, Jerry Ann. They bought into Univar-Maintenance Services Inc. in Ypsilanti, MI, which operates a cleaning service similar to USI.

Now, seventeen years after its founding, Unified Services Inc. has grown from about 125 employees and revenue of $266,000 to a staff of 300 general cleaners, 10 supervisors, 15 managers, four executives and $7-plus million in annual sales. Profits are a steady 6.5 percent of sales. The company operates out of a two-story handsomely scaled old brick and stone 27,000-square-foot building at 2640 Reed Street in a mixed residential and light industrial section on the northeast side. The Davises own their headquarters and lease it to the company. The building backs up to an alley and is sandwiched in between headquarters of The Maids, which now has sales of $150,000 a year, and Consolidated, which produces $4 million in sales and has higher margins than USI because its labor costs are a smaller percent of overhead.

Jerry estimates company sales are in the upper 10 to 15 percent of the 1,500 companies that are members of the main trade association, The Building Service Contractors Association International in Fairfax, VA. USI is among an elite group of about five to six percent of all black-owned office cleaning businesses in the country and among the most successful in the DC area, says Jerry.

Today Jerry and Jean's offices, which stand across the hall from one another, provide an almost sitcom study in contrasts. Each reflects their different personalities. Jerry's is pristine. Papers are arranged on his desk in neat stacks like soldiers lined up for a drill. Jerry's bathroom and adjacent study are spotless. Jean's room is messy. Her desk is cluttered with stacks of paper covering the floor.

They're like the odd couple in other ways. She counts pennies; he spends dollars. He smokes cigars; she smokes cigarettes. She favors steep high heels; he wears clunky wing tips. She is guarded; he is winningly open. She exudes class; he is salt of the earth. She is smart and saucy; he's smooth and savvy. She is the inside person; he's the outside man.

But their oppositeness works because they handle different assignments for the company and complement one another's styles. Jerry is the visionary, who can see and dream, according to Jean. He's a dynamic leader who's supportive of his troops. He's good at getting people revved up and marching. Davis arrives at 10:00 A.M., his presence noticeable as soon as he storms through the front door. His voice booms. He gathers his senior staff: Jean; William T. Troutman, president of Consolidated; Robert Weldon, operations manager; Joseph Jones, vice president of operations, and Jerry's secretary, Estelle. They go over the day's agenda. By noon, Jerry's out the door to meet with a potential customer or a governmental official. He's buddies with Mayor Marion S. Barry, Jr., whom he met through Jesse Jackson's campaign. Jerry returns late in the day.

Jean, who arrives before 9:00 A.M., uses the morning to open mail and answer phone calls before Jerry arrives. It's a deliberate process. She needs to change roles. Jean gets down to the details of paying employees, investing pension money, putting together the budget, administering the office staff and pricing contracts. Her staff queues up outside her door. She switches to her next role of troubleshooter, going over accounts receivable with the company accountant and placating customers. Her phone never stops. Her secretary has put through a call from a building manager who demands to speak to the president. Jerry is out and Jean is eager to help. "This happens all the time and I resent it. They want to speak to the president, but I have to feed Davis all the information in order for him to make a decision." Jean rarely interrupts her workload to eat lunch unless Jerry is free.

At the end of the day, Jean saves an hour to wind down and plan for the next. Today, she's preparing a report for NASA and the Department of Defense which have run a security check on USI employees who clean the Kennedy Space Center. "It's hard at times working with a husband," she says quietly. "A lot of times I do all the work and he gets all the credit. But he's pretty good at telling me what he thinks, though we don't always agree. I love arguing issues. I want to know why he wants to do things certain ways. I really pin him down."

But Jerry has the last word, she concedes as she sits in his office. "What's hardest in dealing with Jerry is getting him to focus on the present. I'll be there trying to pay tomorrow's payroll and all he wants to talk about is the way this company will be in 10 years. Who needs to hear that?"

Jerry comes into his office chain smoking his Dominican Don Diego cigars, symbols of his enhanced status and machismo. He takes a long drag and comments on what Jean has said. "She's right. I'm tired of the day-to-day details. I'm lucky that Jean does a really good job of being the watchdog and doing a lot of the grunt work that I don't want to do or can't."

Others also claim the Davises have forged a special business union. "They never expected extra favors from each other," says Earl Hunigan, Jean's former boss. "Jerry expected Jean to produce in her capacity, the same as everybody else. As long as you understand that and meet Jerry's objectives, he's okay. But they've had their moments, sometimes blowups. Jerry used to have a very violent temper and it was a hair trigger. If he was expecting something to be done and it wasn't, watch out. 'I can't understand why it's not done,' he'd yell. Jean wasn't timid and would shout back. He didn't back off. But she respected him as the president of the company and in the office it wasn't a husband/wife relationship. And he respected her."

Because Jerry craves adulation and harmony more than Jean, she has assumed the role of bad guy that she knows is necessary to run a growing family business. Her criticism isn't only targeted at non-family employees, but also at relatives, including her son-in-law and daughters-in-law.

A run-in with Jerry's son-in-law illustrates how well Jean plays her role. Rick, 49, used to purchase supplies for USI. He had to pay sales tax on some purchases. Jean thought he kept sloppy records. It infuriated her. She needed the records for tax time. Eight months later, she asked again to see the records. Rick still hadn't collated them. Jean went to Jerry to complain but he replied, "Well, I know, but what can I do?" Finally one morning, Jean needed the records. She walked into Rick's office, demanded the records and didn't get them. She bawled Rick out. Rick quietly got up and left. He went on vacation and didn't come back.

It put Jerry's daughter, Jerry Ann, in a tenuous position. She told Rick, "You're my husband and he's my daddy and I intend for it to stay that way." She told her father the same thing.

Rick, who retired from the Air Force as a senior master sergeant with more than 20 years of engineering experience, discovered it difficult to find a niche in the Davises' established family firm and found himself quickly embroiled in family problems. "There was just too much family. All my expertise gained from serving in the Air Force was for naught. I knew about managing people. They wouldn't let me do much."

Rick left and went to work for a wholesale refrigerated foods company in DC as night supervisor. He liked being on his own and not relying on his in-laws. "Davis kept calling me on the sly and asking me to come back. I would come back when I knew I was really needed." Two years later, Consolidated's warehouse manager asked Rick to work for him. He took the job because he knew he wasn't going to be an understudy for Jean and Jerry.

Rick and Jerry Ann, who works for The Maids, rarely see each other during the workday. Jean has been pushing Jerry Ann to assume more responsibility and run the franchise and to increase sales, which she says are a fraction of their potential. But Jerry Ann, who has been runner-up for Maid of the Year, has shown no interest in taking on more. Jean has realized that Jerry Ann is basically a homebody seeking some extra dollars.

Jean is also critical of Davis' granddaughter, Theresa, who is company receptionist for the summer. "Theresa wants more responsibility, but hasn't earned it. She's not dedicated enough. She's careless. She doesn't complete phone messages. I'm not sure if it's her being 20 or a lack of interest. The jury is still out on whether she'll come into the business."

When it comes to Amelia, Jerry's other daughter, Jean is magnanimous, however. She'd like to see her come into the business. Amelia currently works for Lifespring, an EST-type organization, out of San Francisco. "She's great at selling," says Jean. "If she can sell that kind of philosophy, she can sell anything."

Both Jean and Jerry are ambitious and clearly enjoy their success. The company garage houses his and her Mercedes cars. His is the large silver four-door 380 SEL sedan. Hers is the smart two-seater 560 SL silver roadster that Jerry gave her two years ago for their anniversary. They live in a four-bedroom Colonial-style ranch with a swimming pool in an integrated neighborhood in Ft. Washington, MD, a nice residential area in a country club setting. A golf course runs through the subdivision.

Seated at his enormous desk surrounded by signed and framed photos of President Ronald Reagan and other dignitaries, Jerry cuts an imposing figure. Jean strides in. "She's very stylish," Jerry says pointing to his wife who is dressed in a mid-length black and white cotton two-piece dress worn under a buttercup-colored linen jacket. She's tall, thin and handsome with close-cropped hair that highlights her massive forehead and prominent cheekbones.

Jean takes the floor. She speaks sotto voce and chooses her vocabulary carefully while editing every phrase. "Success hasn't been a straight dash to the top," she emphasizes.

The Davises have had to contend with many roadblocks in building their minority business and know that other hurdles will get in the way. Federal Government contracts under the "Set-Aside" 8(a) program helped fuel sales for 11 years. Through it they were awarded the Kennedy Space Center at Cape Canaveral, the Kennedy Center for Performing Arts in Washington, the Goddard Space Flight Center in Greenbelt, MD, and DeWitt Army Hospital at Fort Belvoir, VA.

Then almost as quickly as an about face is shouted, the contracts dried up between 1982 and 1983 after company sales hit $10 million. It was time for USI to graduate. It needed to sink or swim on its own. Most minority businesses are restricted to a five-year term with the possibility of a single two-year extension. Many companies, however, have not built a stable growing company by graduation, which happened with USI. It had been in "Set-Aside" for 11 years when the Reagan administration enacted a new policy that cut the time and the annual dollar volume for companies to remain eligible. USI exceeded both.

After losing its 8(a) status, USI saw many accounts dry up and annual sales slashed in half. Jerry had known the boom was about to be lowered, but didn't expect it to happen so abruptly. He had planned, but not well enough. After he started losing contracts, he should have trimmed his staff immediately. But he worried that if sales picked up, he would be short-handed. "To get sales you need people," Jerry said.

Jerry's son Rob considered his dad's lack of planning a major faux pas. "Dad should have gotten rid of the dinosaurs. If he had, we'd still be the largest minority-owned janitorial contracting firm in the country.

Today, his Army contacts have dried up as most of his buddies have retired. He's lost his edge. This is where my mother comes in. Her dollars-and-sense smarts and marketing skills have helped us win and maintain contracts in the private sector."

Jerry adds that his company can still take advantage of being in a sheltered market for minorities in Washington, though the U.S. Supreme Court's ruling striking down affirmative action Set-Aside programs earlier this year was a further permanent blow to a possibility of preferred treatment.

Trying to sign up new clients meant that the Davises had to go up against larger white-owned firms that could offer bigger cleaning crews and cheaper rates.

USI has acquired clients and cleaned more than 50 buildings representing eight million square feet, but revenue hasn't climbed back to its peak. There are now more than 150 firms in the Washington area that clean offices in what has become a $650 million industry.

Attracting outside capital to minority firms is another major obstacle. It's not all conscious racism, Jerry says. He dons his reading glasses while searching through his top drawer for a recent series of articles on black entrepreneurship that ran in the *Wall Street Journal*. "People aren't used to seeing black folks in business, especially in a family business. It's a new phenomenon. If you present a product or service to white folks, right away they feel uncomfortable. It's true with all small businesses but intensified with minorities. We just don't let it get us down. We keep plugging away."

Dispelling the stereotype of the lazy, incompetent black man also continues to be a struggle, Jerry says. Only recently has the black man been portrayed as an intelligent, upper middle class professional in the media such as on "The Cosby Show." Historically, he was the butt of humor as he danced, sang and shuffled, the court jester on such TV programs as "Sanford and Son," "The Jeffersons," and "Good Times."

Jerry believes he can best help other blacks by setting an example. He graduated in 1977 from the Smaller Company Management Program at Harvard University's Graduate School of Business Administration. He encouraged Jean to enter the program and she graduated in 1982.

Jerry also has become an active member of the office cleaning trade association. He served on its board and was its first black president.

But for all his crusading, Jerry isn't quite sure where he and others like him fit in. He's much more savvy than the self-taught, all-controlling black business founder of the past. Yet he's not a cold-hearted deal maker who wants to build a huge empire at any cost.

Another problem Jerry and Jean must solve is how to attract and keep qualified help at all levels. The recent crackdown on illegal aliens means there are fewer potential janitors. USI has had trouble competing against fast-food restaurants. They've found that most people would rather fry hamburgers all day than clean toilets.

The Davises also have had a hard time keeping qualified white and black executives and getting them to work well together. They try to hire a good mix. "Integration causes them all to do better," Jean says. "It promotes healthy competition." Others disagree claiming that some whites still have a hard time taking orders from blacks.

Still an additional obstacle is that integration has meant fewer blacks buy just ethnic products. Jerry is delighted to see a trend of companies moving into the mainstream by broadening the appeal of their products and services and by buying existing companies that have a wide base. But Jerry acknowledges that it's hard to get a start and to stay in business. He's concerned with the number of black-owned businesses that get off the ground and then sell out to whites who can offer bigger bucks. "It's the white people that have the money. And blacks, historically, have had few role models. Our society is going to have to get used to seeing blacks in business. It's hard for blacks to advance if there's not a network of black people out there to promote them," says Edward W. Jones, Jr., a black corporate consultant in South Orange, NJ. Jerry says that most of his clients are white. "They are the ones who own the buildings."

Expanding USI by acquiring separate, but related operations has presented still other and unexpected problems. Consolidated Maintenance gives the Davises the leverage to buy more than 300 cleaning supplies for USI at a good rate. But in spite of this advantage, Jerry loses business. Some office cleaning firms refuse to buy from Consolidated because Davis owns a competing company.

Because the business has demanded the Davises' complete attention, Jerry and Jean haven't formally decided who will take over. Both talk of bringing Rob into the business but with different goals in mind. Jerry envisions him running the company. Jean sees him in charge of sales.

Only 1.3 percent of black firms are successfully passed down in a family, says Gavin M. Chen, senior economist with the U.S. Department of Commerce's Minority Business Division, Research Development Agency. The largest proportion are in agricultural services, forestry, fishing and mining. But the trend of more blacks starting their own businesses should translate into more multigenerational firms.

Jean wants Rob to work for someone other than Jerry before taking over. Rob doesn't see the need although he doesn't believe in handouts. "Blacks have no right to expect breaks because we're a minority. If we work for it, we'll get it. The thing that will keep blacks from being as successful as their white counterparts is their refusal to assimilate. I hate to use cliches, but 'it's a white man's world.' You have to be able to move, groove and talk in that world."

Jean sees herself as Jerry's natural successor, until Rob is ready. She already knows the type of company she'd operate. She talks of a much more efficient organization with more accounts and specialized departments. "We'd be doing $20 million annually."

But Jean acknowledges that when Jerry retires, he'll want her at his beck and call to go to their officers' clubs to dance or to vacation at their condo in Virginia Beach. For Jean, giving up a career may be tantamount to losing her identity and power. She has worked long and hard to get where she is, typical of many successful black women who have had to hold families together.

Jean remains insecure about how far she's come, whether she can hang on to success and whether Jerry will allow her to run the company. "I feel sort of isolated. Your strength and love are supposed to come from your Significant Other but sometimes he's one of the ones resenting you. A lot of Jerry's friends, many of whom were in the service with him, are married to their first wives who are more traditional and older than I am. Military people are very clannish. I just don't fit right," she muses.

Jean also admits that it would be hard for her to run the company and have Rob report to her. "I don't think I could stop being his mom. We were together a long time before I married Jerry and I have a hard time not telling Rob what to do."

Rob thinks he could work easier under his mother, whom he describes as a communicator, rather than for his father, an order giver. He sees the real tug-of-war for company control between himself and his sister, Amelia, if she joins USI. "She'll be a shark in my swimming pool. She's got Mom's skills, she can swim circles around me."

Rob's not about to do battle. "It will all work out. The money will be there, the toys. I'd have no trouble working under my sister as long as she doesn't take my share of stock. We'd be producing for each other."

Jerry returns from lunch in a good mood. He yells "Hi" to everyone in the hall. He's looking to tell Jean about the four-year $3.2 million deal he consummated with the Air Force to clean Cape Canaveral. Getting the contract took a year. He's ready to move on to pick up new clients. Jerry is happiest selling big accounts such as a $500,000 contract with United Airlines to clean its midfield terminal and jetways to its planes at Dulles or a recent five-year $1 million contract to clean Fort Belvoir Army Base.

Jerry walks into his office and pauses abruptly after taking a look at where Jean is sitting and roars, "You're in my chair."

She doesn't budge from the burgundy leather-tufted wing chair.

He repeats more sharply, "You're in my chair."

She still doesn't budge and continues talking.

Jerry relents and moves to a chair across the room

Jean is thrilled about the deal. She drafted the contract and checked the details.

On a major point they agree: They want to see their black family business survive into the next generation. "Black entrepreneurship is a civil right that should be defended for our families and our race," Jerry says. To do so, both he and Jean know that a family business head needs to gradually bring in the next generation to learn the business and make changes. Jerry philosophizes, "The dynamics of business won't allow it to stand still. If you do, you'll lose your share of the marketplace and eventually the business. Blacks owning their own businesses gives us a chance to control own own destiny."

The way to play the game is to inch along, steal a base, bunt a man down, hit behind the runner, thread a needle—and don't look back.
—Leroy Satchel Paige, 1953

Glen Ellen Winery
Glen Ellen, CA

I see many similarities between mastering the art of winemaking and raising a family of seven. Care, consideration, thoughtful planning and understanding are inherent in both. The ultimate satisfaction comes with the recognition of doing each one well.
   —Bruno Benziger, wine label of Benziger of Glen Ellen Selections

For the Benzigers, success has come faster than Florence Griffith-Joyner running the mile. It was almost overnight. Yet it was well-timed and took hard work, savvy marketing and lots of young, energetic Benzigers pulling together.

J. Bruno Benziger, the patriarch who performed wine marketing wizardry in introducing medium-priced Glen Ellen wines, had previously mastered bottling, pricing and marketing spirits during a 26-year career in his family's import and distributorship businesses, Park-Benziger & Co. Inc. in New York.

Why not transfer those skills to making and marketing wine, he thought?

Wine imports were at an all time high and California vintners concentrated on producing either cheap jug wines or high-priced premium varietals, wines made mostly from one grape, listed on the label. There was an obvious middle market gap.

Bruno's family winery would exploit that gap by producing premium varietal wines that retailed just slightly above jug wine prices and below the expensive imports and domestic wines of small, or boutique, wineries.

There was a stigma at the time of being in that middle price range. The California wine market was a $10 to $15 a bottle segment, appealing predominantly to wine snobs. "Yet, there was this huge inventory of bulk wine in stainless steel tanks with no place to go," said Mike, 34, Bruno's eldest child. "Dad figured why not take what he had done with Scotch, which was bottled in bulk, and duplicate it with wine. My dad's always been comfortable selling on price. He likes to move quality and volume."

Bruno's hunch was right. He found the industry's sweet spot. Varietal wine sales have been propelled by the emergence of the fighting varietal segment, branded varietal wines that retailed from $3.99 to $5.99 per 750 milliliters.

Today, in just nine years and at a time when the industry has seen some sales flatten or decline, the Glen Ellen winery has struck gold. Annual shipments have climbed steadily upward in a growth curve that would please any business owner. Glen Ellen is the third hottest varietal winery in the country with growth up 60 percent to 2.4 million cases in 1988. Glen Ellen wines appear among the country's top 10 in sales on most every varietal wine scoreboard. This year the company expects to produce close to three million cases or 36 million bottles of wine, estimated to be worth between $55 and $70 million in annual retail sales. Industry experts are dazzled. Most vineyards need 10 years to show a profit. Glen Ellen produced a profit in one.

Every year, more than one million new businesses get off the ground in this country, the Small Business Administration estimates. But for every two of the 600,000 businesses that employ more than the owner, one folds.

Bruno, 63, didn't succeed alone. He did so because his son Mike knew how to make great wine, and in this case the son persuaded the father to join him in the business, a role reversal but an increasingly common trend. The son benefits from the father's wisdom and experience. The father, often near retirement, finds a new challenge. They become equals and better friends.

Over the years, Mike has told the story dozens of times about how he and his father started the winery. The anecdotes and wording rarely vary.

After graduating in 1973 from Holy Cross College with a major in political sociology, Mike had his first taste of the wine business as a clerk at Beltramo's, a large 5,000-square-foot wine shop in Menlo Park, CA, just outside Palo Alto. He became enamored with the business, especially as California wines began to come into their own. "I developed a palate in my two years there. A lot of it is subjective."

While working there, Mike squirreled away about $15,000. After two years, he grew restless to learn more about the winemaking process. Using his funds, he traveled through the vineyards of France, Italy, Germany and Switzerland for one year. His father encouraged him and promised him a job when he returned, selling and distributing wines for Park-Benziger.

The trip was a triumph and Mike came back East armed with knowledge and an itch to sell the product. He went to work for his dad to learn how to market. He lasted nine months. He wanted to return to California where the finest domestic wines were being made. He went to work in the cellars of Stony Ridge in Pleasanton, in the East Bay area of San Francisco. Stony Ridge was the perfect training ground, according to Mike.

"We had the worst conditions—primitive equipment, undercapitalization, poor management. In general, it was a reform school for wine. We were always out of money. But I'm glad I got the experience. If you worked at a perfect little winery, with perfect little grapes, what the hell would you learn? If you have to be resourceful, you really learn how to blend and do the nitty gritty jobs." Mike was there 20 months.

At Stony Ridge Mike met Bruce H. Rector, who later would become part of the winemaking team at Glen Ellen and one of the company's few non-family partners.

Mike again became restless. He wanted to be his own boss. "I got really obsessed about finding my own place," he recalled.

Bruno also had become fidgety. At Park-Benziger for more than 26 years, he wanted to start a second career, a nursery in upstate New York.

In 1979, Mike picked up the phone and offered his dad a slightly different option. He asked Bruno to invest in a California vineyard. "Sure," Bruno told him warmly. "Go ahead and see if you can come up with some good property."

Helen, Mike's mother, encouraged him, but she added firmly, "If we're all going to come to California to become winemakers, you'll have to find property with some buildings. We aren't the communal types."

Mike didn't think they took him seriously. "They were throwing bread out on fertile soil."

Every Sunday for 18 months, Mike and his wife Mary packed up their Volvo, bundled up their young daughter, Erinn, and scouted for land up and down the California coast. They found a schoolhouse in Monterey, but it had chicken coops and wasn't fit for living. They found property near Mendocino, but it didn't have running water or electricity. Every so often, Bruno flew out to visit and joined their search.

One day in the winter of 1980, Bruno and Mike went to see a rancher in Livermore, east of Oakland. They had heard about 100 acres in Glen Ellen off London Ranch Road near the Jack London State Historic Park where the writer who penned *Call of the Wild* is buried and where his ranch is open to the public. London, who died in 1916, was an American author from San Francisco who lived 45 miles northeast of that city in Glen Ellen in northern Sonoma County.

Bruno and Mike's reactions to the area were immediate, like an electric current, Bruno recalled. There was land and two potential homes, one of which had been a hotel in 1902 and had apartments so that three married couples could live there. There were already 15 acres of grapes that had been planted by the previous owner, Dr. Patrick Flynn, a cult-type character who had built a small Greek columned structure that resembled the Acropolis along one hill and who was rumored to have planted marijuana on one terrace. The grapes were alive, but had been improperly pruned. The buildings were abandoned except for chickens living in them.

The town of Glen Ellen was bursting with history. Julius Wegner, who in 1868 had built the home of Sonoma's founder, General Mariano Guadalupe Vallejo, had been the first owner of the Benzigers' future winery. He received 120 acres of the terraced property as payment for his carpentry work. In the 1870s, the ranch produced 60,000 gallons of wine and 30,000 gallons of brandy. London was a frequent visitor. In the early 1900s, phylloxera, a plant lice, killed the grapes. The property languished for years.

Bruno and Mike were smitten. Bruno sold his stake in Park-Benziger. All the Benzigers—parents, grandmother and children—pooled their money and plunked down $750,000 to buy a 110-acre ranch, grapes and equipment and hire a staff and consultants.

Making a major change would have meant a cultural shock for most upper-middle-class urban families. The Benzigers had raised their children in affluent White Plains, NY. They would be leaving a 17-room home, membership in a beach and tennis club on Long Island Sound, close proximity to everything New York City offered, and dozens of long-time friendships.

Friends thought they were crazy. "At your age, you are out of your minds," said one of their most outspoken friends. "You are going to go out there and all your other darling children are going to refuse to stay and will leave you." Fortunately, that friend was dead wrong.

What the Benzigers got was a sleepy town with a picture-postcard landscape—a backdrop of emerald green lawns, stately pines and towering redwoods dotting the Sonoma Mountain foothills.

In fall 1980, Mike and Mary and their two older children moved into the property's old winery surrounded by neglected and overgrown vineyards and a crumbling 1868 vintage frame house where conditions were less than ideal. The laboratory became their kitchen. The bottling room their family room.

The rest of the Benzigers came West. Bruno moved out in March 1981. Helen came that summer, followed by Joe, Jerry, Chris and Kathy and their 82-year-old grandmother. They camped out in the larger adjacent main building. When Helen's elderly mother saw her new home she gasped, "Is this what we're going to sleep in?"

Helen, the peacemaker, meekly replied, "It's only for a short time." Crates, boxes and trunks had been opened and unpacked. Everything the family owned in New York had been shipped to California. The furniture was set about haphazardly.

"I don't like this," Helen's youngest daughter Kathy wailed. She cried on her grandmother's shoulder from the moment she boarded a plane in New York to the time she arrived in Glen Ellen.

But the family never doubted its ability. "Maybe I was just dumb, but I thought we'd be reasonably successful," mused Bruno. He never felt like the old guy in the wagon coming over the plains. Only once was he concerned. Two years after starting, money was running down and inventory was depleted. Bruno borrowed $100,000 from Helen's mother.

Through hard work, the Benzigers learned by hit and miss the essentials of farming grapes and transforming them into wines.

In 1981, they planted 10 acres of Sauvignon Blanc. Their goal was to make 4,000 cases the first 12 months. In 1982, they planted five acres of Merlot. One year later, they planted seven acres of Cabernet Sauvignon.

Mike appreciated the area's well-drained soil, consisting of red loam with plenty of rocks and pumice, a combination that promoted deep root growth, added nutrients and flavors to the grapes. The area's hilly terrain, cool mountain breezes and warm sunny days would allow harvesting a wide variety of grapes at different times which would eliminate a major management problem.

There were kinks to be worked out, sore joints, sleepless nights, too much togetherness at times. They mastered the seasonality of their new business. They planted in spring. Nurtured and thinned vines in summer. Harvested ripe grapes in late summer. They sorted and crushed.

They learned to cope with the weather. The fall of 1982 was the wettest in recent years—110 inches of rain between November and April. The rain caused the soil to erode on the steep hills. The family learned the hard way that when it rains late, harvesting is delayed. If it rains too much, grapes may get mildewed.

Mike called in soil experts to give advice on erosion control. They planted permanent cover crops to hold soil in place.

They called in wine experts. They found when it's too cold, grapes may freeze. They learned that more sun in the morning causes the varietal characteristics of a particular grape to be accentuated. A Cabernet becomes more peppery. Cool mornings and late afternoon sun lead to richer, riper flavors.

They ascertained that vines can get stressed if they're worked too hard, but that some stress adds a positive richer character to the grapes. They discovered it takes three years to attain a good grape yield and that the best vines are five to 15 years old.

Joe, the third eldest Benziger child, recalled those first days fondly, spewing forth a kind of book jacket blurb. "They were horrible and they were heaven. I'll never forget it. We stood there with a little book on how to make wine. Page one told us how to grow grapes. You step on them. Page two, you throw the yeast in. What do you do next? You get some refrigeration. We crushed grapes under the headlights of cars. We fermented in the back of old milk trucks. Some of the first wines made, however, were fabulous. A Sauvignon Blanc made in the winter of 1981 won the Best of Show in the Sweepstakes of Sonoma County in 1982. A Chardonnay won runner-up. How did we do it? We had bought some very good grapes. Ninety percent of our success is due to what's done out in the vineyard. We also hired good people."

Mike made contacts with independent growers to add to and vary grape supplies. They bought grapes in bulk. Prices were high then. A ton of Sauvignon Blanc cost $750. A ton of Chardonnay was $1,250. Prices subsequently dropped and would later climb back. Rector, Mike's friend from Stony Ridge, was brought in as a consultant.

Under Mike's direction, the family and a handful of employees including a Mexican field foreman and a mechanic, cleared and planted. They slowly invested in equipment. They bought three 1,500-gallon stainless steel tanks at $3 a gallon in 1981 and three 2,500-ton open top wood fermenters to extract rich textures and aromas. They also bought that year fifty 60-gallon French oak barrels made in place by a Frenchman skilled in the craft. They added two 1,600-gallon and one 3,200-gallon French oak tanks at $4 a gallon in 1984. Next came $1 million of semi-automatic bottling equipment for two lines.

With equipment in place, the family made wine. They fermented, aged and topped barrels to make sure they were always filled to keep oxygen out of the tank. After each lot of wine developed its own characteristics, with the length of fermentation dependent on the type of wine made, Mike and his brothers tasted and blended in wines of different flavors to create special tastes. "Think of it as a lot like cooking," explained Joe.

Joe Benziger, Brian Wilson, Jose Ortiz and Jack Ryno filtered out yeast and bacteria through three systems. Kay Bogard sent wines to the lab for extra checking between filtration. Mark Burningham and Larry Topping bottle aged red wines from 12 to 18 months to increase softness and complexity. They bottle aged white wines from one to six months.

Bruno manned bottling lines, spun caps and set up sales and marketing systems. Even the youngest of the third generation was called on to help. Parents stood their kids on boxes and let them put foil on top of corks. The Benzigers compressed 50 years into a few. The family put in 17-hour days.

Perks were minimal, primarily the joy of working together and living in a peaceful bucolic setting.

Within a year, they uncorked their products, which consisted of Benziger Family Selections of estate wines grown on their property and wines made from grapes grown by other farmers, and white and red table, or generic, wines that Bruno cleverly labeled his Proprietor's Reserve. Usually wineries reserve that terminology for their most expensive wines.

Bruno used contacts back East to distribute and promote the wines. Family members hit the road to push the lines with other distributors and large retailers.

Two years down the road in 1983, they added Cabernet and Chardonnay varietals to the Proprietor's Reserve line.

Wine writers and experts were knocked over. Harvey C. Savadsky, assistant manager of Zachys, a well-known wine and liquor store in Scarsdale, NY, tasted his first Glen Ellen Chardonnays and Cabernets at a tasting at the swanky Plaza Hotel in New York City in 1981 and distinctly remembers his reaction. "There were 100 wineries represented. As soon as I tasted one of Glen Ellen's Chardonnays, I couldn't believe the price. It had an $8 nose for a $4 sticker. This was going to be perfect for the Zachys' customer, who's used to watching prices. We quietly brought in five cases so we didn't alert our competition and the wines took off."

Other retailers stocked the Glen Ellen brands. The New Liquor Barn, the giant chain formerly owned by Safeway Stores in California with 100 stores in California and Arizona, started buying between 1983 and 1984. Vons Grocery Co., a giant Southern California supermarket chain, introduced Glen Ellen wines in 1986. Consumers, often intimidated by high-priced wines and hard to pronounce names, grabbed Glen Ellen off the shelves. Safeway became Glen Ellen's biggest account.

The winery has become a busier hub. Follow Arnold Drive the length of the Sonoma Valley. Take a sharp right and turn left up the narrow London Ranch Road, past living oak and eucalyptus trees. With hardly a marker in view, the vineyard suddenly appears. Terraced kelly green vineyards juxtaposed against steep woods and rocky peaks. Lawns with perfect crew cuts. Planted and potted flowers everywhere. Vivid red roses and geraniums against a Victorian frame guest house. Budding yellow tulips poised and eager to open. A small enclosed swimming pool, surrounded by redwood picnic tables where visitors sip wine and eat lunch.

Further up the main road is the home that Bruno and Helen moved into six years ago—a sprawling one-level redwood and glass retreat.

Walls inside are lined with family photographs recording their schizo-
phrenic East and West coast lives. Next door is a small "love cottage"
their daughter Patsy Wallace Benziger and her husband Tim moved
into when he joined the company fresh from Harvard Business School.
Bob lives in Sonoma. Joe lives in Kenwood.

Back down to the winery at the foot of the property the peacefulness
stops. Here there is little margin for error. This is a tiny facility that
produces tremendous output—8,000 to 10,000 cases of 10 varietal
wines a day, which includes 77 different products in an assortment of
sizes and shapes. Twenty-five double trailers roll in to pick up the cases
and take them to the Glen Ellen warehouse now located off premises in
Sonoma, seven miles away, so that there is enough room to store
200,000 to 300,000 cases. From here wine is shipped to 50 states as
well as to Canada, England, Japan, France and Switzerland.

The warehouse boasts a new fully-automatic bottling line that will
fill more than 20,000 cases a day or 400 bottles a minute, twice the
output of the semi-automatic lines that are kept to meet the unrelenting
demand. The new bottling line will accomplish in four 10-hour shifts a
week what has taken the manual lines six 18-hour shifts. Joe contends
Glen Ellen's new automatic bottling line is among the largest in
Northern California.

"Our main problem," he says, shaking his head for emphasis, "is
that we can't get the wine in the bottles fast enough yet we don't want a
backlog in the tanks. We want to bottle our product fresh. We usually
bottle white wines within a year of blending them. We give reds a little
more time, two to three years."

Not surprisingly, Joe, his siblings and parents love every minute of
their new lives and of their new setting. Glen Ellen has become a zany
mixture of artists living in the hills, bohemians who think they have a
little bit of mystery writer Jack London in them and rich people trying
to escape from hectic big city lives. Yet Glen Ellen, with 2,200
residents, still retains its folksy charm with just a few stores, a gourmet
pizza restaurant, one fancier dining establishment—the Grist Mill, a
single unpretentious lodge, plus the Sonoma Developmental Center in
Eldridge on the outskirts of Glen Ellen.

In Sonoma, the latest amenities of bustling boutiques, wine shops,
souvenir stands, pubs and restaurants meld with yesterday's charms.
Nearby is the posh pink stucco Sonoma Mission Inn. Sonoma County
has become a $60 million-a-year wine and tourist mecca.

The daily grind, the intense proximity to one another and the strong personalities of the players would undermine many families. The Benzigers have more than their fair share of robust shouting matches, brouhahas and rivalries. But they have avoided letting disagreements get out of hand.

"Being successful has helped," says Joe, who explains that every decision made will not make or break the family and the business. They have taken on a challenge that never lets up and which has created clear-cut roles and provides a high in this intoxicating Never-Never Land. For these reasons, the family has no desire to slow down, halt the daily grind and spend their millions. They are always working at the winery, in the fields and at home.

"Why would we stop the momentum when we've got a one in a million opportunity?" asked Mike, the most introspective of the children. He nods at Joe, knowing that his brother agrees. "We're all young and competitive. And we've got too many irons in the fire. There will be plenty of time to cut back in the future. We each goof off one week a year. Joe and Bob have a softball team Friday nights. We get together as a family when we entertain others."

At the same time, success occasionally proves a tough mistress. On a recent weekday, an inferior order of glass bottles slowed the operation to a standstill, then part of the case packing system broke down upsetting Mike, who tried to track down his sister Kathy's boyfriend, a mechanic, to repair it.

But what may be an equally important reason for this family's camaraderie is that the Benzigers are bound by a family pact that stresses a team approach to any project rather than individual glory. Every family member is accountable to the other. Although there is no single anointed leader, family members and outsiders consider Bruno the "boss of the bosses" and that Mike, the general manager, deserves credit for getting into the business in the first place. He is next in line. The winery was his idea and he works hardest.

Bruno represents a different kind of leader than is usually found in a successful corporation, whether or not a family business. He downplays his importance to the company, shrugging off personal compliments and bending over backwards to make sure Mike and the rest of the family get credit. "I came out here as an equal to all the kids. I'm no more responsible than anyone else for our success."

Bruno also knew what it was like to work with a parent. He got his start in business as a part-time office boy in his family's importing and distributing business, founded by his uncle, Meinrod Benziger, and partner, A.D. Park, at the turn of the century.

Bruno was drafted into the Marines and sent to Guam and Iwo Jima. He returned home and went to college at Fordham University. In 1950 he graduated and married his childhood sweetheart, Helen Williamson. Bruno became a steamfitter for three years. But after his younger brother Paul was injured in the Korean War, Bruno rejoined Park-Benziger and became president. He quickly instituted changes. He found a loophole in the Federal excise tax law that allowed him to bottle Scotch for $1 less per bottle than his competitors.

Paul recovered and returned to the business in 1959. His father and his father's partner died suddenly. Bruno and Paul were in charge. They sold off every division of the company except wine and spirits. At the same time, a different branch of the family worked in another family business, a religious books publisher, Benziger Brothers.

Today, Bruno meanders down from his home in well-worn blue jeans, a flannel shirt and torn gray cashmere sweater. Dried mud is caked on his shoes. He grins his boyish grin, bobs his flat-top head of gray hair and makes the rounds on a small red Ford Payloader tractor, "his limousine," according to Mike. His homespun, hands-on management style is more appropriate to this folksy setting than it was to New York's paneled boardrooms and fancy restaurants. He rarely needs a suit and tie and has given most away to his Mexican field hands. "They loved it," Helen says. "Bruno was never into clothes. He used to buy all of his for $200 including his underwear."

Bruno's favorite greeting is a firm slap on the back. His handshake is warmer than his low droning voice. He's a gruff, military-type, an intense man with ice blue eyes set in a dark, tan face. He mingles well with all types of people whether wine snobs or migrant field hands. He's a master at working hard.

Helen Benziger is the matriarch, the glue. She keeps Bruno calm and makes each of her seven children and her more than 120 employees feel special. "She was known in the neighborhood when we were growing up for never turning any one out," said a childhood friend of Mike's. "She was always feeding or putting up someone overnight." She still fills that role today, though often to strangers who are important customers.

On a recent weekend, she's hostess to 14 Vons sales managers, who have come for a tour of the winery and lunch. It's a chilly, windy day. The sky is a splendid blue. Great cotton clouds float across. The president of Liquor Barn, his wife and young son have also been invited from their home on San Francisco's Russian Hill for a tour and lunch.

All visitors are seated in three separate rooms of the guest cottage and fed barbecued chicken, sausages, salad, bread and home-baked ginger cookies and fresh strawberries. "It's important for Helen to sit down and talk with the clients," says Bruno, trying to get her to mingle in the red parlor. But Helen shoos him away. She's too busy refilling platters and clearing dishes. Her only help is from Kathy, her daughter-in-law, Bob's wife.

Every week Helen is handed a typed schedule of who will be coming and when, most often retailers and wholesalers from throughout the country. Somebody from the family must be there to lead tours, host lunches and dinners and be sure that guests are comfortably housed overnight in the main guest cottage or in the family's San Francisco apartment.

Each of the other Benzigers in the business has his or her domain, from making wines to managing employees and promoting products. Each full-time family member draws the same partnership salary of $60,000, sidestepping squabbles over who makes more.

Paul Benziger, 60, who sold the Park-Benziger importing business at the end of 1987, has become the East Coast sales manager and works closely with Bruno and Helen's son, Jerry, and Paul's son, Peter. Paul and Paul's sister, Nancy Connellan, manage the East Coast office.

Michael, who has the intense Benziger blue eyes, is slight, blond and athletic. He's the idea man and order giver, the head of the winemaking team. He's perpetually in motion or involved in several discussions. On a recent weekday in his office, he halts one conversation in English to switch to speaking to a field hand in Mexican-Spanish, as he calls it. "I had four years of Latin and five years of French. Neither helped much. I got out here and found that I had to learn the stock Spanish phrases or I wasn't going to swim with our field hands."

Mike gets up at 5:00 A.M. and writes work orders until 6:30 A.M., heads for the winery to oversee daily operations. On any day, there are interruptions such as television interviews, meetings with distributors and growers and buyers, radio spots, dozens of phone calls and even an occasional audit. He's often there until 7:30 P.M. at which time it's not unusual for him to have a dinner meeting which may last until late at night. He may head for the winery if he's needed to check the bottling or taste a new batch of wine. Once every six months, he does a thorough evaluation of every employee.

Mike spots his dad coming up the hill to the office. He gets fidgety. When Bruno and Mike are in the same room, young Mike clams up. The tension is palpable. Helen quietly bends over and whispers in Bruno's ear to leave the office with her so that Mike may have the floor. Bruno seems startled by the suggestion, but gets up and announces, "Mike will tell you what you need to know."

Bruno and Mike usually meet three or four times a day when both are at the winery, though they infrequently sit down to brainstorm. Each knows what he has to do for the family business. Exceptions are when there's a problem or when they partake in their Tuesday morning partners' meetings.

Mike is Bruno's alter ego and confidante. They share goals. Both work for the long term. "They're both stubborn and Mike never lets up," says Helen.

"Mike and Bruno were always at odds when he was in college," says Philip McGovern, one of Mike's childhood friends who's now head of a construction company in New York. "Bruno was real strict. But I think that Bruno has had a growing respect for his son."

Another friend, Steve McGowan, head of a marine engineering and design firm in Westport, MA, concurs. "I never would have thought that this family could work together, especially Mike and Bruno. They're all strong personalities. Having an idyllic lifestyle up there helps. Yet Mike and Bruno are a great father-son combination. However, I still question how anyone can work with a father?"

A father-son business relationship often proves the most difficult. Whether or not father and son can work together in business usually depends on the two men's prior personal relationship. Unfortunately, the classic scenario is for a father to be too protective of his son and try to map out the son's life, says Dan Bishop of the National Family Business Association in Los Angeles.

There are exceptions, sometimes eased by the father and son's ages and the life cycle of the business. When a son is between 23 and 33 and a father is in his 50s, the men are usually physically and intellectually strong and capable of contributing to the business and sharing authority and rewards, says John A. Davis, assistant professor of management and organization at the Graduate School of Business Administration at the University of Southern California.

Mike also works with his wife, Mary, a tall striking blonde, who heads the shipping department and collects sales information. Mary enters the living room of their home on a Saturday afternoon. She's in a bad mood after misplacing her car keys. She is three months pregnant with their third child and is hot and tired after spending the day at a family christening. Mike turns and remarks that Mary's had to cut back her hours with the new baby on the way.

Mike also acknowledges that everybody in a family business has a different set of goals and doesn't necessarily work as hard as he does. "That's okay. I know it's tough when a hobby and work become one. You can become pretty rough to live with." Mike looks away. "We were married in 1974 after graduating from college and divorced 1½ years later. We went our separate ways and did things we should have done before we met each other." They remet after Mike moved back to California and remarried. Mike finally gets up from the sofa to ask Mary a question. There's a quiet understanding between the two.

McGovern, Mike's childhood friend, worries about the next generation of Benzigers. "They've got a product and they've got some recognition. But some of the brothers and sisters only work hard if you put a whip to them. They don't have the same love for the business as Mike and Bruno."

The second eldest Benziger child, Bob, is the personality man in the family, the quintessential smooth talker. He is the national sales manager who joined the company in 1981 and first sold for Glen Ellen out of New York. He got his start running a retail wine and liquor shop near White Plains with his brother Joe. Bob's wife Kathy is the family decorator, who helped furnish the guest cottage on Bruno's shoestring budget.

Joe, the cellar master, enters the kitchen on a Saturday morning and slaps his big brother Bob on the shoulder. "How are you doing?" Joe is the family handyman. He works closely with Mike and Bruce and is responsible for aging the estate wines in barrels and checking that there's always enough available tank space. Joe's wife Diane was company caterer until their second daughter was born.

When Glen Ellen was started, another brother, Jerry, helped build the winery. He stayed in California until 1986 and then switched sales jobs with his brother Bob, who was eager to relocate to California.

Christopher began working for the winery in July of 1988, and concentrates on promoting one of the firm's newest labels, the Benziger of Glen Ellen Selections.

Helen talks excitedly about her daughter, Patsy, and son-in-law Tim, who came West to work in the winery. Patsy was a part-time nurse who promoted Glen Ellen wines in her spare hours. Tim has been made a partner and named the winery's professional manager because of his freshly-minted Harvard MBA. His first job has been to organize and coordinate sales and production. Once this is accomplished, Tim will spend 20 to 25 percent of his time looking into new ventures such as a possible microbrewery, a small regional beer-making operation, and food line. "Excuse my Latin," Mike says candidly, "but Tim will be taking a flying fuck at the moon."

Before going to graduate school, Tim worked for the food division of American Home Foods, a subsidiary of American Home Products, a pharmaceutical company that manufactures Woolite.

Tim is articulate and sharp. He thinks the winery still has a way to go to operate efficiently. "We need to find out why people are buying Glen Ellen wines. We need to find out what our image is out there, what our strengths and weaknesses are." He also thinks that the partners have to make group meetings more productive and decide on one leader. "The line of decision making is just not efficient. There are serious conflicts that arise between two strong bosses. I can be the bridge between both Bruno and Mike, until a single senior management leader is selected. But I do feel I am stepping into a minefield at times. I'm willing to take a chance. This is a fabulous opportunity."

In hearing this comment, Mike, who respects Tim's opinion, says abruptly, "I'm going to send him back to school to cool his heels."

Kathy is the only Benziger not working in the business. She's in a management position at a hotel in San Francisco.

The Benzigers never have hesitated to fill in the gaps where needed. Rector became a partner in 1986 after serving as a consultant for several years. He worked part time at the Nichelini Winery. He went to South America to study winemaking, returned to attend the University of California at Davis and majored in fermentation arts. He went to work for the Monterey Peninsula winery and then operated the Napa School of Cellaring, a non-profit winemaking school. He next worked at the Stony Ridge winery where he met Mike.

In addition to finding the best grapes from which to make Glen Ellen wines, and blending and tasting, Bruce also has become a referee between Mike and Bruno. "I help keep the lines of communication open," he says. Mike nods.

Mike heads across the hall to Mark Storenatta's office. Mike needs some industry figures from Mark, who's been with Glen Ellen for three years as chief financial officer. He handles finances, makes projections and works with the banks to secure loans. Mike sinks into a chair in his office and taps the desk with one finger. "What do you think we should pay the new guy to work the automatic bottling line?"

The partners meet every Tuesday in the conference room of the guest house which is electronically hooked to the New York office so that Paul and Jerry can participate. The meeting begins. Either Mike, Bruno or Bruce reviews the minutes. The floor is thrown open for discussion which centers on grape sourcing, sales, production and new business. "We have our good arguments but we never vote," says Mike. "And we don't end the meeting until all issues are resolved unanimously. We do this by either compromising or wearing the bastards down." A meeting can take up to eight hours.

Another non-family member, Bill Thompson, who is the company accountant, is evasive about explaining how the company could become more cost efficient, but eager to show off the fermentation and crushing equipment, the grounds and the spate of offices that have been computerized to track depletions and new orders.

Bruce Rector's right-hand man is Charlie Tsegeletos, whose babyish pale face and bright dark eyes belie that he's worked in the industry since 1981. He started at Hacienda Wine Cellars and became the winemaker at T. Augustini Winery in 1984. He describes the conditions at Glen Ellen as "absolutely ideal. We're able to pull grapes and wines from all over California. My goal is to buy the best fruit so we make the best wine and we've got that opportunity," he explains standing in his lab in front of a long wood table covered with beakers and bottles. He tinkers with blends, yells in suggestions to Bruce.

After he mixes and sips, he notes the taste and comes up with a formula for the right blends, marking them on a clipboard. "We want wines to be consistent with our style. Is it flowery? Is it vegetal like a Brussels sprout or pea? If it's not fruity enough, we look to components and decide how we can change it. We can't use all the components right away. We have to save some for throughout the year. We aim to please our customers as well as our own palates."

Kay Bogart, the company's enologist who has studied the science of wine and winemaking, bounds into the kitchen on a Saturday morning for coffee and chitchat. She came to Glen Ellen from Callaway Vineyards. She had graduated from Davis three years before and is delighted to be affiliated with a booming business where she has responsibility. She arrives six mornings a week at 6:30 A.M. and checks the bottling line and the wines to be sure they're distilled properly. She stays until 5:00 P.M. and earns $25,000 for a more than 60-hour week.

Seconds after Kay leaves, Terry Ritz dashes into the kitchen to warm up, grab a cup of coffee and rest her voice. She runs the tasting room on Saturdays, a pleasant change from her daily grind as a bank teller. She describes wines to visitors who number as many as 500 on a busy Saturday. She's part of a tasting team that may sell more than $300,000 a year in wine, T-shirts, postcards and books. "This is pure gravy for the company," says Bob. "We've got the space, the inventory and the captive audience."

A national staff of 11 salesmen and 10 brokers help sell Glen Ellen wines. Doing so has become easier, family members explain as they pull out a Glen Ellen star—a white Zinfandel Proprietors Reserve that won a gold medal at the 1987 Orange County and Sonoma County Harvest fairs. "Now that we're hot everybody wants to buy our wines," says Joe.

Joe rises to his feet. "I've got to go," he mumbles. Visitors have assembled outside and Joe must conduct tours. Many of the visitors will stay on to have lunch later to be served by Helen and Bob's wife.

Glen Ellen is like the "Little Engine That Could," a small winery that huffed and puffed in an uphill battle to keep up with its larger and more established competitors who are moving into its middle-market segment. Their names shoot up on crude wooden signs everywhere as a visitor drives through the Sonoma Valley and over to Napa. Robert Mondavi Winery, Sebastiani Vineyards, Gundlach Bundshu Winery, Chateau St. Jean, St. Francis Vineyards and Winery, Kenwood Vineyards. Upstarts appear at every other turn, ready to shake up the industry more—Smothers Brothers Wines, now defunct, B.R. Cohn Winery, Ferrari-Carano Winery.

The family welcomes the competition. "Napa Ridge, Fetzer Vineyards and Round Hill have all helped us forge a legitimate new category whereas before we weren't always taken seriously because we were the only ones in it," says Mike.

To compete, Glen Ellen has introduced several newer lines at different price points: M.G. Vallejo, a less-expensive line averaging $4.99; a more pricey and limited Imagery Series of $12 to $16 wines, bottled aged in black glass with artist-designed labels and packed in a three-bottle wooden crate; and The Benziger of Glen Ellen Selections of $8 to $12, with labels that play up the family's role.

On one wall in the study of Mike's contemporary redwood house on six acres hangs the original artwork for the Imagery Series. Bruno spews forth his opinion of the abstract artwork. He points for emphasis. "Can you believe they think that's good?" he asks rhetorically within earshot of several of his kids.

"That's the way Bruno is," sighs Bob.

"We like to evoke a reaction and be controversial," interrupts Mike.

The team is also moving into the champagne market. By 1990, it plans to retail the sparkling wine for $7.99 to $10.99 a bottle.

Glen Ellen is reluctant to reveal profits. "We're a closely held business," Mike says. "Our profits are solid on paper. We've got a good velocity of money. I'm a wealthy guy for only about 30 seconds, however. The money goes through the system fast. We know we can't double growth every year. We've always been on a roll. A lot of our decisions now are based on risk."

Industry sources and friends of the family confirm that Glen Ellen is doing so well that it's "printing money." Mike reveals that retail sales will hit $55 to $70 million.

Jean Michel Valette, with the San Francisco investment banking firm of Hambrecht and Quist, Inc., says that wineries producing between 50,000 to 150,000 cases and more than one million cases a year, such as Glen Ellen, will be the most profitable. They realize a 46 percent pretax return on the dollar versus the industry average of 13 percent." Valette bases his information on a 1988 Touche Ross & Co. survey.

Always looking ahead, Glen Ellen is devising long-range strategies as a cushion against several predicaments. Grape growers and other farmers vie against developers for land. Grape prices are fluctuating and have tripled in the last year. Consumers are quaffing less, though better, wines.

Throughout the region and in the nearby Napa Valley, the popularity of "God's country" has pitted farmers, environmentalists and developers against one another as the number of wineries keeps growing throughout California. Between 1982 and 1986, wineries in Sonoma increased from 109 to 142, according to The Wine Institute, a San Francisco trade association.

As Michael stares out at his vineyards, he is keenly aware of changes taking place in the valley and the invasion of commercialism. "I'm betwixt and between on this issue. On one hand, I think the land should be protected for the best possible use, which is grape growing and keeping the backwoods feeling. On the other hand, I think there's a lot of marginal land here where grape growing isn't feasible and if it's not developed you could have a lot of people going broke."

With California varietal wine marketers facing an increasingly tight grape market for the most popular varieties, Mike says that only those wineries with either extensive vineyard holdings or long-term grape contracts with other growers will be in the best position to maintain competitive pricing in the next few years. Only Glen Ellen's premium estate-bottled reserve wines are produced from its own vineyard.

To make sure Glen Ellen winery has an ample supply of grapes in the future, the Benzigers have four people scouting up and down the state. The winery obtains grapes from about 260 different growers with whom it has medium to long-term contracts. "We like to purchase from numerous areas so if bad weather damages one crop other sources will serve as a buffer," Mike says. "It's important to be flexible in this business. For that reason we don't own vineyards, a lot of property. We're a little winery that could pay itself off at any time. We'd rather pay for things as we go along. And that includes grapes."

The Benzigers raised prices slightly on existing brands in March 1988 to match escalating grape prices. They raised wholesale prices about five percent or $2 per case on the 750 milliliter Proprietor's Reserve Cabernet and Chardonnay and three percent on the white Zinfandel and Sauvignon Blanc. The family is adamant about not losing customers with too big a price jump, afraid that a lot of importers are going to launch popularly priced varietals which look and taste like California wines in the next couple of years.

In addition to stiffer competition if the winery has to move up the scale and go into higher-price wines, Glen Ellen could also run into problems once contracts run out and grapes become harder to get. Bigger wineries like Gallo may beat them on price.

The Benzigers believe grape prices will fall because farming and making wine are cyclical. Joe explains that several top California varietal winemakers fear that the market could even be flooded in the early 1990s by an influx of cheap Chardonnay grapes from the central region of California. Bob Benziger contends that the additional planting activity around the state will stabilize grape prices over the long term, a boon to the wineries.

For now, Glen Ellen's swift success has made it more attractive to potential domestic and foreign conglomerates, who are buying wineries in Napa and Sonoma in order to diversify. About 70 percent of all California wineries are still family owned, says Phil Hiaring, Jr., editor of *Wines and Vines*, a San Rafael, CA, magazine. But consolidation continues. For instance, Nestle S.A. of Switzerland bought Chateau Souverain and Beringer Winery which encompass Los Hermanos and Napa Ridge. Grand Metropolitan P.L.C. of Great Britain bought Almaden, Inglenook and Beaulieu. Guinness P.L.C. of Great Britain owns Sonoma Vineyards and San Martin.

Observers disagree how corporate ownership affects the quality of wine and whether such investments are fiscally sound. Coke used to own Monterey Vineyards, but sold it when profits proved disappointing. Robert M. Parker, Jr., editor and publisher of *The Wine Advocate*, says that maintaining quality depends on the specifics of the situation. "A family-run winery has a wonderful romantic sound, but if it's undercapitalized it can be as bad a situation as a faceless corporation running it and not caring. There are cases where quality has slipped."

Mike says Glen Ellen hasn't had many offers to sell and the family never would consider doing so now. "We are not an attractive investment to many people because Glen Ellen doesn't own anything except for a brand and what makes the brand go is the family behind it. You can't buy a brand and a family at the same time."

Although Mike doesn't see negative effects on the wines that corporations produce, he thinks that family businesses have the edge. "We can make decisions in a hurry. There is more flexibility, more dedication. We don't have to answer to anyone. We also have the labor and loyalty that's needed to survive downturns and we can increase our volume by shaving our margins. What I'd like to do," he jokes, "is put up an enormous billboard and say that we're the last of the family-owned wineries."

When Bruno steps out of the picture, which may be in three years, Mike expects the family to turn to him to head the winery. There are undercurrents that a leader in the second generation may have a harder time mustering the troops. Kathy, Bob's wife, says she worries about how Mike dominates.

On the other hand, Tim thinks Bruno's exit offers advantages. "We'll be a young company, all under 40. We'll get closer and more structured without him. There will probably be a real reckoning when Bruno pulls out. Then things will settle down." Also, the family is talking about diversifying in the future, perhaps marketing other beverages or food. But for now, the Benzigers are sticking close to their core business which is growing so fast the company can't afford to become overloaded with new projects.

Mike has planted the seeds of success which he'd like to bequeath to his three children. But with nine children in the third generation and four more on the way, Mike acknowledges that there could be even greater succession problems than when he takes over. So far they don't perturb him. "Cream rises to the top," he says.

On a recent Saturday in late April, a distant cousin, Peter Benziger, wanders up the winery's winding driveway. He has come to meet his relatives for the first time. Peter, a tall and bookish-looking market research executive from Greenwich, CT, was in San Francisco on business. He telephoned his relatives after his mother, also a Helen Benziger, had spotted the other Helen's name and picture on a Glen Ellen label.

It's a pleasant reunion in the cozy parlor of the guest cottage. Peter and Bruno trade family tales, gossip and sip wine. Bruno is eager to learn about Peter's father, Xavier, who worked for Benziger Brothers, the religious books publisher, but for only three years. "What's he doing now?" Bruno asks. "He's retired," Peter replies.

Peter proceeds to explain that the business was torn apart by family squabbling—two brothers siding against a third, Peter's father, Xavier, who decided the solution was to sell to his brothers. A cousin subsequently took over the company and overextended operations as the demand for religious publications waned. The company was sold to a large family business, Macmillan Publishing Co. of New York in the 1960s and is now part of Macmillan's Glencoe Publishing Co. division in California.

As Bruno's children wander in and out of the room, they pick up bits of conversation. Some consider the characters and details fascinating, but too remote from their place and time to be of consequence.

Mike is quick to note that his family has never known bad times, though he acknowledges they are likely to occur as the business grows at a slower pace. "Those are the times we're planning for."

For those willing to listen, a good lesson may be learned, one as obvious as the first sip of an exquisite 1974 California Cabernet. The success of a family business and the cohesiveness of a family are ephemeral unless a number of ingredients are blended in.

The Benziger family had a good moral foundation. Parents had taught children the value of getting along and working hard together. Parents and children knew the value of the dollar. Nobody would earn money from the business unless they worked for it. Nobody would earn more than the others. They only had time to work, not to fight.

Once sales took off, the Benzigers didn't let success derail them. They plowed back most of their profits into the company, paid themselves modest salaries and marked up their wine less than the traditional 100 percent. They bought more equipment, hired more staff, improved quality.

But the most important ingredient was that they never lost respect and love for each other. And Bruno and Mike have beaten the odds of a father and son working well together because in this case, the son brought his father into the business.

J. Bruno Benziger died in his sleep of heart failure at age 64 on Monday, July 10, 1989. Six months before he died, the family had drafted a formal written succession plan naming Mike, the eldest, chief executive officer.

POSTSCRIPT:
BACK TO THE FAMILY

"... Most Western cultures have norms regulating family behavior that discourage parents and offspring from openly discussing the future of the family beyond the lifetime of the parents."
—Ivan Lansberg, "The Succession Conspiracy,"
Family Business Review

Last Act, Final Scene: A LOOK INTO THE FUTURE.
The board room.

An aging founder sits at the head of a conference table ready to address the board. Around the table are seated two respected community leaders, two executives of major conglomerates who live in other cities, the company's professional manager, its outside attorney and the founder's two children, a son, 35, and a daughter, 30, both of whom work in the family firm. The mix is perfect—an odd number of players and enough outsiders. So is the chemistry. This group is determined to make the company succeed financially and into future generations.

The meeting is special. Everyone knows the agenda. Tension is palpable. The founder rises slowly, clears his throat and announces, "Bear with me please. I have made my decision, though it hasn't been easy. Giving up my business is like giving up a third child." Everyone laughs. The heirs-apparent fidget nervously. They know their father has agreed to retire. Today the board will vote on the founder's choice for a new chairman and on his succession plan, which he has shrouded in secrecy.

267

The founder had numerous options. He could choose his son or daughter to lead the company. He could take a more novel route and rotate the chairmanship between his children, split the company into divisions so that each heir has a power base, or could acquire a new business as another way of creating separate domains. He could choose neither heir and tap his professional manager to run the firm. Or he could play it safe, sell the company and stop succession as a way to insure a secure financial future for his family and avoid intrafamily rivalries.

If he sells, he must decide on the best settlement—a tax-free stock exchange, an all-cash deal or an earn-out.

These are some of the issues every family business owner will face in his lifetime if he wants to protect his family and his business. In *Corporate Bloodlines: The Future of the Family Firm*, we have zeroed in on these and other issues by journeying into the lives of 14 families and their family businesses to discover why some make it, but so many fail. Success and failure do not occur by happenstance. Common threads hold healthy families and healthy businesses together.

A majority of family members in a family business must share a warmth, love and feeling for each other and the business, which they usually have inherited from the matriarch of their clan. The family members pass on this sense of belonging and harmony to their heirs-apparent, says Leon A. Danco, the "dean" of family business study, who set up the Family Business Center in Cleveland 26 years ago in order to counsel owners of closely held firms. Danco operates the Center with his wife, Katy. Many families and their family businesses, however, aren't able to do these things because of pressures inherent in family dynamics, the business world and society, Danco says. Rivalries, greed, social climbing and poor or little planning tear apart families and their businesses.

Nevertheless, despite the odds, the prognosis for passing on a family business looks good because of two concurrent trends. The idealism and liberalism of the 1960s and early 1970s have given way to tougher, more pragmatic attitudes and standards and more professionalism in the 1980s. Family businesses have been strengthened. Second, family businesses may be the last holdout in corporate America where paternalism is alive. Many large businesses have cut back on amenities once considered sacrosanct. Eastman Kodak Co., formerly known as a "home away from home for its employees," has eliminated its bowling alley and billiard rooms, dinners with dance bands and guaranteed jobs. Kodak chairman Colby Chandler explains, "The principal object is to make the company more agile, more competitive and more flexible."

When the ingredients of professionalism and paternalism are blended in a family business, the upshot is the best of all worlds. The family business becomes a utopia where owners create the lifestyle and work world of their choosing and where family members and employees thrive, Danco says.

According to *Time* Magazine in a 1986 poll conducted by D'Arcy Masius Benton & Bowles, men and women were asked: "If you could have your dream job what would it be?" The most popular choice was to own and manage their own business.

Third-generation Hasbro Inc., a $1.3 billion public company and the world's largest toy manufacturer, has created a feeling of extended family as it has added divisions, employees and layers of management. The atmosphere at the company is relaxed and casual. Chief executive Stephen Hassenfeld and his younger brother Alan G. Hassenfeld, president and chief operating officer, genuinely like each other and have divided responsibilities. Whenever they are in the Pawtucket, RI, headquarters, the Hassenfeld brothers dine with employees from all levels in the new huge brick-walled company cafeteria, which has become a corporate town hall with its painted pillars, pastel-colored tiles and huge cut-out metal wall characters in primary colors.

The Hassenfelds also have turned other sections of the Rhode Island headquarters and factory and their New York showroom, where the movie *Big* was shot, into a veritable Disneyland, a menagerie of classic and new toys whose names ring familiar. G.I. Joe and his troops. Mr. Potato Head with a new bucket of parts. Maxie, the girl with the beautiful hair. At Hasbro fantasy prevails, allowing everyone to work seriously at play.

We live in a mercurial world. Regardless of the economy and political and social climate, there always have been, and will be, family businesses, started by entrepreneurs who take an idea, money and build something permanent. Many entrepreneurs won't succeed. Those who do and pass on their legacies to successive generations have followed many of these strategies.

1. **State and establish the goal of the family business.** Family business consultant and attorney Gerald Le Van suggests having the family prepare a written **mission statement** and a **code of**

conduct regulating personal behavior. Is the business to support a certain lifestyle—a country club membership, fancy cars, a big house—or is it to make a profit? Sometimes it can do both. Sometimes owners also have ethical, social and political goals. The former head of Hasbro established a Children's Foundation, which funds innovative projects for children nationwide such as outfitting a mobile medical/dental van to reach homeless children throughout New York City.

2. **Decide whether the business should be continued into a successive generation.** Some family business chief executives never appoint successors. Many family business heads work an average of 42 years in the same slot, or well into their 70s and even 80s.

3. **If the business is to continue, objectively analyze each heir-apparent's qualifications before he or she joins.** Set up strict criteria of acceptable credentials, similar to those used to hire non-family employees. Don't alter this credo for in-laws, cousins, nephews, nieces or long lost relatives. Potential family employees should be interviewed in a suit and tie or dress and heels. Interviewing should take place at the office, not in the family living room.

4. **Don't force heirs to join.** It won't benefit their development, happiness or the business. If you want to encourage joining, speak positively about the business at home and at work. If the heirs hear only about problems, such as long hours, low pay and theft, there is less likelihood they'll join.

5. **Insist that heirs acquire practical outside experience before joining the family firm.** Most owners falsely assume they can teach everything that's needed. Heirs also may be in a hurry to reach the top. They need to mature away from the family and business, establish their independence, develop a true sense of what they are worth and learn to compete for promotions and communicate with a boss. When they do come into the family firm, they are better trained, bring outside experience and a fresh perspective on how another business operates. They'll also have more credibility with non-family colleagues. Once in the business, heirs should be realistic about where they will start and how they'll advance.

In a study conducted by John L. Ward, professor at Loyola University in Chicago, 30 percent of the 80 family business heirs questioned had worked outside the family business before joining full-time and said it was beneficial. Of the remaining 50 percent, more than half said they regretted not having worked elsewhere first. One novel solution to working elsewhere is the "swap program" established by the National Family Business Council in Chicago. Sons and daughters are "loaned" to other firms to broaden skills. The Jewish Young Men's Apparel League in New York helps its members train their sons or daughters away from the family firm for at least eight to 10 years.

6. **Define responsibilities and assign a job for which the heir is qualified.** Keep jobs from overlapping when several heirs work together. Differentiate jobs with titles and written descriptions. Set up an organizational chart with a clear chain of command. Make sure there's only one boss. When there is a leadership change, apprise all employees. If rivalry develops, consider creating a division, dividing the company, or buying another company such as Hassenfeld Brothers Co., the forerunner to Hasbro Inc., did. Founder Henry Hassenfeld bought the Empire Pencil Co. in Shelbyville, TN, to establish a separate turf for his older son, Harold, while his younger brother, Merrill, Stephen and Alan's father, stayed on to head Hasbro.

7. **Set hours, salary, increases, vacations in advance.** Pay should reflect market-level salaries so a job is viewed as competitive to any outside position. Equal compensation among heirs is not required as long as salaries are perceived as "fair." Perks should reflect performance. Family members should be prepared to work harder and longer and to set an example for non-family.

8. **Re-evaluate an heir's performance on a regular basis in the same way that employees are evaluated in non-family businesses.**

9. **Establish a policy of how to deal with unproductive or incompetent family members.** Find them a new job in the company that appeals to their strengths or get them more schooling or training. If all fails, encourage them to find another job. If they don't leave, it will undermine family relationships and business operations.

10. **Set budgets, make projections and plan. Remain flexible.** Too many family businesses are afraid to change, clinging to old ideas and old business cultures.

11. **Carefully position a scion's office.** Put a family member in the center of activity so that he gets to know employees and they view him as accessible, understands the workings of the company and is privy to information.

12. **Introduce family members to key outside contacts.** Take them along to meetings and on business trips. This helps build heirs' credibility and helps outsiders understand that a transfer of power is in progress.

13. **Schedule regular intergenerational family meetings to encourage dialogue so that everyone is exposed to the same information at the same time.** This helps air problems and get them resolved. These meetings also make it more difficult for an owner to be secretive. Once a year, plan a retreat for family and key non-family employees. Bring outside consultants.

14. **Try to avoid role carryover from home to office and vice versa.** If disagreements develop among family members at work, resolve them immediately.

15. **Define the roles of other family members not active in the business.** Family business expert Paul C. Rosenblatt of the University of Minnesota points out that one of the most sinister problems undermining family businesses are spouses who feel physically excluded but emotionally included. Unfortunately, most owners use their spouses as sounding boards for business problems which gives the spouse a false sense of influence. On the other hand, more young owners are giving qualified spouses jobs in the company. More husbands and wives work together successfully as equal partners.

16. **Do estate planning while the owner is alive, otherwise the business may die with him. Estate planning is for more than minimizing taxes.** It's to provide for continuity of the business, protection of the spouse, equitable treatment of heirs, which doesn't necessarily mean the same treatment, explain consultants at Hubler-Swartz of Minneapolis. Family business owners need to stipulate in advance what will happen in the case of a divorce or a disability.

Most incorporated family businesses issue only common stock and usually only one class of common stock that's held exclusively by the owner, says Charlotte K. Ray of the Family Business Foundation Inc. in Baton Rouge. In many cases, shares are transferred equally to heirs without differentiating between those active in the business and those not. Some families divide stock into two classes, voting and non-voting. Those active in the business get the voting stock and have control. Those on the sidelines get non-voting stock.

The 1986 Tax Reform Act that changed personal and corporate income tax rates did little to affect estate taxes, but Congress amended the Internal Revenue Code a year later and enacted section 2036 (c). This closed a major avenue of freezing an estate and lowering a founder's taxes. The provision has been dubbed the "anti-family business section" of the Code. Formerly, an owner could convert his common stock to preferred. This left him with dividends, and, if he wished, voting control. By converting his common stock into an equal, but fixed dollar amount of preferred stock, he lowered his estate taxes below those that would have applied if his common stock had continued to appreciate.

The company issued the owner's children new common shares which appreciated in value as the business grew, or alternatively the owner sold or made a gift of the remaining common stock. When the owner died, his assets in the business were frozen at the date of the transfer of stock so a spouse or heirs paid taxes based on the company's value at that date rather than on the company's appreciated value. The IRS eliminated this benefit because it believed family business owners were abusing the preferred stock category by retaining voting control.

Estate and tax attorneys say it is unclear whether 2036 (c) is applicable if an owner/parent does not convert his common stock to preferred, keeps voting stock and gives away the non-voting stock.

The easiest estate planning tool may be for an heir to take over the business and pay off the former owner in cash. There are other legal options:

—A buy-sell agreement can be drafted that restricts the sale or transfer of stock. The stock must first be offered to family members active in the business and then to other family members or employees before it is sold to outsiders. A formula agreed upon in advance is used to value the stock. An independent appraiser, a trust company officer or an investment banker, can make the evaluation, usually based on book value and a multiple of earnings. Or, the family may agree among itself what the business is worth, though if members want to sell, they will need to call in a third party to make a more objective assessment.

—Interest in a business can be bequeathed to a spouse to avoid estate taxes because of the unlimited marital deduction or through tax-free gifts of $10,000 per annum. Upon the spouse's death, the next generation will have to pay a tax on their inheritance. Children are also entitled to $10,000 tax free each year during an owner and parent's lifetime. The number of children does not matter. The $10,000 exclusion doubles to $20,000 if a spouse joins in the gift.

—Another option is to sell the business to heirs over a specified period of time to reduce the value of the owner's estate. Any profit on the sale to heirs is subject to an income tax at the current capital gains rate of 28 percent. This tack weeds out heirs who aren't interested in paying for their equity.

—Set up an employee stock ownership plan that will benefit family and non-family employees. It has become more difficult for family businesses to comply with ESOP requirements because of changes in the Code in 1984 and 1986.

—Set up a testamentary trust which is funded with common stock for the children to become beneficiaries. When the founder dies, a trustee runs the company until any minor children reach an age when they can take over the business. Voting control is held by the trustee. This trust is also a good option for family members who have no interest in running the company day to day or for a warring family who needs an objective mediator. But one tax attorney, who routinely advises closely held businesses, says the trustee should have control for less than five years.

—Set up an annuity sale by using a life expectancy chart to determine the size of tax-free income payments to the owner that continue until his death. The annuity consists of the tax-free payments based on the value of the business and a taxable interest element, which makes the sale similar to buying an insurance policy and using the business to buy the premium. At the time the business owner dies, payments usually stop, though some policies stipulate that a spouse or heirs may get money on which they will have to pay a tax.

—Set up a trust for family members to remove them from business operations while still providing funds for them to start new ventures.

—An owner can buy life insurance in the amount of his estate tax bill which is income tax free to the estate.

—Set up a charitable foundation as a way to keep non-active family members out of daily business operations and make it either a volunteer or paid position. The amount given away may not exceed 50 percent of the value of the company. It may, however, be hard to get such a foundation to comply with the tax rules.

17. **Prepare for succession, the hardest step in operating a family business, but what will ultimately determine whether the business survives or fails.** Succession planning takes about five years. If an owner fails to plan, heirs may lose interest or not develop skills necessary to take over the business, says Peter Davis of The Wharton School. Succession works best, Davis says, when an owner is between 50 and 60 and the heir is in his 20s to 30s. Succession is easiest when there's one child or only one interested in taking over the business. How will the owner step down? Will he phase himself out gradually or immediately?

Experts disagree regarding what they think is the most effective solution. Family business consultant and attorney Gerald Le Van believes in a period of "creative disengagement." The owner cuts back his work over a two-to-three year period, comes in a little later, leaves a little earlier or only works a few days a week, but retains a title and income. This unclean break may confuse employees and clients who aren't sure who's the boss. Family business experts Leon A. Danco and Nancy Bowman-Upton both think a clean break is best, allowing a successor to run the firm autonomously. Danco cautions, "It has to be labeled as a 'Renaissance' rather than an end."

Le Van reports, however, that the chance of getting a business head to stay away after retirement is slim. "About 85 percent of those who retire keep their offices and continue to 'wander around' the office." Nevertheless, as soon as possible, the former boss should be sent on a long vacation. He'll most likely find that the business doesn't fall apart or go bankrupt in his absence.

Once in charge, the heir must improve the business to reflect the times, the industry and the economy. "Every entity, whether biological, social or economic, survives on inputs of new information," says William Monahan, head of the Sociology Department at St. Louis University. "The same is true of a family business. You can't count indefinitely on the family as the best source of information."

As successive generations assume control and there is more family, rivalry among relatives complicate a family business. Problems can be most difficult when two adult brothers, close in age, plan to join the family firm and both are qualified. A solution, according to Lawrence Kutner in a *New York Times* article, is to encourage the brothers to leave home for college or a first job so they develop separate identities and have time to resolve childhood conflicts. Siblings with an age span of more than five years, are less likely to develop rivalries but they are also less likely to become close.

18. **Hire a professional manager, pay him well, give him autonomy but monitor closely his performance, especially if it's the company's first professional manager.** Consider giving him a percentage of the company in non-voting or phantom stock. Phantom stock reflects how well the company performs and is doled out in cash based on the number of "shares." Because it is "phantom" or "pretend," the shares do not dilute the owner's equity.

19. **Hire an outside board of directors that includes an odd number of directors.** Outsiders should have no prior connection to the family and no self-interest in the business. This excludes the family accountant, lawyer and banker. "This is important, particularly during a crisis in selecting a successor," said Samuel C. Johnson, Chairman of family-owned S.C. Johnson & Sons, Inc., in an April 9, 1989, *New York Times* interview. Have the board meet regularly and be paid competitive directors' fees. Provide liability insurance or a surety bond.

20. **Take the company public so it is accountable to the family and shareholders.** Ben Benson of Laventhol & Horwath says that family businesses that are public and well managed are the most successful because of the professionalism and caring. But the number of family businesses who have reached this level is relatively small, Benson says. Danco doesn't see the need for family businesses to go public. "Pride is far greater than share-

holder pressure. Going public for a family firm should be a last resort." Sometimes private family matters can undermine public companies, as in the case of R.P. Scherer Corp., a $241 million Detroit gelatin-capsule maker. Heiress Karla Scherer Fink is fighting to sell the company, thus challenging Scherer's CEO, who is her estranged husband, Peter R. Fink.

The only certainty in our economy is change. The only constant is family business. The future of the family firm mirrors what is happening in a society that is harking back to the past, a time of close-knit immigrant nuclear families with good values and ethnic pride, who started small enterprises to make a living and worked hard.

As we enter the 1990s, the country has rekindled this trend and begun to build a new era of families living and working together in tight communities. But this time there will be differences. Families are smarter, more innovative and more enlightened. Businesses are sharper and better managed. The combination is indomitable.

SELECTING AND USING A FAMILY BUSINESS CONSULTANT

Some family businesses have sufficient internal resources to resolve day-to-day and long-term work problems and pass the business on to successive generations. These businesses are characterized by members that communicate well, have compatible senior management, warm healthy relationships between older family members who are willing to let go and younger scions, skilled, enthusiastic and patient about taking the reins.

But most family businesses aren't so blessed. Many could be saved if they used a professional consultant. In order for change to take place, however, the consultant must work with the company's power source, usually the head or founder, as well as heirs and employees.

1. How do you find a consultant when the field has only recently become professionalized and interdisciplinary? Trade associations are a good source. Most family businesses are affiliated with trade associations that have become sensitive to the issues in a family business. The trucking association is an example. Call colleges, many of which have set up entrepreneurial and family firm institutes. Ask lawyers, accountants, bankers, colleagues in family businesses.

2. How do you evaluate a consultant? Some family business consultants come from the mental health field. Some come from

organizational development backgrounds and others are the "technocrats" with specialized training in management, law or accounting. All these disciplines contribute something important and exclusive. But alone, none of them can completely analyze and treat a family business. A trend is emerging in the field that integrates the disciplines, called "quarterbacking," according to Gerald Le Van, the family business consultant.

3. Check the consultant's credentials. Get references. How many family businesses has he worked with? What size were the firms in terms of revenue, employees and industry ranking? What was the consultant's success rate? After how long?

4. Find out fees, how much time is involved and what is the approach? Will it be individual and/or family treatment? Some charge $2,000 to $3,000 a day and the most sought after, like Leon A. Danco, charge $18,000 a day. Check to see if these sessions are covered by insurance? Is there a charge for the initial office evaluation? Is all client information kept confidential?

5. After the first session, ask the consultant to define the problem, and if he can solve it and over how long a period? Choose your consultant with the idea that if you don't like him or her, you switch. Chemistry is crucial. There must be trust and respect.

6. The next session should involve a family assessment. Everybody in the family should be interviewed, individually and by birth order about the family and the business. What do they like about the business and family? What do they dislike? Next "outlaws" in the business should be interviewed about the family and business.

7. The consultant should question key employees from the top down. How do they view family members and the business? Who do they think should run the firm? In a succession, do they think they can transfer their loyalty? How would they respond to a professional manager?

8. Assess communications with the consultant. How does the family generate information? How is it shared between family and family and between family and non-family?

9. The consultant should assess the firm's culture. What are its values? Are they and the goals realistic? Does the company need to grow, change and head in a new direction?

10. Once the consultant has gathered this information, the family should begin to strategically plan for a two-to-three-year

stretch. Where is the industry headed? How does the company fit in? How quickly can it respond?

11. The family should draft a long-term family mission. It should answer such questions as: Is the ultimate goal a good life? To maintain the family name? To manufacture a product or offer a service? The process of working together is as important as the result.

12. Discuss with the consultant the pros and cons of an outside board. Who should be on it? For how long? Pay? What will be the extent of control? Will board members have veto power over the head?

13. Get a written report from the consultant of what changes need to be made and how they can be put into action. What is the company doing right, as well as what is it doing wrong?

14. After about three months, organize a family retreat. Select a distant place for two or three days. Gather the family and key employees. If a board has been set up, bring members along. Come prepared with a variety of topics to discuss. Should young family members first work elsewhere? What kind of career counseling should the company offer? How can the boss's spouse be kept out of decision making? How can some family members be stopped from abusing perks? Talk about the present state of the business and its future.

15. Be sure the consultant organizes periodic refresher sessions. Join organizations to gauge how the company compares to the competition. Some cities have family business support groups such as Minneapolis, Los Angeles, Chicago, Miami, St. Louis. Don't hesitate to scrutinize operations when a new generation takes over.

Family Business Consultants and Institutes

This list is by no means conclusive, but a sampling of academicians, psychologists and business executives.

Jeffrey A. Barach
Professor
A.B. Freeman School of Business
Tulane University
New Orleans, LA 70118

James Barrett
Managing Director
Cresheim Company Foundation
P.O. Box 27785
Philadelphia, PA 19118

Benjamin Benson
Director of Family Business Consulting Service
Laventhol & Horwath
2 Center Plaza
Boston, MA 02108

Daniel Bishop
National Family Business Association
18246 Rancho Street
Tarzana, CA 91356

David E. Bork
Coda Inc.
201 N. Millstreet
Suite 103
Aspen, CO 81611

Robert H. Brockhaus
Institute of Entrepreneurial Studies
3674 Lindell Blvd.
St. Louis University
St. Louis, MO 63108

Frank Butrick
Independent Business Institute
Box 139
Akron, OH 44309

Center for the Comparative Study of Social Roles
Helena Znaniecki Lopata
6525 North Sheridan Road
Loyola University
Chicago, IL 60626

Center for the Family
Susan Golden and Mary Whiteside
617 East Huron
Ann Arbor, MI 48104

Leon and Katy Danco
Center for Family Business
P.O. Box 24268
5862 Mayfield Road
Cleveland, OH 44124

John A. Davis
Assistant Professor of Management and Organization
Graduate School of Business Administration
University of Southern California
Los Angeles, CA 90089

Peter Davis
Director
Division of Family Business Studies
The Wharton School
University of Pennsylvania
427 Vance Hall
Philadelphia, PA 19104

Nancy Drozdow
The Wharton School
Center for Applied Research
University of Pennsylvania
3508 Market Street
Philadelphia, PA 19104

W. Gibb Dyer Jr.
Assistant Professor of Organization Behavior
School of Management
Brigham Young University
789 Tanner Building
Provo, UT 84602

Family Business Dynamics
Edith L. Perrow
New Haven, CT

Family Business Institute
Neal Wehr
1 Campbell Avenue
Branford, CT 06405

Family Business Management Services
Donald J. Janovic
2967 Attleboro Road
Cleveland, OH 44120

Family Business Resource Center
Deborah Menashi, David Paradise, Michael Sales
19 Crescent Avenue
Melrose, MA 02176

Family Firm Institute
Roderick W. Correll, Executive Director
P.O. Box 476
Johnstown, NY 12095

Roger A. Ford
Director
James Madison University
Center for Entrepreneurship
College of Business
Harrisonburg, VA 22807

Georgia Institute of Technology
Mike O'Bannon, Senior Research Scientist
Office of the Director of the Georgia Technical Research Institute
Education Extension Department
Atlanta, GA 30332-0385

Genus Resources
Tom Davidow and Richard Narva
148 State St.
Boston, MA 02109

Mark Granoveter
Professor of Sociology
State University of New York
Stony Brook, NY 11794

Barbara S. Hollander Associates
Barbara Hollander
1174 Harvard Road
Pittsburgh, PA 15205

Hubler-Swartz & Associates Inc.
Mary D. Korman, Thomas Hubler, Stephen Swartz

701 Fourth Avenue South
Suite 810
Minneapolis, MN 55415

The Institute for Family Business
Leslie B. Kaddis, M.D., Ruth McClendon, Ruth Scott
P.O. Box 190
Aptos, CA 95001

Rosabeth Moss Kanter
Harvard Business School
Soldier's Field Road
Cambridge, MA 02163

Florence Kaslow
1900 Consulate Place
West Palm Beach, FL 33401

Ivan S. Lansberg
Assistant Professor of Organization and Management
Yale School of Organization and Management
135 Prospect Street
New Haven, CT 06520

Robert E. Lefton
Psychological Associates Inc.
8201 Maryland Avenue
Clayton, MO 63105

Gerald Le Van
President
Family Business Foundation Inc.
Four United Place
Suite 201
Baton Rouge, LA 70809

Harry Levinson
Levinson Institute
375 Concord Avenue
Belmont, MA 02178

Amy Lyman
4128 Amaranta Ct.
Palo Alto, CA 94306

John L. Nash
President
National Association of Corporate Directors
1707 L Street
Suite 560
Washington, D.C. 20036

National Family Business Council
John E. Messervey
60 Revere Dr.
Northbrook, IL 60062

National Small Business United
John Gallen
Executive Vice President
1155 15th St. N.W.
Suite 710
Washington, DC 20005

Performance Improvement Associates
  Mardy S. Grote
  75 Wells Road
  Lincoln, MA 01773

  Peter B. Wylie
  1666 B. Euclid St.
  Washington, DC 20009

Paul C. Rosenblatt
Professor of Family Social Science and Psychology
Rm. 293
McNeal Hall
1985 Buford Avenue
University of Minnesota
St. Paul, MN 55108

Matilde Salganicoff
The Family Business Consultancy
556 North 23rd Street
Philadelphia, PA 19130

Jeffrey A. Timmons
Professor of Management
Babson College
Wellesley, MA 02181

Nancy Bowman-Upton
Streich Professor of Family Business
Center for Entrepreneurship
Hankamer School of Business
Baylor University
Waco, TX 76798

Marta Vago
Clinical and Business Therapist
1421 Santa Monica Blvd.
Santa Monica, CA 90404

John L. Ward
Ralph Marotta Professor of Free Enterprise
Graduate School of Business
820 North Michigan Ave.
Loyola University
Chicago, IL 60611

Abraham Zaleznik
Harvard Business School
Soldier's Field Road
Boston, MA 02163

Selected Bibliography

Alcorn, Pat B. *Success and Survival in the Family-Owned Business*. McGraw Hill, 1982.

Ambrose, David M. "Transfer of the Family-Owned Business," *Journal of Small Business Management*, January 1983.

Barnes, L. and S. Hershon. "Transferring Power in the Family Business," *Harvard Business Review*, July-August 1976.

Barzini, Luigi G. *The Italians*. Atheneum, 1964.

Berry, Wendell. *Home Economics*. North Point Press, 1987.

Benoit, Ellen. "The Family that Buys Families," *Financial World*, June 30, 1987.

Bork, David. *Family Business, Risky Business*. American Management Association, 1986.

Bowman-Upton, Nancy. "Family Business Succession: Issues for the Founder," Hankamer School of Business, Baylor University.

———. "Family-Owned Businesses: Challenge of Survival," *The New Adventurers: Entrepreneurs Surviving and Growing*, University of Southern California, 1987.

———, and J. Clifton Williams. "Interesting the Children in the Family Business," Hankamer School of Business, Baylor University.

Brenner, Marie. *House of Dreams*. Random House, 1988.

Burack, Elmer H. and Thomas M. Calero. "Perils of the Family Firm," *Nation's Business*, January 1981.

Burt, Nathaniel. *First Families: The Making of an American Aristocracy*. Little, Brown & Co., 1970.

288

Chandler, David Leon. *The Binghams of Louisville*. Crown, 1987.

Clifford, Ronald K. Jr. and Richard E. Cavanagh. *The Winning Performance*. Bantam Books, 1985.

Cooper, Wyatt. *Families: A Memoir and a Celebration*. Harper & Row, 1975.

Cornfeld, Dave L. and Lawrence Brody, "Estate Planning for Shareholders of Closely Held Corporations," in *Missouri Corporation Law and Practice*, from the Missouri Bar, 1985–86.

Crane, Margaret. "How to Keep Families from Feuding," *Inc.*, February 1982.

Cross, Theodore. *Black Capitalism: Strategy for Business in the Ghetto*. Atheneum, 1969.

———. *The Black Power Imperative*. Faulkner Books, 1986.

Danco, Katy. *From the Other Side of the Bed*. Center for Family Business, 1981.

Danco, Leon A. *Beyond Survival: A Business Owner's Guide for Success*. Center for Family Business, 1978.

———. *Inside the Family Business*. Center for Family Business, 1980.

Davis, John A. "The Oedipal Drama in the Family Firm: Rage or Stage," Graduate School of Business Administration, University of Southern California. Unpublished paper.

———, and Renato Tagiuri. "Bivalent Attributes of the Family Firm," Graduate School of Business Administration, University of Southern California and Graduate School of Business Administration, Harvard University. Unpublished paper.

———. "The Influence of Life Stages on Father-Son Work Relationships in Family Companies," Graduate School of Business Administration, Harvard University, 1982.

Deal, Terrence. *Corporate Cultures: The Rites and Rituals of Corporate Life*. Addison-Wesley Publishing Co., 1982.

Dyer, W. Gibb Jr. *Cultural Change in Family Firms*. Jossey-Bass, 1986.

Edmond, Alfred Jr., "Reginald Lewis Cuts the Big Deal," *Black Enterprise*, November 1987.

Farmer, Val. "Broken Heartland," *Psychology Today*, April 1986.

Goldwasser, Tom. *Family Pride*. Dodd, Mead & Co., 1986.

Greeley, Andrew M. *The Irish American*. Harper & Row, 1981.

Hartman, Curtis. "All the Right Moves," *Inc.*, January 1988.

———. "An American Tragedy," *Inc.*, May 1986.

———. "Family Business," *Inc.*, November 1984.

Hershon, S. "The Problem of Management Succession in Family Businesses," Graduate School of Business Administration thesis, Harvard University, 1975.

Howe, Irving. *World of Our Fathers*. Harcourt Brace Jovanovich, 1976.

Israelowitz, Oscar, *Guide to Jewish New York City*. P.O. Box 228, Brooklyn, NY 11229. O. Israelowitz, 1983.

Kent, Calvin A., Donald L. Sexton and Karl H. Vesper, ed. *Encyclopedia of Entrepreneurship*. Prentice-Hall Inc., 1982.

Kinkead, Gwen. "Family Business Is a Passion Play," *Fortune*, June 30, 1980.

Lansberg, Ivan, ed. *Family Business Review*, quarterly journal of the Family Firm Institute. Jossey-Bass. Vol. I, Nos. 1 and 2, Spring and Summer 1988.

Le Van, Gerald. "Passing the Family Business to the Next Generation—Resolving Family Conflicts." Unpublished article.

Levinson, Harry. "Conflicts that Plague Family Businesses," *Harvard Business Review*, March-April 1971.

Loyola Business Forum, Graduate School of Business Alumni Association, Loyola University, Vol. 4, No. 1, Summer 1983.

McKnight, Gerald. *Gucci: A House Divided*. Donald Fine, 1987.

Morrison, Ann M., Randall P. White, Ellen Van Velsor and the Center for Creative Leadership. *Breaking the Glass Ceiling*. Addison-Wesley Publishing Co. Inc., 1987.

Muson, Howard. "Generations," *The New York Times Magazine*, Nov. 29, 1987.

Nelton, Sharon. *In Love and In Business*. John Wiley & Sons, 1986.

———. "Making Sure Your Business Outlasts You," *Nation's Business*, January 1986.

Prokesch, Steven. "Rediscovering Family Values," *The New York Times*, June 10, 1986.

———. "When the Relatives Fall Out," *The New York Times*, June 11, 1986.

———. "Keeping Control Gets Harder," *The New York Times*, June 12, 1986.

Reginato, James, "All in the Family: Heirs Apparent," *Avenue*, September 1987.

Rosenblatt, Paul C. "Family Inc.," *Psychology Today*, July 1985.

———, Leni de Mik, Roxanne Marie Anderson and Patricia A. Johnson. *The Family in Business: Understanding and Dealing with the Challenges Entrepreneurial Families Face*. Jossey-Bass, 1985.

Rutigliano, Anthony J., "When Worlds Collide: Problems in Family-Owned Businesses," *Management Review*, February 1986.

Sexton, Donald L. and Raymond W. Smilor, ed. *The Art and Science of Entrepreneurship*. Ballinger Publishing Co., 1986.

"Supermarket Format Propels Bookstop," *Chain Store Age*, December 1987.

Timmons, Jeffry A., *The Entrepreneurial Mind*, Brick House Publishing Co., 1989.

Ward, John L. *How to Plan for Continuing Growth, Profitability and Family Leadership*. Jossey-Bass, 1987.

———. *Keeping the Family Business Healthy*. Jossey-Bass, 1986.